THE IMPACT OF RACE

THE IMPACT OF RACE

Theatre and Culture

Woodie King, Jr.

APPLAUSE
THEATRE & CINEMA BOOKS

The Impact of Race
Theatre and Culture

Library of Congress Cataloging-in-Publication Data
King, Woodie.
    The impact of race : theatre and culture /
by Woodie King, Jr.
    p. cm.
    ISBN 1-55783-579-9
    1. African American theater.
    2. Black theater.
    3. American drama—African American authors—
    History and criticism.
    4. Drama—Black authors—History and criticism.
    I. Title.
PN2270.A35K54   2003
792'.089'96073—dc21   2003004948

APPLAUSE THEATRE & CINEMA BOOKS
151 West 46th Street, 8th Floor
New York, NY 10036
Phone: (212) 575-9265
Fax: (646) 562-5852
Email: info@applausepub.com
Internet: www.applausepub.com

Sales & Distribution

NORTH AMERICA:
    HAL LEONARD CORP.
    7777 West Bluemound Road
    P. O. Box 13819
    Milwaukee, WI 53213
    Phone: (414) 774-3630
    Fax: (414) 774-3259
    Email: halinfo@halleonard.com
    Internet: www.halleonard.com
UK:
    Roundhouse Publishing Ltd.
    Millstone, Limers Lane
    Northam, North Devon
    Ex 39 2RG
    Phone: 01237-474474
    Fax: 01237-474774
    Email: roundhouse.group@ukgateway.net

For
Elizabeth van Dyke

Acknowledgements

I would like to thank some people who helped make this book possible:

First, Carol Cupril, who worked on the computer to put pages and words together; Glenn Young and his wonderful staff at Applause Books; and all the brilliant actors, writers, designers, and theatre craftsmen who work in the Black theatre.

Contents

FESTIVALS

LETTERS

APPENDICES

Foreword

Woodie King is a most excitable man. His enthusiasms—and there are many—keep him busy (but not conflicted) trying to catch up—and keep up—with himself. His subject is always Black Theatre, and it's hard to shut him up once he gets started.

This book you're holding is pure Woodie King (as much as can be captured on page), consisting of history, commentary, criticism, polemic, propaganda, special pleading and a little bitching—and more than you need to know about bureaucrats, and Liberals, and foundations, and group sales, and Black folks who tend to buy their tickets at the last moment, and white folks who know more about being Black than Black folks do. All of this comes jumping off the page straight at you on the tide of Woodie's passion.

Logic is nice, but Woodie King, being a Black man, needs something more than structure and correctness to make his point to a world that seldom listens. Ordinary English is a little too slow to keep up with the overload that burdens his mind, so Woodie resorts to jazz as a method of attack: getting to the point a little ahead of the beat, letting one thing lead to two things—wherever the melody, or the madness, takes him.

It could hardly be otherwise, since the controlling narrative—Black Theatre—is itself little more than a figment of a dreamer's imagination. Still, the more it doesn't exist, the more we love it and defend it, and argue about it, and fight over it, and promote it, and tell ourselves great big lies about it existing—mostly in the eye and in the heart of the beholder— what it means and what it's all about and why its presence is absolutely essential to our status as a people.

9

Theatre for us is often a form of Black Magic, more intuition than institution. A dramaturgical sleight of hand where even the prestidigitator is always a little surprised when it works. Woodie sees it all, knows it all, and loves it all—I doubt if anybody can explain what it is, and what it is not, better than he can. Sometimes he seems the only one who really does, which means he spends a lot of time talking to himself.

Woodie, by conviction as well as color, belongs to Off-off-Broadway; but he knows Broadway, its culture and its cash flow—from beauteous to banal to bullshit, and back again. On Broadway, he's a very small fish in a very large pond; Off-off, he's a big fish in almost no pond at all. He walks a tightrope with an acrobat's foot and a con man's tongue. And if he falls, he always manages to land on somebody else's feet. A gambler, a hustler, a braggart, and a scholar, Woodie wants you to read this book almost as much as he wants you to invest in his plays.

Someday we will prevail, and we Black folks will understand why we must ultimately come into control of the images we want the world to know us by; we will come to respect and depend on our own Black Theatre, which will have something more to offer than genius and raw gumption, good intentions and fly-by-night productions. We'll have stable, respectable, black middle-class institutions owning and operating their own theatres from one end of the country to the other. Our playwrights and our performers will join our musicians and our athletes as carriers of the message of black artistic excellence. But, till that time, we have our Woodie Kings—with no visible means of support, struggling to keep all the right things in line and the wrong things from happening.

Read this book, and join him.

— Ossie Davis

The Impact of Race
on Theatre

The American Black Theatre Movement. It's alive and it's every-where. It's everywhere because of forerunners like the Karamu Theatre, Langston Hughes, Canada Lee and the American Negro Theatre. Because of those people we're able to see that past, to know some of the things that have gone on before and not be too afraid to try something ourselves. Before I actually went into theatre I spent more time in the library looking for photographs of Blacks in theatre than I spent in school. So when I got to the point that I really wanted to go into theatre it really didn't matter too much where I got the training—I already had a history of what came before to guide me.

The Black Theatre Movement started for me in 1961-62 in Detroit at a place called the Concept East Theatre, which I founded with David Rambeau and some other brothers. We all got together with a thousand dollars; we all put up a hundred dollars each. There were no foundations at the time. One thing we found out early—you had to know how to direct, how to make sets and lights. Everybody had to know how to do everything. Running that little theatre in Detroit was a great learning experience.

Few Black people were actually involved in running theatres when I came to New York, even though there were bars and churches vacant everywhere. Cliff Frazier and I set out to start a theatre. It's funny because we went to the Church of Saint Marks in the Bowery and asked the minister if we could have the parish hall to do some plays. We started Theatre Genesis in 1963-64.

One man can't totally run a theatre in New York and be totally successful because the system has ways of cutting him down.

Black theatre has failed to develop directors. The Frank Silvera Writers' Workshop actually has a directors' workshop. I know our theatre is developing them. At New Federal we do six or seven plays a year and I try to get as many different directors coming in as possible to work on plays; it gives the theatre a different personality. When a theatre takes on one dominant personality it's a problem.

The early Sixties Black Theatre movement came out of some work Baraka was doing up in Harlem and down in the Saint Marks Playhouse. Right after that he went uptown and started the Black Arts Repertory Theatre and wrote a position paper called "Revolutionary Black Theatre: What It's All About." That inspirational paper and that feeling in Harlem helped, indirectly, a great many Blacks across the country. The white establishment was so afraid of Baraka they'd do anything. They'd just give money away. Anybody who said they didn't like Baraka got a grant.

What we failed to do, though, was distinguish Black Theatre from mainstream theatre. A white person who bought a ticket for *Guys and Dolls* and *Brownsville Raid* saw both of these pieces of work as Black theatre. He didn't see any difference in paying $12 for *Guys and Dolls* and $6.95 for *Brownsville Raid*. He wanted *Brownsville Raid* to be just as flashy and full of music as *Guys and Dolls* because he wanted to be entertained.

In trying to get the word out, to get the Black Theatre Movement out before the public, we didn't make that distinction. We didn't distinguish that "something" for a lot of Black people. A lot of our mothers would come to New York and see *Hello Dolly* on Broadway and go see *Unfinished Women* and deal with them on the same level; they wouldn't see the difference. "It's got Black people in it so it's Black theatre."

How do you produce plays, black plays, in this system? It's one of the most corrupt systems in the world. You don't really know it until you get into it. It can cost more to produce a "non-profit" play in New York than one for profit! For example, not that long after I arrived in New York you could do a play with commercial investments in an off-Broadway theatre for $60,000-70,000. But that same play in a non-profit theatre might have cost $100,000.

What you find out — and I'm saying this with caution, but I think it's true and I feel very strong about it — is people who work in non-profit institutions are basically lazy because they know they're going to get a check every week whether the play is a hit or not. In the commercial theatre, if it's not a hit, you don't get paid, you don't make anything. So they will sell you a ticket.

Commercial theatre in New York is controlled by the theatre owner on Broadway. If you deal with off-Broadway, it's controlled by *The New York Times*. No matter how much you may think you can get through by not using them, the Times knows if you open a play for $75,000, they're going to get $25,000 of that in ads. The theatre knows when you open a play on Broadway that they're going to get $45,000 a week and a percentage of the gross. They don't care whether you have two people in the house or two thousand. That's the system we're operating under. You can do an all-black play on Broadway with ten characters, and there'll be twenty-five union white people making more than those actors, sometimes three times as much. And that's what's really frightening about this system.

I used to read magazines like *Theater Arts* and all kinds of books that said "Negro in American Theatre" this, or the "Negro in American Theatre" that, and somewhere in the mid-Sixties that started changing to "Black Theatre Movement" and "Blacks in Theatre." It was mainly because plays like *Anna Lucasta* up until then had been directed and produced by whites. Blacks in Black Theatre Movement changed that to where Black people in plays projected unity. I point to theatre groups, producing organizations like the Frank Silvera Writers' Workshop — just staging plays — and places like Concept East in Detroit and Free Southern Theatre, which deal exclusively with the audience in their development.

There's a change in our attitude from the mid-Sixties in terms of white people. During the mid-Sixties, Black actors in Detroit felt they were able to coerce white theatres into doing plays where they could play the leads. Then in the mid-Seventies you couldn't coerce them anymore because they felt they no longer needed you. Blacks were and are expendable in most white institutions. It wouldn't matter if our Black Theatre put on plays and turned away hundreds of Black people. If that play doesn't appeal to white critics, then that play won't get white audiences.

One of the greatest fallacies in the theatre is the "crossover audience." If Black people packed a theatre for three or four months and paid to see it, white people would come and see that play whether you were in one of the worst ghettos anywhere. The paradox is, however, it must get a great *Times* review and have the money to *stay* open those three or four months. I don't think anyone should develop a play or a film because of its "crossover potential."

Black businesses sustain themselves because they have a product that Black people need. Black artists create the spiritual and cultural nourishment Black people need.

Over the past 100 years, from Henry O. Tanner to Romare Beardon, the need to own Black Arts has been obvious. However, it has been wealthy whites or museums collecting the works of these fine artists. In more recent years Blacks have been collecting the work of Black artists. A piece of Black art can be placed on the living room wall or in the new office of a Black business. But how can we deal with a piece of performing arts like dance or theatre? Can we place it in our new office? No, we must experience dance or theatre as a spiritual or cultural abstraction. However, we're not sure who we are spiritually or culturally. To begin to deal with this void we must begin to relate to the spiritual and cultural reality of our existence on this planet.

The Black Artist in performing arts or plastic arts looks on his life as one totally lacking in the material sustenance exhibited by the Black Businessman. When the Black Artist picks up a *Black Enterprise* magazine listing the earnings of the top 100 Black Businesses, he wonders how each businessman relates to Blacks in the arts. Does he buy Black Art? Does his company give grants to Black Theatre companies or Black Dance companies? He surmises they don't support Black Art because most Black Art is owned by white collectors; they don't give grants to Black Theatre companies and Black Dance companies.

What is the problem here? Does the Black Business believe the arts are needed? Without question! But many worked for years to get to the point of placing acceptable products on the market; some got in the public eye through white acceptance. Many more are one of the top 100 Black Businesses by accident. They aren't sure if they'll be able to sustain a position. They're afraid of abstractions like art and spirituality. Artist and performing artist are feared.

Black Artists, on the other hand, believe too much in the power of the Black Businessman. They don't know that in many of the top Black Businesses white accountants and white attorneys are the decision makers — including decisions on what piece of Black Art to buy or what Black Theatre company to support. They don't appreciate that Black CEO's and COO's are golfing, vacationing, dinner partying, and associating with their white counterpart. Black Artists don't realize that they must constantly invite (cultivate) Black Businessmen to openings, screenings, and arts related ideas (events). Just as white donors, sponsors, and contributors are wooed, Black Businessmen must be treated the same way. Black Artists must let Black Businessmen know what a painting costs, what a $2,500 contribution means to a Black Dance Company or a Black Theatre Company. Exactly what would it mean if at least ten of the top 100 Black Businesses gave $2,500 to twenty Black non-profit organizations each year?

Black Theatre Companies don't have a base group of wealthy individuals to act as donors, sponsors or contributors. These companies depend on Federal, State, and City support. This support adds up to about 40 percent of overall cost of operating, about 30 percent coming from box office and concessions. That's all! They're always operating at a 30 percent deficit because of the lack of donor, sponsor, contributor support. That's real!

Both the Black Artist and the Black Businessman must remove all abstractions. Abstractions tend to be easy fronts, it's so easy to say a company grossed $50 million; it's so easy to say a play cost one million to produce on Broadway. It's very difficult to say it cost a company $50 million to gross $50 million, especially if it's not on the American Stock Exchange. It's also pure bullshit to say it cost one million dollars to produce a play and not talk about the ten to fifteen years an investor hopes to be earning on that investment.

On the other hand, tax deductible grants and contributions can be made to non-profit Black Theatre companies because that company corroborates that business's or individual's spiritual or cultural existence.

The Impact of Race

Yes, Black Artists need the support and they need the visibility. But one can lead to the other. If an artist gets visibility by a Black Business, that can lead to support by individuals who buy that company's product. If an artist gets *support*, he can *create*. The exchange for the Businessman can be spiritual, cultural, and a corroboration of his spiritual and cultural self.

Every man, woman, or child needs this part of him or herself. It's not a Black or white thing. Romare Bearden, Jacob Lawrence, Hughie Lee Smith, John Biggers, Benny Andrews, Dance Theatre of Harlem, Alvin Ailey, ETA, National Black Theatre, New Federal Theatre, Amas Repertory Company, Karamu Theatre, The Ensemble Theatre Company, Lorraine Hansberry Theatre, Jomandi Theatre Company, AUDELCO, Studio Museum of Harlem (to name just a few) represent the best as artists and institutions providing cultural and spiritual sustenance. Yet, not one of these artists or institutions is supported primarily by Black Businesses.

A few Black Artists have created a product that the public needed and Black Businessmen have been known to create art. In each such case I can think of, the creators became extremely wealthy and vanished. Wealth and art aren't mutually compatible; neither are business and wealth. Many of the top 100 Black Businesses in this country are just breaking even. The CEO's and the COO's are in debt way over their heads. It's important that Black Businessmen know that Black Artists are aware of these financial realities.

From the so-called Harlem Renaissance through World War II artists had patrons. The patrons were wealthy white people who loved the primitive nature of Blacks who were artists. It was impossible to exist during that time without a patron. But as described by Langston Hughes, Zora Neale Hurston, Jean Toomer, Wallace Thurman, Jessie Faucet, Alain Locke, and Paul Robeson, these patrons represented another form of slavery. They controlled the writings of these artists as well as their bankbooks. Between the two world wars, a few fellowships were given to Blacks through the Rosenwalds and the Carnegies. Black Businesses were rare when it came to patronage.

Aleia Walker, the daughter of the hair millionairess Madame C. J. Walker, supported many of the artists through the Twenties. She gave both money and support. Her favorites were Langston Hughes and Countee Cullen. She also provided food and shelter in her famous salon called The

Dark Tower (now part of the Schomburg Center for Research in Black Culture). In the Fifties, patronage for Black artists dropped to an all time low, never recovering. The Black Power movement and Black consciousness among Blacks of the Sixties created this gulf between the white patron and the Black Artist. State and City support appeared, thus rendering the old form of patronage obsolete. That support was a direct result of the riots and turmoil in the urban ghettos. But these funds were administered by liberal whites who had only a sociological knowledge of Blacks and Black artists.

Blacks do support their spiritual institutions. Across this country, East to West and North to South, churches abound. The church has been supported by Black people since slavery. According to Dwight Cook, a noted director who grew up in the Baptist Church, "Our entire social structure is built around and nurtured in the church." Black Artists have always been supported by the church. Our arts were reflective of our daily lives and thus reflective of our spiritual selves. Spirituality and culture were inextricably connected. Towards the mid 18th century, Europeans changed all that. To this day church related arts aren't looked on as an important part of our lives. So we ask the question: Will our churches support Black artists, Black Theatre companies? The answer is, without question, yes!

Look at the five-year run of *Mama, I Want to Sing*. As a result of church support, Vi Higgensen, the creator and producer, grossed $8.3 million in 1988 to become one of the top 100 Black Businesses. Note the large number of church groups coming out to support Black Theatre and dance companies. Black Businesses don't, in general, gather together their employees for a theatre party. And, as stated earlier, Black Artists don't woo the Black Businessman. Black Artists feel more comfortable seeking out the support of Black ministers and the Black church.

Being Black is extremely complicated; being a Black Artist or a Black Businessman is a nightmare. To comprehend it one must realize we're less than 300 years out of slavery. Our language as well as our entire way of life was taken away from us. We went into European institutions (transplanted to America) to become re-educated. We're part African, part European and part American; our training as artists and businessmen are as such. Our constituency represents about 15 percent of the American population. We're going to find it extremely difficult to make a profit as businessmen or as Black artists reaching only 15 percent of the American population. We, therefore, make our product—art or otherwise—to cross over. Some of the 15 percent refuse to buy or deal with a product that homogenized. In both cases our economic existence is based on what white America earns and what white America spends.

What exactly does a Black Artist need from Black Business and Black Businessmen? Black Artists need for Black companies to purchase art for their offices and lobbies. Black Theatre companies and dance companies need Black Businesses to make yearly grants; they also need CEO's and COO's to join the Board of Directors of the non-profit institutions.

What does Black Business need from Black Arts? They need art, dance, music, and theatre as a cultural and spiritual nourishment. They need an art where the mystery of creating it has been removed. They want to visit the painter's studio, the theatre company in rehearsals, and the rehearsals of a new dance piece by Alvin Ailey. And the Black Businessman must be as welcome here as the artist would expect to be at the businessman's plant. Why has collaboration never happened? Many believe it has great deal to do with ego needs; realization of ideas and achievements as individual accomplishments. That means, *I want to do it alone because I want the credit alone.* In the Black world one must step on a lot of little people in order to achieve wealth. Black Artists and Black Businessmen who've worked on projects for years aren't eager to share the credit of the project's creation. These are artists and businessmen who don't necessarily need wealth but need corroboration of individual accomplishments.

Black Businesses and Black Arts must look to a world market for the sale and the distribution of art and product. The growing Japanese presence in this country seems to be an obvious market for Black Art and Black performing groups. *Mama, I Want to Sing* toured the Far East. The entire tour of this Black gospel show was sponsored by Mitsubishi. African countries are making overtures to our jazz artists and our dance companies. These overtures are coming directly from African Businessmen.

Ultimately, it all boils down to Blacks helping each other. Black Business and the Black Arts, Black Arts and Black Business. The common denominator is obvious. Our markets are wherever Black people happen to be; they're everywhere. The Black Theatre in London should be brought to America by Black Business. The best Black Theatre and Dance in Africa should be brought to America by Black Business. And, without question, the best Black Theatre and Dance in America should be taken to Europe and Africa by Black Business. This kind of tie-in promotes the Black Business and its products, nationally and internationally. Moreover, when Black Art and Black Theatre are past the development stage, they happen to be tremendously profitable.

In South Africa, in the mid-Seventies, Athol Fugard's *Sizwe Banzi Is Dead* and *The Island* raised consciousnesses. In Nigeria, Wole Soyinka's *The Road, The Lion and the Jewel, Madmen and Specialist* were all highly favorite plays. In the Caribbean, Derek Walcott, Trevor Rhone, Yvonne Brewster redefined the artistic vision from the Caribbean diaspora. Black Theatre tries to give the world an honest picture of exactly what's happening with Blacks on a day-to-day basis; we very seldom depict the past in our work. We try to recreate and redefine the present. Note: I said "recreate and redefine" the present. So many of us are so disappointed with what's happening out in the world. We all *use* Black Theatre as a haven; and in this haven we create our illusions, our reality, and our world. Since Black Theatre is everywhere, our haven may be in a Black Theatre professional situation, a Black Theatre community situation, or even in a Black Theatre department in a major university.

So many of our Black students are in school simply to get a degree; they're not about change anymore. They don't care at all about institutional survival; they care about self-survival. Why is that? It's because wherever we are we're surrounded by a white power structure that attempts at every moment to dominate and direct world culture. This domination may be through economic control or through political control. They start with youth in general; Black youth in particular. Across the United States, the most prestigious universities are those that are most Eurocentric. That can also be said about the most prestigious American theatres. So, what do you do if you're in Los Angeles, or New York or San Francisco trying to manage a theatre that reaches out to Black people, when all the major distributors of information see only the Mark Taper Forum or Lincoln Center? Who's going to take the time to understand you? Where are the foundations deeply rooted in *your* history?

White Americans support their institutions by subscriptions, by donations, contributions, etc.; through the media, through images, they tell Blacks we're nothing! Yet, our political and cultural situation here in America has been a beacon for most of the darker people of the world. South Africans' cry for freedom is a reverberation of American Blacks lashing out in the turbulent Sixties. The content of so many of our better plays explores a road that screams for change; many of the plays even explore exactly what that change might mean for individual freedom. Reexamine the work of Baraka, Bullins, Alice Childress, Ron Milner, Jack Jackson, Charles Fuller, J.e. Franklin, and August Wilson and you'll see artists working for change.

Whether Blacks are on a university campus, in a resident non-profit theatre, on Broadway, the politics of Black "being there" causes traumatic repercussions. Witness, if you will, the small budgets allotted Black Studies and Black Theatre departments at major Eurocentic universities; witness the so-called "peer panels" making recommendations to Federal, State, and City funding agencies for Black institutions and the small amounts granted to non-profit Black Theatres; witness the paucity of professional Black Theatre productions on Broadway. If not for the fine work of August Wilson, Black Theatre on Broadway would be nonexistent.

What is the situation in New York? Why can't we get Black images on Broadway?

The political situation in New York is dismal; the number of Black elected officials is at its lowest. Black artists really have no political clout on a local or national level; no one's fighting for the survival of Black theatrical institutions. A new breed of politician entered the arena in the Seventies, gained some credibility in the Eighties through the rhetoric of politics and barely hung on to office in the Nineties. For lack of a better definition, they were integrationist. Black Artists believed the politicians in the Sixties and Seventies. They then integrated into a system that's really about the destruction of the culture of the darker people of the world. The distribution of information about Black cultural activities is so distilled, so homogenized, that by the time the information reaches grass roots people, these integrated politicians look like buffoons. Blacks who work and operate from a grass roots level tend not to pay much attention to the integrationists, whether they're politicians or artists.

Those few Blacks capable of financing Black Theatre productions on

Broadway are also, for the most part, integrationist. These people would rather invest their money where there are greater possibilities for a return. They believe Wall Street to be a safe place. These people are not so interested in Black images for themselves and their children but in images that will please whites. With this as a backdrop, what can be done to keep Black institutions alive with, at least, some degree of artistic quality? Though I'm using the political situation in New York as an example, it holds true across the United States. We must support local non-profit Black Arts institutions.

The Negro Ensemble Company was one of our finest Black Theatre institutions. I could go into great detail on how this organization struggled to survive. From its inception with *Song of the Lucatanian Bogey*, *River Niger* and *A Soldier's Play* it struggled. Yet, its politics were very clear; its artistic health compared to that of similar white institutions was robust without question—but its demise seemed always imminent because of financial instability.

My own New Federal Theatre has been around for thirty-two years producing hits year after year, introducing new playwrights, reestablishing older playwrights. The productions at New Federal Theatre: *Black Girl* by J.e. Franklin, *What the Winesellers Buy* by Ron Milner, *The Taking of Miss Janie* by Ed Bullins, *for colored girls...* by Ntozake Shange, *Showdown* by Don Evans, *Steal Away* by Ramona King, *When Chickens Came Home to Roost* by Laurence Holder, *The Dance and the Railroad* by David Henry Hwang, *Paper Angels* by Ginny Lim, *Long Time Since Yesterday* by P. J. Gibson, *I Have a Dream* adapted by Josh Greenfeld, *Williams and Walker* by Vincent Smith and *From the Mississippi Delta* by Endesha Ida Mae Holland, *God's Trombones*, *Good Black Don't Crack* by Rob Penny, *Robert Johnson: Trick the Devil* by Bill Harris, *Do Lord Remember Me* by James de Jongh, *Checkmates* by Ron Milner. Yet, New Federal Theatre may not be around much longer because of financial strangulation.

National Black Theatre, The Billie Holiday Theatre, The Black Spectrum Theatre, The Roger Furman Theatre, and The Harlem Theatre Co. are all Black institutions desperately trying to survive in New York City. This financial crisis holds true for institutions outside of New York like ETA Theatre Foundation in Chicago, Karamu Theatre in Cleveland, Freedom Theatre in Philadelphia, and St. Louis Black Repertory in St. Louis.

The Impact of Race

In the face of such financial adversity, how did these institutions last so long? Look at the leadership; what's driving the leadership? It's certainly not money! Most of these theatres are barely capable of getting through a season, yet, the institutions are still here; making contributions to world theatre. The institutions are still here because the managers and artistic directors came of age during the Fifties and Sixties; we had "isms" — Communism, Marxism, Radicalism (the Radical Left), and Nationalism.

We must find "isms" again because our Blackness isn't enough. Our Blackness is simply the surface of *how* we *appear* to ourselves and to *others*. We must have some sort of political direction. We must believe in something; we must have a sense of our value beyond money.

In the Forties, Black Artists discovered the overwhelming power of the written word. The late writers Abe Hill, Theodore Ward, and Langston Hughes helped in guiding the Black Theatre. In the Fifties, Lou Peterson, Alice Childress, William Branch, Lofton Mitchell, and Lorraine Hansberry took on the mantle and created works considered classics today. Financial strangulation but certainly artistic health. Under all the financial constraints the Black Theatre nurtured Sidney Poitier, Harry Belafonte, Hilda Simms, Lou Gossett, Estelle Evans, William Greaves, Julian Mayfield, Ruby Dee, Ossie Davis, Helen Martin, Gertrude Jeanette, etc. I don't want to make this a shopping list but I do want you to know that, even though suffering financially, Black Theatre made outstanding individual contributions to the American cultural scene. Yet, America still can't see itself supporting a Black cultural institution.

Even in the Black universities Black Theatre flourished under financial constraints. Pioneers like Dr. Randolph Edmonds, Dr. Ann Cooke, Owen Dodson, and The Fisk Jubilee Singers. These pioneers sent graduates out into the world to carry our message through acting, directing, playwrighting, and song. The major question now seems to be: Who will step into the shoes of our past pioneers?

We must look on the contributions of our Black pioneers with gratitude; some of these pioneers spanned three or four decades; Paul Robeson, James Baldwin, Langston Hughes, Lorraine Hansberry, etc. The politics of Robeson and Hansberry leaned to the Radical Left; James Baldwin leaned to Nationalism; Langston Hughes stayed out of politics altogether (so he thought).

Woodie King, Jr.

The politics of the Radical Left seemed to be a more moderate form of Communism. It captured the imagination of the Black cultural elite in the Forties and Fifties. This Black cultural elite seemed to have an overriding need to integrate with whites of similar cultural and political persuasion. Younger Blacks of the Sixties saw an integrationist philosophy at work. With the highly visible Black Power Movement and the Nationalist Movement, whites in the Radical Left turned to Blacks in the Radical Left for answers about these "new" Negroes. Blacks in the Radical Left didn't "know" these "new" Negroes; they'd avoided them over the years of struggle. Blacks in the Radical Left believed Nationalism would soon fade away. They really hated much of the literature and the art of the Sixties as well as the politics. Many refused to work in the Black Theatre; many *could* not work in it. Some of these conflicts are well described in Harold Cruse's *Crisis of the Negro Intellectual.* Note James Baldwin's conflict in the Fifties with Richard Wright in Baldwin's essays "Alas, Poor Richard" and "Everybody's Protest Novel." The conflict between the Negro Ensemble Company (downtown) and The New Lafayette Theatre (uptown—Harlem). It was simple: Negro Ensemble Company and its artistic director came out of the Radical Left and New Lafayette Theatre and its artistic director came out of the Black Power Nationalist Movement.

Political ideas on the road to full citizenship in the American Way of Life vary so radically that one must read about them: The conflict of Booker T. Washington vs. W. E. B. DuBois; W. E. B. DuBois vs. Marcus Garvey; Mary Church Terrell vs. Ida B. Wells; Malcolm X vs. Dr. Martin Luther King, Jr. Yet, the contributions of these pioneers and the institutions they represented are so major it would be impossible to talk about the struggle for freedom and justice without noting them.

It's interesting how non-profit theatres seem to need commercial success for both media visibility and financial stability. The commercial theatre needs time and greater artistic input and has a great need to cut escalating cost.

One can certainly feed off the other. In many cases serious non-profits have worked successfully with commercial producers. The New Federal Theatre, in its first ten years of existence, moved non-profits into commercial arenas with great success. For example, *for colored girls...* brought in about $150,000 to our theatre. But earnings shouldn't be the purpose of the non-profits; it should be about the development of the artist.

For example, our productions of *Black Girl* by J.e. Franklin, *What the Winesellers Buy* by Ron Milner, *The Taking of Miss Janie* by Ed Bullins, *Prodigal Sisters* by J.e. Franklin and Mikki Grant, *Showdown* by Don Evans, and *Checkmates* (optioned by NFT but not produced) by Ron Milner moved into commercial arenas.

Negro Ensemble Company did do *Ceremonies in Dark Old Men*, *River Niger*, *First Breeze of Summer*, and *Home*. Amas Repertory did *Bubbling Brown Sugar*.

Let's talk of financing productions moving from non-profits to commercial theatre: In 1969, A *Black Quartet* cost $30,000; *Behold Cometh The Vandercellans* cost $35,000 in 1971; *What the Winesellers Buy* cost $75,000 in 1974; *for colored girls...* cost $250,000 to open on Broadway in 1976. Today each of these productions would cost close to ten times the original cost. Investors' earnings haven't increased equally. Therefore, those people cannot invest; they don't have the money.

The commercial theatre is controlled by theatre owners and what's called local presenters. A non-profit producer must have some kind of relationship with theatre owners or local presenters. That relationship, at one time, could have been based on the artistic quality of the work (defined by audience responses and reviews). Now it's based on the amount of money the non-profit producer brings to the table, the amount the theatre owner can get in rentals and his crew. The local presenter needs an easy sell (something with a major star from television), or an extremely inexpensive show.

If we look at shows wherein the quality has been questioned, like *You My Woman, Not My Wife*; *Beauty Shop*; *Mama Don't*; *Wicked Ways*, etc., it will be those same theatre owners and local presenters who make substantial incomes. Most of those productions were writer/director/performer-driven with non-union cast. It's very important that we distinguish non-profit producing organizations from the individual director/writer/actor; the very high quality of an August Wilson play on tour to a Chitlin Circuit play.

Traditional non-profits and traditional commercial theatre producers need each other. So, what's the problem? *First*, it would have to be *each producer needs to satisfy the artistic ego*—whoever has the financial clout will insist on having the artistic clout. Each small New York non-profit gambles between $135,000 to $150,000 that its artistic vision is correct; if it's correct (critically and popularly) that non-profit doesn't want the commercial producer changing the play in the pick-up. Most of the time that's exactly what happens. *Second,* commercial producers are almost always white. Their first thought is how will white audiences like the play? The commercial producer will spend every advertising dollar available in white media. Commercial producers always assume the non-profit's hit is an accident. He'll show them how it should really be produced.

The commercial theatre, which is controlled by the League of Broadway Producers and Managers, should be levied an extra dollar per ticket and that amount would be given to non-profits. Non-profit producers need to be union-protected just as playwrights, directors, and actors are.

No matter how we say it, commercial theatre is in the business of making profit for its investors; they're in the business of selling $55 tickets. In that ticket price is $20 worth of advertising to get individuals to buy that ticket. Most of the time they need a media "star" to sell.

The non-profit theatre is in the business of developing artists. Minority non-profits go to Federal, State, and City funding sources for primary funding. Donors, sponsors, and contributors are, as I've said, a misnomer in Black Theatre. Like successful white theatre artists, Black artists who develop their craft in Black non-profits should try to give something back. Unlike commercial producers, non-profit ticket cost is about $35; very little in that amount is for advertising. We expect funding from grants and corporations to make up 33 percent of our total production cost. *It does that for white non-profits.* It doesn't come anywhere near that for Black Theatres. Thus, we never have money to pay our artists or to pay for advertising.

Yes, we both need each other. Yes, non-profits have worked with commercial producers in the past. Should we merge the non-profit and commercial theatre? Definitely not; whoever finances the production will have the clout.

A study in methods of non-profit producing can be noted in the Lloyd Richards / August Wilson / Yale Connection. (Note: I didn't include the

Eugene O'Neill Theatre Center because I don't think all of August Wilson's plays were read there.) This connection is, first, with a genius director who captured the imagination of the white power brokers in the American Theatre. Second, August Wilson seems to be a writer with a passion — nothing less than a mission!

Lloyd Richards took the Wilson plays on a journey; that journey can be defined as artistic — giving the play time; giving the playwright time to rewrite, to restructure, etc. But most of the time that isn't the case. It's simply to get more reviews, more publicity, to get the right set of actors working together, etc. And, yes, it's prestigious to have a Pulitzer Prize winner in your season, in your city, and the critics do come out en masse. Thus, the not-for-profit!!

Finally, let's examine the role of playwright, director, actor, and non-profit producer in the journey from not-for-profit to commercial theatre.

The playwright makes very little money in the not-for-profit. The play-wright gets 5 to 10 percent against a $37,500 advance for a play in the commercial theatre. In general, the playwright wants the merger.

The director gets very little money in the not-for-profit. However, in the commercial theatre there's the SSDC fee — as much as $45,500 for a Broadway play and 2 percent of weekly box office gross. The director usually wants the merger.

The actor is protected by AEA. In the non-profit theatre an actor's salary can be anywhere from zero to $600 per week. In the commercial theatre, the salary can be anywhere from $600 off Broadway, per week to $1,500 on Broadway, per week. An actor usually wants the merger.

The original producer usually is a non-profit organization; the need for visibility and cash are always in the forefront of his mind. However, the commercial producer knows this and will promise the non-profit producers the world. Yet in most cases he'll lose all artistic and financial control. In the end he seldom gets what's promised. The experienced non-profit producer usually won't want the merger. If he has a good contract with the writer, he can control the merger and the fee coming into the theatre.

Black Theatre and so-called Ethnic Theatre attract audiences that, as a rule, aren't "Broadway" audiences. Organizations have been set up to reach this new audience but few have found any success. This isn't an audience that reads *The New York Times*; it's not an audience that follows theatre as religiously as we might like; it's not an audience a producer can count on, unless he's willing to produce a certain kind of play; and finally it cannot afford to spend seventy-five dollars for an evening out, not to mention dinner and taxis. I know there are cheap seats available, but that's exactly what that audience doesn't want. Its whole life has been a series of cheap seats.

The audience that the Black Theatre and the Ethnic Theatre attracts is looking for comfort and relaxation. This means they want to feel welcome in the theatre. And I found this to be true in our audience from 13 to 60 years of age. We artists sometimes forget that the rules and regulations we take for granted can be unfamiliar to our new audience. In some cases, little things like responses to what's happening on stage can cause undue embarrassment in traditional theatres. In other cases it might be leaving at the intermission of a bad play, thinking it's over. If we're not going to make our audience feel comfortable, why should they be bothered?

Non-profit Black Theatre shouldn't be subject to the same union rules as theatre for profit. Our audience cannot support theatre owners, *The New York Times*, and union rules designed for profit theatre and based on what white Americans can afford to pay for a seat.

Cost of productions have risen, but not the income of ticket buyers. There are people in this country who can not pay $60 per seat; and you can't keep on producing the same kind of theatre in N.Y.C.; there's a new audience here. The old audience doesn't live here anymore.

America's economy is based on its political climate. Indeed, the social conditions in this country are directly related to its politics. Therefore, the cultural arts — including theatre, dance, music, and film — flourish and regress according to the economic and social conditions. Art is political, both in its production and in its distribution. We Black artists are as controlled in our art as we are in influencing social and economic change.

In the Sixties and Seventies it was politically expedient to support the founding of The Harlem School of the Arts, The Negro Ensemble Company, The New Lafayette Theatre, The Dance Theatre of Harlem, The Free Southern Theatre, and so forth. Why? Because the country was in turmoil and we Blacks didn't believe in the American Dream anymore. And no amount of rhetoric from our politicians could make us believe. To stop the destruction of the cities, we were given token handouts, handouts which supported many whites who happened to be experts in the administration of the politics of art. Then, in the Eighties, these very same people were the ones suggesting these cultural programs be cut or merged into white-controlled organizations which, by virtue of their supposed administrative skills, should save taxpayers their hard-earned money.

Our problems, our crisis, is that we want our art appreciated by white Americans and, frankly, they don't want it. When they reject it, we then want to sell it to our Black brothers and sisters. It won't be bought; it cannot, because the sale's price is based on what white Americans pay, not on what Black Americans can afford. What white America really wants is Willie Best, Mantan Moreland, George Jefferson, and a minstrel clown dancing for Ronald Reagan and George Bush (both father and son).

Politically speaking, if white Americans accept our art, they, in a matter of speaking, accept us. And they're not ready to do that. If our art is to their taste, they'll have one of their artists imitate it and then sell it back to us, the original creators. It's important to note here and now that because of our economic and social condition we're easily influenced by money and class status. One or two of our race are raised to great heights and we're eager to attain the same status. We've been down so long that anything looks like up.

We writers, actors, dancers, painters, filmmakers, know we're good at our craft. We had the turbulent Sixties to move us socially; we had the Seventies to sharpen our economic understanding of our work. Federal, city, state, and even some private foundations helped us to this current place in American art. Now, what's left except total acceptance into the American mainstream of all aspects of its art? The question, then, is: Will we Black Americans be accepted?

Back in the day the Reagan Administration tried to tell us something by cutting all social art (read Black Arts) programs by as much as 50 percent. For Reagan it seemed important that we return to the image of our happy-go-lucky selves. We didn't need to be trained or disciplined for that. At millennium, the 9/11 tragedy is moving art subsidy to privatization. Privatization is also the way of depriving without racial backlash.

Woodie King, Jr.

Because America is basically a racist society and steeped in European tradition, white Americans won't support, in any great degree, real indigenous American Art. Therefore, individual contributions from white Americans to Black artists and Black institutions will never be substantial. The few Blacks who are in the 50 percent tax bracket are giving to our Civil Rights organizations. Black arts are at the bottom of a very large pile which includes education, religion, poverty, hunger, housing and high employment.

It's sad to reveal what other governments contribute to their arts: Canada contributes three times as much; Great Britain, five times as much; Denmark, seventeen times as much; and France contributes twenty-six times as much as our government. Perhaps they understand the politics of art.

The best thing for the stability of the arts is a partnership with business, individuals, and our government. Black arts are void of the first two — business and individuals. It's very sad that our Black businesses don't support our Black artists or our Black institutions.

Sometimes I think that we, like legendary bluesman Robert Johnson (who was poisoned by a jealous husband in 1938), must have made a pact with the Devil to work in the so-called professional theatre. We ethnic and multicultural people are trained in Eurocentric institutions like the University of Massachusetts, Wayne State, New York University, Stanford, UCLA, City College, etc. What we all have in common are histories, from birth to adulthood, that are common and yet very unique. What some of us believe is that we have the answer to Black, Latino, and Asian problems in America. As individuals *we do not*. The theatre I produce isn't an answer to America's problems but, to varying degrees, a response to these problems. But whether I produce an Asian, Black, white or Latino play, I won't go outside that culture for its artistic vision.

At New Federal Theatre, we work under certain restrictions imposed by the union, by Actor's Equity. We must also face certain implications in our application to the National Endowment for the Arts or New York State Council for the Arts. Beyond the restrictions of unions and grant-makers are the challenges of working with actors, technicians, and designers who happen to be minorities but think European, as a result of their educational process and the society.

The Impact of Race

As multicultural artists here in America, our work as a whole tends to be ignored. It's very simple — if mainstream America accepts our work, they accept us. They're not yet ready to do that. Traditional acceptance hasn't been acceptance but control. Control always depends on who signs the checks. Control on Broadway is usually through the managers and the financiers. What little influence we can exert as artists — director, writer, actor — comes from gains made by that artist's union. Critics are part of mainstream America. The newspapers, magazines, and television outlets they represent aren't really about changing the perception of the media they represent. Why are there so few black journalists covering culture in major white media? Because they'd speak on both black and white culture? Do any of us really foresee a black writing regularly on Lincoln Center, Kennedy Center, the Metropolitan, the Mark Taper in Los Angeles?

There are no relationships between my theatre and the commercial theatre except that in New York City the same critic covers both *and* the audiences don't really know the difference between what I'm doing and what Broadway and off-Broadway are doing. Ticket prices at my theatre are $30, ticket prices Off-Broadway about $55, ticket prices on-Broadway about $75. Most of the non-profit theatres have built a small and local constituency over the years; that constituency also attends productions at other non-profit theatres. If, by chance, we should accidentally get a "good" review, the general public that generally patronizes only mainstream theatre will buy our tickets.

People of color do support our theatre. To sustain this support we must remember not to price the audience away from us. We must not bullshit that audience — our aesthetics, our cultural commonality must be within the truth of our characters, we must really love our people. Our people are everywhere: here, in the Caribbean, in Africa, England, etc. We can support our own art and we must see our audience as part of a global community.

One could spend a lifetime trying to solve the many problems hindering the growth of Black Theatre at the present time. I believe the only people who can solve these problems are those who work in Black Theatre, who love it, who've given their lives to its fulfillment.

My own theatre, the New Federal Theatre, like most theatres across the country which deal in minority theatre in general and Black theatre in particular, is faced with unbelievable hardships, not only in terms of the financial problems but also a scarcity of directors and playwrights— who've given up the theatre because they couldn't make a living in it.

New Federal Theatre has been able to exist because of the generosity of the Henry Street Settlement. We produce three plays a year, and because we believe in making opportunities available to people who work in the theatre, the same directors and actors seldom appear twice in one season. We're an open and a tolerant group. In our company are students who have come to New York to work as actors, directors, and technicians. Those interested need only send us a résumé to schedule an appointment for a new beginning.

Ghetto Art and Energy

"Consider one small island known as the Cultural Arts Program, sponsored by Mobilization For Youth in this city. It has been a refuge and inspiration for creative, underprivileged kids whose talents had too long remained hidden in the smog of the streets. They have written and produced their own films and plays; their dance group has staged notable performances; their painting and choral groups have stirred impressive efforts."

— From a New York *Post* editorial

I graduated from Will-o-Way School of Theatre in 1962 and after a series of events in Detroit—starting Concept-East Theatre, producing and directing and acting in ten to fifteen new plays, meeting Langston Hughes, etc.—I headed for New York City in early 1964 in a play by Rev. Malcolm Boyd. Because we thought our Blackness and our culture must be embraced, we worked in Black Theatre.

The year 1964 was a fervent time to be in New York City. Black Power! Black is Beautiful! Nationalism! Malcolm X killed! The Harlem riots of 1964. *I am a witness! I was there!* (James Baldwin said it in *The Fire Next Time* and *Notes of a Native Son.*)

I am in New York City in 1964 at a time when all of these things were happening. Certainly Yankolovich's *New Rules in a World Turned Upside Down* applied to these times. But my advantage was, I had produced, written, and acted in Detroit for over six years. Yes, I was in the right place at the right time! However, Black Artists must always be in the right place at the right time.

33

The Impact of Race

The play that brought me to NYC was *Study in Color*. We toured through the Episcopal Society for Racial and Cultural Unity. We played Episcopal churches across the U.S. When we arrived in New York we played at St. Mark's Church in the Bowery on Second Avenue. It was there, one block away, that Black artists like James Earl Jones starred in *Blood Knot*. St. Mark's Playhouse produced *The Blacks*, LeRoi Jones' (Amiri Baraka) *The Slave* and *The Toilet*, *Day of Absence* and *Happy Ending* (produced by Robert Hooks, written by Douglas Turner Ward), and eventually that theatre housed the Negro Ensemble Company.

A block away, jazz clubs like The Five Spot had Thelonius Monk, Miles Davis, Max Roach. In the same area, Café La Mama, Slugs and all played to full houses. Television and videocassettes had not yet taken the audience.

In 1966 Robert Hooks (a leading actor at the time) was asked to run a training program for young Blacks, Hispanics, and Asians. He didn't want to interrupt his career. He recommended me.

At 26 years of age, I became the director of a training program in the arts at MFY with a budget of $575,000. These programs within "The Great Society" were designed to fail. However, ours didn't fail. I designed it based on the structure of my drama school in Bloomfield Hills, Michigan.

We trained young people in:

    Dance — Rod Rodger

    Drama — Ed Cambridge, Cliff Frazier

    Music — Garrett Morris, Eva Texter

    Art — Jay Milder, Peter Martinez

    Film — Where young people first made their own

We exposed our students to world culture:

    30 to Rome

    50 to Exposition 1967 in Montreal

    40 to HemisFair 1968 in San Antonio

In the 1970/71 season our program moved to the historic Henry Street Settlement. It was at Henry Street that I formed a separate producing theatre, New Federal Theatre. We needed a place for our training to work.

For the first six years of New Federal Theatre, admission was free. NFT also had one hit per year for seven years in a row. *Black Girl, What the Winesellers Buy, The Taking of Miss Jane, for colored girls...* About 95 percent of the plays we produced were new plays; 75 percent of those new plays were written by Black playwrights.

In 1969 I produced *A Black Quartet* (four one-act plays by Baraka, Bullins, Caldwell, and Milner) off-Broadway for $30,000; in 1988 *Checkmates*, a four-character play by Milner cost $850,000 for Broadway. The budget for an off-Broadway production of *Checkmates* was $350,000. The income of the people who put up the money for *A Black Quartet* in 1969 didn't increase twenty times so that they could invest in *Checkmates* in 1988. For a producer to go out and raise that kind of money, when those who invest are so strapped financially they can hardly exist, takes a special kind of playwright-producer relationship. First, the play must connect to some sensitive chord within the producer's psyche. Then it must, in some way, attempt to connect to the Black theatergoing public in particular as well as the traditional audience in general.

Why will I produce certain playwrights? Avoid others? Probably the commonality of experiences, or language. Those are intangibles. It has something to do with taste; with culture; with vision. Can the intangibles be taught like the craft of playwrighting? I'm not sure. Yet, I am sure one comes to producing through an acquired taste for Black art and Black culture. Producers may have taste and culture but lack vision. Also, the vision of the playwright may not be the same as the vision of the producer. We hear about that happening a lot in Hollywood.

How does a playwright connect with a producer? First, the playwright must visit a lot of theatres; study the repertory of those theatres that interest him. Find out a theatre's personality (it's usually the personality of the artistic director). If the writer is honest he'll soon realize where his work fits. On the other hand, producers roam the country, visiting readings, workshops, listening to other writers talk; in search of that innovative new voice, the new visionary—someone to tell him something he's already known, but in a language, a style, and an arrogance entirely new.

To understand our program, you must understand the community it represents. Its residents are the classic urban American mixture—Jews, Puerto Ricans, Blacks, Chinese, Italians, and many others, brought together by choice, by the immigrant tradition, poverty. Only one out of five adults has completed high school. Blacks comprise only 10 percent; yet three quarters of the public school children are Black and Puerto Rican.

As I write, we're in the midst of the fourth major disorder this week. The first two were intramural. The second was directed at the Police Department's Tactical Patrol Force, which represents the thoughts and feelings of the establishment exclusively. When the Tactical Patrol Force visits our neighborhood, the only piece of equipment they don't bring is a tank. Within this tension, the Cultural Arts Program is producing plays, films, dance concerts, music concerts, and art workshops in the streets and amphitheatres of the Lower East Side, the most unusual community in New York City. Our arts program isn't interested in the arts and culture projected by Doris Day, Rudolph Nureyev, or Andy Warhol.

The Cultural Arts Program of Mobilization For Youth (MFY) began in the summer of 1965 to give young people in the area a real chance at professional experience and training via the arts as they relate to everyday life. This was appealing because it said in essence that there's an art form in the ghetto. And since I believe this form, and its content, is a thousand times more eloquent, more relevant, and considerably more useful to the nation than anyone is willing to concede, I was drawn to this program. Actually, it goes beyond the ghetto because there's a kind of *first anger* in the film, music, art, and drama—and I think it's tough and honest enough to make us see that this art form is relevant to all of us. That's how it's always been in this country: the new citizen, angry because it's not the way he dreamed it would be, but come hell or high water he's going to make it that way. Those are the fellows that revive our art, our nation's self respect. What we're trying to do down here in the Lower East Side of New York is turn bricks into sentences, suppressed intellectual energy into art. (In the near future, Rap and Hiphop will be instrumental in defining the culture.)

Our first project was the play *Dope!* by Maryat Lee. The play was performed on the streets of the neighborhoods that breed the narcotics problem. While mothers hung out of tenement windows and young boys lounged on fire escapes, many who'd never even seen a play before got their first taste of theatre that related to their lives. In fact, *Dope!* was so real to some members of the audience that they got up on the stage to dance during a party scene and later hissed at the hero when he started to take a fix. They, you see, knew something about the hero's life that the hero didn't know. And they wanted that young man to make the right decisions. An old woman junkie begged the hero not to take the drugs, telling him to look at her, see what dope had done to her. I was reminded of something Malraux wrote in *Man's Fate*: "We hear our own voice with our throat, we hear voices of others with our ears."

In the beginning our important programs were theatre, modern dance, choral music, and fine arts. We added a film unit because it gives young people a sense of immediate visual results from group participation. We're also aware that an instrumental music training program is necessary. There's a need for a community orchestra that can understand the richness and beauty of both black music and Spanish music.

We have sixty young people in this program, two teachers for each twelve students. These teachers are top professionals, performers, and artists. Through them, the young people can see where they can go and what can happen to them when they get there. I try to select men teachers who project strong masculine images or women teachers who think young. The students respect working professionals. They can use those images as a substitute for what they lack at home: often, in the ghetto community, it's the father. In our program, the teachers must know their Black history and Spanish history. In the ghetto where we work, we want people to feel a tremendous pride in being Black or Puerto Rican.

All decisions are made by the group doing the project. If it's a film, then the young people in the film department decide on the content and direction of that film. These discussions, often heated, last for about a week. In this way, the content will always be directed toward the social problems of the community in which the youngsters are living. For example, one year the drama group wanted to do Odet's *Waiting for Lefty*. However, they changed the play from a taxicab strike to a rent strike. Even though it wasn't Odets, it was an exciting piece of theatre. The people of the community related immediately to the play's problems.

We don't justify our program solely on the grounds that it provides underprivileged youngsters with vocational training and some promise of future security. The concentrated study of cultural arts disciplines will provide a practical knowledge about performing arts, and be helpful to those who might later become interested in a related profession in theatre, television, costume, or set design, in administration of programs concerned with the arts, in commitments to other arts or crafts, or in any effort, expression, or observation that may be enhanced by heightened esthetic sensitivity.

But we're also interested in using dance training, music training, theatre training, and film training with the highest possible standards as vehicles to help these trainees develop into responsible, resourceful professionals. We expect them to learn to communicate ideas and feelings, to learn to approach simple problems creatively, to understand that to accomplish worthwhile things often requires patience and persistence more than inspiration. We expect them to learn that the human body and the human voice are the vehicle and instrument of the spirit and intellect; that suppressed intellectual energy can be expressed creatively rather than physically. And we expect them to appreciate that the cultivated primary human instrument is capable of enormous power and subtle expression.

What We've Done and Where We're Going

We began with street theatre. We wanted plays that could speak to ghetto audiences, that, in the language of the ghetto, would deal with issues meaningful and important to its people. We wanted plays that accurately said what the actors were really thinking as youngsters living in the ghetto. Along with *Dope!* we put on *Charades on East Fourth Street. Charades* is tough. A policeman is held captive by a Lower East Side gang. The gang members debate the fate of the cop in a succession of violent scenes. The arguments used by the gang members were actually taken from discussions and interviews held by playwright-in-residence Lonnie Elder with the youngsters. When *Charades* made its official off-Broadway debut at the New Dramatist Workshop, a reviewer from *Show Business* lavishly praised the acting of MFY youngsters. MFY brought the play to Expo '67, when the Cultural Arts group was invited to present its outstanding works at the Youth Pavilion. *Charades* was a new kind of theatre with a new breed of actors and a new voice. It's the theatre of our own violent, vengeful times.

Later, street theatre moved away from the young and angry to become Broadway-in-the-street. The New School started a course called "Introduction to Street Theatre," $70, strictly middle-class. We hope to find other new directions that are as relevant as street theatre used to be.

Our program pioneered filmmaking by the young. It all started when the Brooks Foundation of Santa Barbara gave Mobilization a $10,000 grant to start a film workshop. The group began shooting after a few weeks of preparation. Occasionally, members asked the advice of professional actors, directors, and cameramen who were on call, but they did all the actual work themselves.

What came out at the end of ten weeks was *You Dig It?*, a largely auto-biographical account by drama group member Leon Williams, 17, who wrote the script and played the lead role. Under the direction of Richard Mason, the film was shot in the streets and alleys of the Lower East Side and on sets designed and built by the MFY Fine Arts Group.

Even before it was completed, the film was generating excitement; once it was released, the response snowballed. Lincoln Center premiered the film; WABC-TV presented a screening and discussion; Expo '67 invited MFY to show *You Dig It?* at the Youth Pavilion in August of 1967 and HemisFair '68 invited us in August of 1968.

Everywhere, the film was praised. Somehow, these youngsters who'd never before made a film had connected with a subject very close to their own lives. Using their talents as artists, they brought off a film which has been applauded as "an exciting and significant contribution to the stream of creative work now emerging from urban ghettos."

The Game, a film made by Roberta Hodes with youngsters of MFY's Cultural Arts Program, earned a Plaque of the Lion of St. Mark at the Venice Documentary and Short Film Festival.

The film was based on a play be George Houston Bass, a young Black playwright and former member of the Cultural Arts staff, who went on to a scholarship at the Yale Drama School. Shot entirely on the Lower East Side, *The Game* focused on a group of Black and Puerto Rican teenagers chanting children's games, which mimic their own world and the whole of society. MFY had a hard time keeping up with requests for showings and stories about the film.

A third film, *Ghetto*, directed by Richard Mason, won the young director a position as associate producer of the WABC-TV program, *Like It Is*.

We also started a dance group. They, too, performed at Expo '67 and HemsiFair '68. Some had never danced before joining the MFY Company.

Rod Rodgers, the professional dancer and choreographer who was the group's first instructor, explains that he tries to build on the natural movement of these youngsters and therefore created mostly jazz and primitive dances for them. *Primitive Suite*, for example, was an abbreviated version of a 45-minute ballet originally choreographed by Rodgers for an Afro-Cuban dance company. *Jazz Piece* was a provocative work which asks, "What do you expect us to be like?" and challenged the audience's stereotype of the Black dancer.

The group was enthusiastically received by the dance community. Several of the dancers entered professional careers. Evelyn Thomas, one of the original group members without any previous training, won a dance scholarship to the Julliard School of Music in competition with other dancers from all over the country. It remains a dance group that finds its artistry in the poverty and violence which mark the lives of its own performers. This is a crucial, ongoing component of the MFY Cultural Arts Program, to help articulate the voice of the ghetto.

Racism cannot be fought at a distance—it must be met face to face.

The only way that the young Blacks and Puerto Ricans that I work with feel that racism can be destroyed is through communication—by putting a painting or a picture before the eyes of white America, one so real that she cannot mistake its contents.

Our young people make films that they've written, produced, directed and edited. There can be no mistake on what the problem is. The films strive to communicate with white America.

The films are art, and art may be one route to the solution. A kind of first anger in the art and the films may be just tough enough and honest enough to save us all.

Communication must take place. For the whites as for the Blacks, even the safe community where people try to live in harmony, try to respect each other, will find that danger lurks for them if the next block, or the next town, is abandoned to the junkies and thieves.

One must pass through Harlem to get to Westchester.

Searching for Brothers Kindred — Rhythm & Blues of the Fifties

Remember the Good Old Days!
Moonglows, Flamingoes,
Orioles! Coasters, Dells, Harptones, etc.

Why have we nostalgically graduated towards groups in our search for Blackness? Rhythm and Blues? Even gangs, and families? We've always felt saddened by their disappearance, by their death, by their downfall. We remember when so-and-so used to sing with the [fill in the blank] group, when someone else was killed by the [fill in the blank] gang, and when the [fill in the blank] family moved out of town. Is it because they are all a part of us?

With Rhythm and Blues groups, the companies or labels like Roulette, Atlantic, Mercury, Chess, Gee, Dootone, Vee Jay, King, Chance, Bluebird, Okeh, Specialty, Natural, Jubilee, End, Herald-Ember, Federal, Rama, and so many smaller labels which were really subsidiaries of the larger labels, did not treat the progression as a graduation for a new Black music. Right off, you should know that we all know who was responsible for the exploitation.

They thought they knew more about our Blackness than we did. And that they were the ones who'd manage, produce, and sign us to contracts that not even they could understand. And they'd pay us one-cent royalty and we seldom got that. Ertegun, Feld, Ram, Shiffman, Wexler, Leiber, Stoller, Dowd, Levy, Treadwell, Bacharach, Asch, Lomax, Freed, etc. And we let them do it! If this isn't true, all the groups were happy. They all got a fair count. None were insane, alcoholics, or junkies. Little Willie John, Frankie Lyman, Hudie Ledbetter, James Sheppard and Clyde McPhatter, one of the founders of the R&B movement, did not die broke and heartbroken. These people who came to control our music also exploited our street gangs and destroyed our families. And it's all because we let them. We let them because we didn't understand why we were together in the first place or the value of what we created.

In the early Fifties our rhythm was a studied mannerism. We lived by it. Some called it names like cool, hip, fine, pimp, game, etc. Our dress helped to define it. Shoes, pants, shirt, and hat. Our friends also defined us by their association with us. We were all peacocks; our rhythm and our lives existed in direct relation to our sexual prowess. If we'd made a baby by the time we were 15 or 16, we were given the title of *men* or *women*. It was important that our progression from boys and girls be ahead of us.

Our blues at the time was our need to ignore the reality of our situation. The situation was as unreal as our existing reality. Blues, which Ralph Ellison has described as suppressed intellectual energy expressed physically. What we'd learned in the early Fifties was to express all those problems we had at that early age, all those problems we knew existed with our mothers and fathers, our sisters and cousins, our aunts and uncles; what we had learned was to hide it from that other world in another lifestyle. The ability to hide it was our rhythm. The knowledge of it was our blues.

Our rhythm and our blues. Rhythm and Blues. That's what our groups were called in the Fifties. If we look back to the Forties and on back to the Thirties, we know Ma Rainey, Bessie Smith, Hudie Ledbetter, and Blind Lemon were progressions to the present. To move out of that, out of a definition of it, we moved into the Sixties, into the rock and roll of it, and on into the soul of it. But now, looking back to my formative years of the early Fifties, most events remembered are Rhythm and Blues benchmarks. This is a memory; a benchmark. I will try and recall Gwen Lewis of that period. When I think of the music of the period, I think of her. She was my starting point.

42

She lived in this America. The Detroit of the automobile. Her family was not all together. A father was missing. Her cousins or uncles and most of their lives were affected by the steel mills and the automobile plants in that city. She lived on the northend. There were other ends like the southend, westend, eastend. These ends only meant that Black people, at that time, moved no further in that direction. In this northend, Gwen lived on Chandler and Oakland. She loved R&B music. She especially loved Billy Ward and the Dominoes.

Later I'd return to the area. It would be after high school nearing 1957. I'd carry with me a melancholy mood; a forced loneliness. I'd be searching for little signs that would indicate that I had not existed and would not exist in vain. This mood of the time was so evident among most of us. We were at the end of one movement and at the beginning of another. We who'd finished high school at such great odds were now trying to find some indication that the next step was in us. How do I remember that end of 1956? No, not by graduating high school, but by a record of The Heartbeats, "A Thousand Miles Away" as sung by James (Shep) Sheppard. It was one of the big hits of 1956. Its emotional and religious impact touched me directly because I wanted all my women friends to be reincarnations of Gwen Lewis. I wanted to suffer her loss.

You're a thousand miles away
But I still have your love to remember you by

We all suffered Shep's loss in the dawning Seventies, after the Black revolution of the Sixties. Shep was killed by gangsters.

ITEM: *Variety*, August 2, 1972:

N.Y. POLICE EXEC TIES ROULETTE RECORDS WITH MAFIA:
LEVY DENIES IT.

Allegations that Roulette Records is linked to organized crime have been made by William McCarthy, Deputy N.Y. police commissioner for organized crime control. McCarthy, speaking on the Victor Reisel show on WEVD, N.Y., Monday

night (7/31/72) said that Tommy (Ryan) Eboli, a reputed
Mafia Figure who was killed in gangland style in Brooklyn
a couple of weeks ago, was general manager for sales and
promotion for Promo Records, a distributor in Paterson, N.J.

McCarthy said that Promo Records was interlocked with
Roulette Records since both companies had the same president, Morris Levy, whom he did not name.

McCarthy said that Eboli's salary was $1 per week.

In the early Fifties, the South wasn't far behind. It had been the South
of Jackson, Mobile, Baldwin Springs, and Bessmer, Alabama. I tell you this
now because I want you to understand our common ground. Mine was
1949. At that time I was 11 years old. And at that time in Detroit, there'd
be movies at the Grant Theater on Russell Street. There'd be R&B shows at
the Echo Theater on Oakland. There'd be Barthwell's Ice Cream, and there
would also be discoveries in an unheard of area of the northend which only
us 11-year-olds knew existed. To us, as I look back, it must have been something like Columbus discovering America.

The family (our group) consisted of my mother and I, my aunt and her
two children, cousin Errol and cousin Gwen. We lived on Oakland and
Euclid in a very small three-room apartment. Our family worked for white
people. All our neighbors worked for white people. The pimps and the
hustlers and the singers did not work for white people, we thought. So, in
all honesty, we children had two roads cut for us. We'd be like our parents
or we'd be like the pimps, the hustlers, or the R&B singers.

A man would come by about once a month. He'd been a friend of my
aunt's husband. They went hunting together in years past for possums and
coons. He was very sad but his laughter would affect us all. He carried a
lot of photographs from World War II. He'd show them to us and we'd ask
questions. There were many dead bodies in the photographs. Sometimes
the man would cry and tell us through tear-filled eyes to stick together. My
mother always offered him a drink and he always refused. I wanted to tell
you about "Golden Teardrops" by the Flamingoes but when I hear the
lyrics I think of the man with the photographs and his tears.

Woodie King, Jr.

Golden Teardrop
I remember when/you
Fell/ from the eyes of my love/

The Grady Family lived across the hall. Mister and Mrs. Grady, the daughter, and James Grady. James was 13. He had a paper route. He delivered the Pittsburgh *Courier* and The Michigan *Chronicle*. He had money. He'd take us to the Echo Theater to see the R&B shows. He could sing bass. He could sing "Sixty Minute Man" just like the Dominoes. He knew Little Willie John and Sugar Chile Robinson who lived near us. James' sister was older. She had large piles of records. She'd play "Crying in the Chapel" for hours. Then she'd play "Baby, Please Don't Go." She had an old gramophone and she'd wind it very slowly so that the music would *sound good*.

But "Crying in the Chapel" was her favorite. She said listening to it was like being in church.

You saw me crying in the chapel
The tears I shed were tears of joy

The records had cost her 49 cents each. She didn't mind spending that much money because she was in love with Sonny Till. She had all the Orioles records: "It's Too Soon to Know"; "Baby, Please Don't Go"; "Forgive and Forget." She'd let us sit and listen if we were very quiet.

Gwen Lewis was my girlfriend. She was my girl simply because that's the way I wanted it. We never talked about it; we talked about other things. My friend James taught me how to kiss Gwen. He'd demonstrate by kissing her, telling me to watch.

Our group was James Grady, my cousins, and a boy named James Mathews.

Gwen Lewis and I would walk home from Breitmeyer School. She was upset on this last walk because Clyde McPhatter had said he was going to leave Billy Ward and the Dominoes. Her two favorite songs were "The Bells" and "Have Mercy Mercy, Baby." She'd sing "The Bells" like Clyde:

There were four black horses
With eyes of flaming red...

I'd tell her I was scared of songs about death. We would sit on her porch and we'd hold hands. She'd always sing to me like in the movies. She'd deliberately imitate some white singer singing to a guy in a film. We'd end up laughing.

One day, not long after that walk, she moved away. I went to her house. It was empty. No one knew where the family had moved. James tried to help me find her. But she left no signs. She was not part of any group. She was alone.

Now try and understand the loss of a first love. It was the end of a created fantasy world of tomorrow. Our ghetto contained us. We dreamed beyond it. Most of us selected a secret someone to transcend the place with. I selected Gwen Lewis — selected her too soon and without her knowledge or my knowledge of it. Do you understand what your first loss was like? By definition of things past and forever lost to one who never had anything to lose, a relationship is golden, a companion is forever. If the loss is a first loss, it will move you to a group that you can merge into. It did that for me. If you wore Mr. B. (Billy Eckstine) shirts, Stetson shoes, Dobbs or Knox 20's, Hi-lo Shirts from Hot Sams, gang warred with the Shakers, danced at the Madison, rollerskated at the Archadia, you probably know what I mean. A group was necessary; a group was golden. I want to believe that the R&B groups came together through the same understanding. Why else would I listen to them and enjoy them so?

School was a discovery. At 11 years old and straight from Alabama, the Detroit school system awaited me. The system welcomed me by putting me back to the first grade. It was not uncommon to put Black children from the south two or three grades behind. The Southern school system was supposed to be so terrible. I was at the mercy of this system as most Black children are. Most of our fathers and mothers couldn't speak for us. My mother couldn't talk to white people. It's part of what we've come to understand as the *perpetual lie*. The white person is lying, the Black listener knows it. The white liar becomes vicious for being caught at lying. To counter that, the Black listener refuses to refute the white liar or even to look him in the face. So, at 11 years, I was in the first grade. I know now it was because I spoke *Black English* and had learned to exist in another rhythm. But the next five years, I attended summer school and I came out ahead of the system. It was due to the help of one teacher, a Mr. Finger.

He was an art teacher at Breitmeyer. I loved art. I loved to draw Cisco Kid, John Garfield, and Black horses. Mr. Finger would teach me in his spare time; always taking the class to places like the Art Institute and urging us when we formed singing groups. He'd often say, young man — I wonder if he ever knew my name — young man, *we have to stick together as a Black group, as a Black family.*

Julius Williams was the terror of the school. He was 16. He enjoyed fighting teachers and singing in class. He had a singing group and a gang. When the teacher left the room he'd always sing, "One Mint Julip" by the Clovers.

One of his best friends was a member of the Five Jets. They became very popular for a tune called, "I Got It." It was rumored that after Julius graduated from Moore Intermediate School for Boys he joined the Shaker Gang. It was also rumored that he made a record with the Royal Jokers.

In the years 1952-55 we listened to the onslaught of R&B music. We didn't call it that until some years later. But we did try to sing it and some of us were successful. Many groups were split by the Korean War. Members of singing groups and gangs were drafted or joined. Families were heartbroken when relatives were killed. As boys came home others joined or got drafted. They all said they were going to kill some Koreans. Very few felt they'd be killed.

ITEM: JANUARY, 1952,

DETROIT'S NEGRO POPULATION WAS 300,000

We moved to the East Side. I had to leave behind my group. All the gains I felt I'd made at that young age had to be left behind. I thought the world would end for me. I'd never find Gwen Lewis. Why did we have to move, I thought, right at the time I was so popular; right at the time all the students and teachers knew that I really existed? And most importantly, right at the time I was appointed captain of the safety patrol? Surely, I thought, there'd be no streetcars as far as the East Side. No Grant or Echo Theaters.

We lived on Heidelberg Street between Elmwood and Ellery. We had the downstairs flat. Upstairs lived the Brown Family. Mr. and Mrs. Brown, their son Lincoln and the daughter, Juanita. Juanita would be murdered a few years later in Brooklyn and her killer wouldn't be found. Next door, on our right, lived the McNeal Family. The family consisted of four brothers and three sisters. Ernest McNeal became one of my best friends. On our left, I remember a Mr. and Mrs. Cooper. I remember he was a master at poker, Tonk and Blackjack. My uncle and Mr. Cooper were partners. They'd travel miles to find a card game. I mention the people, as I knew them — part of a family.

At Smith School, next to Franklin Settlement, I met Leonard Brown, Willie Jackson, and John French. We were members of the Settlement. And after the Settlement closed at ten o'clock, we hung out at Herndon's candy store on Elmwood. Our days and our evenings were discoveries of the games, the girls, and the music there. The northend was far behind. And as Langston Hughes has told us, when one is on a borderline, *the distance between here and there is nowhere.* We all could sing. We sang in the lounge of the Settlement and we sang on the corner in front of Herndon's candy store. Ernest and John could sing better. Ernest was a tenor; he could sing "Blue Moon." John was a bass; he, like James Grady, could sing "Sixty Minute Man." I was a Clovers' fan. I'd sing lead on "Yes, It's You." We'd make our piano intro with our voices and go into it:

> Whaaa aaahh
> Makes my love come tumblin' dooownn
> Makes a lover from a cloown

Most of the groups that rehearsed at the Settlement had all been together for a long time. The relationship went beyond the mere singing. The Diablos used to rehearse "The Wind" there long before it was recorded. It's one of the most beautiful R&B songs ever recorded. And Nolan Strong's high lead voice is one of the most beautifully controlled tenors in R&B music.

> Wind/ wind
> Bloo-ooh wind

And Nolan would rap to the girl, telling her how beautiful it *had* been. Then, he'd sing to us again:

Woodie King, Jr.

I know she has gone
But my love lingers on

Marvin Black who lived down the street from me at Heidelberg and Elmwood rehearsed at the Settlement with his group. He changed his name to Marv Johnson when he left his group. Marv was one of the best. In 1959 when Motown exploded onto the scene, he was one of the first artists to be signed. Another group was The Detroit Emeralds, who sang at some of the dances. Mitchell, one of the members, ran a restaurant on Vernor Highway owned by his parents. Even though most of the group lived on the northend, they had an east side sound. (Yes, groups sound different from different sections of a city.) They were guided by Chico Hamilton. One of Chico's younger brothers was in the Emeralds.

Later, in my high school years at Cass Tech, Chico Hamilton would become very famous as a basketball player. But in 1954 he quit suddenly and disappeared. The white and Black press bemoaned his departure in the sports section. You see, he'd been named high school All-American in his first year on the team. In the late Fifties and early Sixties he re-emerged as Ronnie Savoy—a very talented R&B record producer and songwriter. He owned a recording company in Newark, New Jersey. He produced hit records for the Drifters and the Fantastic Four. And he was one of the first brothers to write music for television commercials. I met him again in the beginning of the Seventies and the years between 1954 and 1971 seemed indistinguishable. Poet Norman Jordan has told us, *In the last days/ all things return to what they were.*

Our after-school activities were basketball and music. Miller High School was in the area and most of the team basketball players were members of the Settlement. They were the best. Their photographs in action appeared in the Michigan Chronicle every week. They also had the best coach, Will Robinson. He was Black and he didn't take no shit. Every kid on the east side wanted to go to Miller High School after immediate school. The five of us vowed we'd go to Miller. We did everything together; we were such good friends. At the time, our world seemed destined to last forever. Ernest was the best fighter. John French was also feared everywhere because the French family's reputation went with him, with us. On this east side house parties on Friday and Saturday evenings were our glory.

49

Ernest and John could dance. Leonard, Willie and I were the pretty boys. We pranced in our Hi-Lo's shirts, expensive Stetsons and Stacy Adams shoes, Knox and Dobbs hats. We were not yet 15 years old but we were living adult lives. As Langston Hughes has told us, *In the quarters of the Negroes/ a nickel cost a dime/ living 20 years in ten* . . . Our dream was to own a Cadillac and to pimp like Ted and Adolph.

In our house parties we searched for dark corners for our slow grinding. Our music at these parties was The Chantels' "Maybe," The Flamingoes' "I Only Have Eyes For You" and "Golden Teardrops," The Spaniels' "Goodnight Sweetheart Goodnight," The Harptones' "Sunday Kind of Love," The Turbans' "When You Dance," The Clovers' "Blue Velvet," The Crows' "Gee," The Moonglows' "Most of All" and "We Go Together," and The Penguins' "Earth Angel." Our house parties and our music couldn't exist without each other. The house parties were in basements and the lights would always be down low. We'd dance our slow grind or we'd dance our slow bop. It was always slow and cool. We hadn't yet been contaminated by *American Bandstand*. House party streets were Kirby, Hastings, Burns, Benson, Elba, Mt. Elliot, Canton, Meldrum, etc. One's reputation must precede him; girls must be expecting him. One must expect revenges to be met from another house party incident. Our girls went by names like Candy, Kay Williams, Leona, Margie Craighead, Tuttie, Carol Hinton, Lodie, Fruittie, Liz, Beverly, Tootsie, Willie Mae, Johnnie Mae, Marie Lewis, Dumpty, etc.

At our house parties we loved to hear Hank Ballard and the midnighters sing:

> Work with me Annie
> Better git it while the gittin is good

The Midnighters told us about ourselves. Things that we all understood because of the simplicity of it. We loved the Five Royales singing, "Crazy, Crazy, Crazy":

> I got a girl named Millie
> Millie, she act so silly

Looking back, as we often do, before the Midnighters changed their name to the Midnighters in 1954, they were known as the Royales. Don't you remember "Moonrise," "The Shrine of St. Cecelia" and "Every Beat of My Heart?"

> With every beat of my heart
> There's a beat for you

So we'd laugh and push each other and our girls would laugh with us. Other times we were so cool, we never said a word for the duration of a party. The mood set by the record would direct our actions.

The singers had a total image. We didn't define them by any one single song. We'd seen them at the Warfield Theatre, the Madison Ballroom, and the Echo Theatre. In the basements, when we danced to "Crazy, Crazy, Crazy" and "Think," we also danced to "Baby, Don't Do It" and "Help Me Somebody." Our singing groups had a total image, be they The Clovers, The Drifters, The Spaniels, The Coasters, or The Penguins.

When we added rhythm to our blues, we did it so that our existence would be less of a burden than could be detected by the casual observer. The observer could not see no hope, had no understanding of our confusion. But we all felt it within us, even the observer if he was Black. It couldn't be hidden by marcelled heads, diamonds, Cadillacs, clothes, or white girls. And our blues singers kept telling us in no uncertain terms that we were blue. We couldn't lie and pretend otherwise. What Bessie Smith, Billie Holiday, T. Bone Walker, John Lee Hooker, Dinah Washington, and Johnny Ace told us, we had to deal with internally. But we didn't have to deal with those things — those blues externally — if we could create an alternate. The rhythm became an alternate.

The group and the rhythm became easily identifiable. Their *sound* and their *rhythm* became their trademark. I cannot show you the background of the R&B groups, the choreographed steps, the doo-wah-wo-ooh sa ra, the harmony. It cannot be defined. Philadelphia had its sound and rhythm as did Chicago, New York, New Jersey, Indiana, and Detroit. In trying, I'll just say, movements were choreographed and comedy routines perfected, for every song. The Royal Jokers, for example, were known for throwing an imaginary bee on each other, then dancing and gyrating until it was found. The Spaniels were known for Pookie Hudson's lead and Gerald Gregory's beautiful bass. They were at their best in the million-seller "Goodnight Sweetheart Goodnight," where Gregory would come in with that beautiful bass:

Dat-dah-da-da-dah

Pookie would come back with:

Mother, oh and your father wouldn't
Like it if I stayed here too long

The Harptones, on the other hand, found their sound and rhythm in Willie Winfield's interpretation and projection and in an emotionally created harmony. Try and remember this one:

I'm through with my old love
I loved her through and through

That's the way the group would start and in perfect harmony. Then Willie Winfield would come in:

I want a Sunday kind of love
A love to last past Saturday night

In each case the sound and the rhythm are distinct. One is a New York sound and the other is a Gary sound.

We were blue in the early Fifties. The Second World War had ended only a few years earlier and the Korean War was now taking away our loved ones and splitting our groups. The automobile industry had taken those that could not *qualify* for the war. The streets were left to those of us under 15 years of age. We didn't know what to do with them. The effect of this street existence changed many of our lives in our later years. It moved us towards a materialistic approach to survival. We worshipped the automobile, the home, the clothes, the pimp, the prostitutes, the hustler, the doctor, the lawyer, the teacher, etc. Aspirations to things we couldn't see or understand were viewed as strange. Even, after the revolution of the Sixties, many of our parents view our work as strange. How can that which cannot be understood by them be important? *When did you stray into that profession?* they ask now. Then, they asked if it was part of the church or looked to see if white people had put an OK on it. And the years between 1953 and now are short if you were 40 years old then. How could they grow if they were already grown? They ask (as do many white people), how can you remember all those R&B groups and all those songs but can't remember any of the teachers who taught you? The question is deep if not profound. Deep in the sense that teachers did not teach and songs and groups did as they related directly to events that we felt important.

I cannot forget Clyde McPhatter and the Drifters' "Whatcha Gonna Do?" because at the time it was popular, Ernest McNeal, Willie Jackson, and I were caught deep in Chilli-Mac territory looking for some girls we'd met at the Madison Ballroom. As we approached the corner of Davison and Lumpkins we heard them singing as pretty as Clyde and the Drifters themselves:

Now whatcha gonna do about half past eight

We were drawn over to them; forgetting that they were asskickers. We asked them if they knew "Adorable" and "Money Honey." They knew all the Drifters' songs. They even knew some of the routines because the group had recently appeared at the Olympia on Grand River. We sang on the corner with them for over two hours. McNeal sang lead on "Money Honey."

We stared laughing and shaking hands. Willie Jackson started right in on "Adorable":

Adorable, adorable, adorable, adorable baby
You're so adorable, sweet as can be

As Africans, our music is sacred because it's spiritual. It has remained our common ground through 300 years of struggle and survival in this country. No white teacher can teach this; no gang can overpower it.

The Impact of Race

The fighting groups at the time were the Shakers, the Jokers, and the Chilli-Macs. The notorious families were the Noble Bothers, The Logan Brothers, The Mitchells, The McNeal Family, The Johnson Brothers, and the French Family. Any altercation with any of them meant bloodshed. Not only were they bad, they had a reputation to uphold.

White boys were killers too. They were named Santini, Bioggi, and Cusimino. Once a thing started it was kill or be killed. The police were always on their side. They'd go against the Black community while looking for the Black gang. So there were very few Black-white confrontations between families or gangs.

The Lord and Master of the Shakers was Maurice. That's all anybody ever called him. He was known across the city. His number two man was James Moody. James Moody was my friend. We met at Smith School. He lived with his mother on Joseph Campau Street until he was 13 years old. He moved away and at 16 he was number two man in the Shakers. Moody was found murdered in the trunk of his Cadillac in the beginning of the Seventies. I don't remember the leader of the Chilli-Macs.

Tadpole loved music as much as he loved to cut people. Everytime he got money he'd play the jukebox in Webster's for hours, listening to the same two records over and over again. "Smokey Joe's Café" by the Robins and "Play It Cool" by the Spaniels.

We all would gather around the jukebox and sing along with Tadpole on the Spaniels' record. We'd harmonize in the deep yeeeeeeeaaAAAHHH oooOOHH Saaa-Rah!

In the last stanza Tadpole would imitate Louis Armstrong, doing the whole thing with the white handkerchief.

Understanding the gang, like the group, was a necessity. It was our protection. In it we found the friends that we didn't have at home. But in it we had to prove ourselves—prove that we were men when in reality we were boys. We'd drink more wine than our enemies, drink more whiskey, and now we must shoot more heroin. But our progression was based on materialistic things and controlled by the same people who produce, manage, and distribute the R&B music. Why not? Weren't the gangs and the groups the same people in the final analysis? After all, the same Tadpole of the Jokers was the same Tadpole of the Five Dollars.

And so the Chi-Lites, the old Temptations, Smokey and The Miracles,

The Dramatics, Stylistics, Delfonics, Four Tops, Black Ivory, Detroit Emeralds are rhythm and bluesing us about the Gwen Lewises we lost years ago. Only they know us; only they can sing to us. With that rhythm we can hide the fact that we know white people are determined to control this world forever. But they can only do this by exploiting our need to survive. And by saying what we hold in our hands is just around the next corner.

Jazz

According to Webster's New World Dictionary, Jazz is a kind of music, originally improvised but not also arranged, characterized by syncopation, rubato, usually heavily accented rhythms, dissonances, individualized melodic variations, and unusual tonal effects on the saxophone, clarinet, trombone, etc.

If you want to understand Black theatre, you must understand the music that inspires it, sustains it. Rhythm & Blues, decidedly; Blues, absolutely; and of course the highest form of the art—Jazz.

The musicians that best exemplify the improvisational, the creative, and the innovative characteristics of jazz are Louis Armstrong, Robert Johnson, Duke Ellington, Count Basie, Billie Holiday, and Charlie Parker. These musicians are closely followed by Bessie Smith, Jelly Roll Morton, Fats Waller, and Dizzy Gillespie.

The people who listened and danced to the music itself defined the rules. Each time a musician played that musician had to be innovative in his delivery. He had to improvise on themes for the many different kinds of dances created on the spot while he played. This improvisatory nature of the music became a standard form in jazz. It, at times, is called "vamps," "riffs," and even, in the case of Louis Armstrong, "scatting" and "breaks."

Jazz has always been an art form for the people of a particular community and not only the Black Community. It originally developed out of marching bands. These bands would become a part of a parade that generally occurred on a festive occasion. Eventually spectators would become familiar with the band and/or individuals in the band. Jazz developed from blues music; blues music offers hope to listeners and dancers. People could listen as well as dance. Albert Murray calls it music for "Saturday Nite Functions." Because of Mardi Gras many of the quartets, quintets, and bands began in New Orleans. Later blues musicians came out of Kansas City.

Louis Armstrong came out of New Orleans, Storyville. Armstrong set the standards for jazz musicians. He played trumpet. However, playing the trumpet was only a portion of his gift. He was a singer and actor. His records sold millions, especially his renditions of "Mack the Knife" and "Hello, Dolly." He appeared on stage as well as in films.

"There is no jazz musician regardless of instrument and no jazz singer today that does not owe their first debt of gratitude to Louis Armstrong," according to drummer Gene Krupa. "Louis did it all, and did it FIRST." As a young ghetto kid, Armstrong played the bugle and cornet. He played in a marching band. As he calls it, "front lining" with bugle, cornet, and trumpet.

While still in his early 20's he joined the Joe "King" Oliver's Creole Jazz Band. According to Grover Sales' *Jazz, America's Classic Music*, "Oliver's trademark was the rollicking rough-and-tumble jam that got dancers moving."

Louis Armstrong recorded the first authentic jazz in 1923 with King Oliver's Creole Jazz Band. He emerged from King Oliver as a first-class soloist. In 1925 he joined up with Sidney Bechet. In 1924, Armstrong was encouraged by his wife, pianist Lil Hardin, to join the Fletcher Henderson Orchestra. It was the most prestigious Black orchestra at that time. It was in Henderson's orchestra that Armstrong's versatility became known all over the country, especially in New York and especially among other musicians. "The guys never heard anything like it," said Duke Ellington. "There weren't words coined to describe that kind of kick...Everybody on the street was talking about the guy."

According to Grover Sales, "His tone was open, spacious, and impassioned, the daring escapades in the high register as generous and unforced as the throbbing low notes. His occasional use of a cup mute lent a clouded beauty to the warm vibrato—his unerring sense of time and placement of subtle accents got the most swing from the fewest notes." Louis Armstrong was able to accomplish all of this through the artistry of his music. His group, The Hot Five and The Hot Seven as well as his work with Earl "Fatha" Hines are lasting treasures. His work on "West End Blues" is classic and set standards for jazz musicians for years.

Early music by Louis Armstrong was clearly what Albert Murray calls music for the Saturday Nite Function. It was music for dancing and having a good time. In later years Armstrong sang and clowned, trying to show a good time to audiences and dancers. To that end his influence on younger blues men was incredible.

Robert Johnson, a bluesman from the Mississippi Delta, traveled from jook joint to Saturday Nite Functions playing and singing the blues. The documentary film "The Search for Robert Johnson," narrated by John Hammond, Jr., traces the musician's effect on a new generation of young white musicians, including Eric Clapton, Ry Cooder, and The Rolling Stones. Again, according to Webster's New World Dictionary, Second College Edition, the Blues is "Negro folk music characterized by minor harmonies, typically slow tempo, and melancholy words, i.e., it's the form of Jazz that evolved from this music."

Robert Johnson is the most influential bluesman of all time and the person most responsible for the shape popular music has taken in the last five decades.

Robert Johnson was born May 8, 1911, in Hazelhurst, Mississippi, to Julia Dodds and Noah Johnson, the man with whom she'd had an affair in Mr. Dodds' absence. However, little Robert didn't stay there long. Still a babe-in-arms, his mother took him and his baby sister, Carrie, and signed on with a Delta labor supplier. After a couple of very hard and unsettling years in migrant labor camps, they were living in Memphis with, and as, the family of Charles Spencer.

In his early teens, Robert Spencer took an interest in music. His initial attraction to the Jew's harp was soon supplanted by the harmonica, which became his main instrument for the next few years.

The guitar became an interest during the late Twenties. He made a rack for his harp out of baling wire and string and was soon picking out appropriate accompaniments for his harp and voice. Leroy Carr's 1928 "How Long–How Long Blues" is recalled as being one of his favorite songs at that time.

Robert's private life got serious about this time as well. A good looking boy, he had little trouble making himself popular with the girls.

The Impact of Race

The jook joints (a place to dance, drink, and have a good time), the road gangs (low paying job or prisoner) and lumber camps set the stage for Robert Johnson.

One of the most wide-open, musically active towns in the Delta in those days was on the Arkansas riverside, and it became Robert's home base for the rest of his short life.

All the great musicians of the area came through Helena. Sonny Boy Williamson II (then known as Little Boy Blue), Robert Nighthawk, Elmore James, Honeyboy Edwards, Howlin' Wolf, Hacksaw Harney, Calvin Frazier, Peter "Memphis Slim" Chatman, Johnny Shines, and countless others performed in Helena's and West Helena's many night clubs and hot spots. Robert had his chance to meet and play with them all—and he did—and left his mark on most of them, too.

The lyrics of his songs are as legendary as his guitar playing. In his "32/20 Blues," he says his .38 Special isn't a gun for defense because it "... is most too light." Or his "Kind Hearted Woman"... "studies evil all the time [but she would] do anything in this world for me." Still on another song like, "If I had Possession Over Judgment Day," his lyrics are:

> I roll and tumble
> I cried the whole night long...

Robert Johnson's music is full of hell symbols and his lyrics are always confronting the devil. For example, in "Me and the Devil Blues," he sings:

> Early this morning he knocks on my door...
> I said, Hello Satan, I think it's time to go

Or even his master work, "Hell Hound On My Trail":

> I got to keep moving
> Blues falling down like rain

Robert had made friends with a local woman, who happened to be the wife of the man who ran the Jookhouse at Three Forks. In fact, she'd come into Greenwood to see him on Mondays. It's rumored the husband of this woman poisoned Robert Johnson.

He died on the Saturday night of August 13, 1938, at the age of 26.

Robert Johnson was 14 years old when Bessie Smith was recording master blues tunes like "Hateful Blues," "Workhouse Blues," and "Poor Man Blues." At 14, Bessie Smith made her debut as a dancer in Chattanooga and went on to become a leading recording star for Columbia Records, and ultimately became "Empress of the Blues." She used some of the finest musicians of the time, including Fletcher Henderson, Louis Armstrong, and Clarence Williams. She died tragically in 1937 as a result of an automobile crash. One year before Robert Johnson was killed.

From New York City Edward Kennedy Ellington a.k.a. Duke Ellington launched a fifty-year career, beginning in 1925 as a band-leader and composer. In 1927 he recorded a series of blues, including "The Black and Tan Fantasy," "Creole Love Call," "The Mooche," and "East St. Louis Toodle-oo." He became a distinctive piano voice with these compositions.

Duke Ellington was able to make a symphony orchestra swing. At the time everyone said it was impossible. His composition, "It Don't Mean a Thing If It Ain't Got That Swing," perfectly expresses the genius of Ellington's contribution to American music. According to Albert Murray in *Stomping the Blues*, "Music which isn't sufficiently dance-beat oriented isn't likely to be received with very much enthusiasm by the patrons of down-home honky-tonks, uptown cabarets, and the ballrooms and casinos across the nation." Ellington's music was both dance oriented and concert sacred. Europeans love to listen to his music.

Duke Ellington was able to direct his orchestra as well as his musicians as if they were a single unit. Over and over again his instruments were arranged to correspond to human voice. Many of his compositions contain call and response utilizing tonalities in the keyboards, strings, brasses, and woodwinds. According to Albert Murray, "Sometimes, as in *Diminuendo in Blue* and *Crescendo in Blue*, not only do the trumpets and trombones extend the shouting and hey-saying voice of the down-home church choir, but they also take the lead in doing drum work and drum talk at the same time."

In the late Twenties, Ellington the arranger, composer, conductor, piano player, and urbane matinee idol took what had been created up to that time and expanded it. Ellington counterstated and extended what had been done with orchestras. "Invention comes from people of special talent and genius, not from those who are circumscribed by routine," according to Albert Murray. Ellington became the first authentic jazz composer to write and record extended works beyond the traditional three minutes. Before Ellington, jazz musicians wrote or orchestrated songs. During his long career, he created, composed, wrote, and arranged tone colors and a special set of emotions for Sidney Bechet, Johnny Hodges, Ben Webster, Barney Bigard, Cootie Williams, Harry Carney, Paul Gonsalves, etc.

The Duke came to his place of recognition via Washington, D.C. and New York City. He started studying piano at the age of 8 and by the time he was out of high school he was fronting his own band in the D.C. area. By the mid-Twenties he had his own orchestra and was gigging in New York City. For five years he reigned over the celebrated Cotton Club. While at the Cotton Club, Ellington wrote hundreds of scores for the changing floor shows. Eventually his music was broadcast nationwide on the "Cotton Club Radio Hour." The average person could listen as well as dance to Ellington's music. In the *Smithsonian Collections of Classic Jazz* revised volume 5, Ellington's work is listed an astonishing eight times!

One of the interesting aspects of jazz music is the continuing influence of one musician on another. Louis Armstrong and Duke Ellington had a tremendous influence on the jazz singer Billie Holiday. Some critics call Billie Holiday the first artist in all of jazz, not just the first woman or the first jazz singer. Her voice was influenced by the tenor saxophone long before she met and worked with Lester Young. She described her singing style as combining "the blues feeling with the jazz beat." Like Ellington, Billie Holiday's music is about instruments, i.e., her voice could be an entire orchestra. "Sometimes there was the soft wail of a saxophone, then the piercing, sharply defined blast of a trumpet," one jazz critic said. However, her voice had none of the volume and majesty of Bessie Smith. Yet, she sang a song which, more than anything sung by Bessie Smith and other female blues singers, became a musical protest against racial discrimination. This song was "Strange Fruit." The "Strange Fruit" hanging from the tree was the body of a lynched Negro. Billie's voice was a mere whisper. Beautifully nuanced, and intimate as it was on "Strange Fruit," her voice would have been unimpressive without the invention of the microphone.

She made her first recordings with Benny Goodman's band in 1993. In 1936, she cut several records with pianist Teddy Wilson that featured the first collaborations with tenor saxophonist Lester Young. Together, Prez and Billie made some of the finest vocal/sax recordings in jazz history. It was during that time she became know as Lady Day, the great vocal stylist.

The three phases of Billie Holiday's musical career began in 1939 with "Strange Fruit," the second phase began in the mid-Forties when she recorded with string, including her own composition, "Don't Explain," and the third phase in the Fifties when she'd been almost destroyed by alcohol and drugs. However, in each of the three, Billie Holiday exemplified the improvisational, the creative and the innovative characteristics of jazz. She did this by going inside the song and magnifying the song's meaning. She could drag a phrase or bend a melody. With that kind of ability she brought a unique emotion and intimacy to very bad songs. According to Albert Murray in *Stomping the Blues*, "The great and lasting distinction of Billie Holiday is not based on her highly publicized addiction to narcotics (a show-biz rather than a blues-idiom phenomenon) but on her deliberate use of her voice as an Armstrong-derived instrumental extension." When comparing Bessie Smith's "Do Your Duty" and Billie's "Do Your Duty," we can hear how unique and different Billie Holiday is. Yes, Bessie Smith recorded her version of "Do Your Duty" in 1933 and Billie's version was recorded in 1949, sixteen years later. However, it was not the time difference but the uniqueness of Lady Day's interpretation.

Charlie Parker a.k.a. "Bird" loved to listen to Lady Day's "You Are My Thrill." When he and Dizzy recorded "Billie's Bounce" honoring her as a great jazz artist he left a lasting tribute to the Great Lady.

As a young aspiring musician, Parker listened to and tried to imitate Lester Young on the alto sax. However, according to Ron David in *Jazz for Beginners*, "Little Charlie, a self-taught alto sax prodigy, didn't realize that jazz in the Forties was played in only a few keys, so the obsessive little genius learned to play every song in every key by the time he'd reached his mid-teens. Without that 'mistake' there might never have been any such thing as bebop."

Charlie Parker was born August 20, 1920, in Kansas City. He died March 12, 1955, in New York City. I am specifically giving the dates of birth and death in this case because he accomplished so much in only thirty-five years. But he also quit school and left home at the age of 15. By the time he was 17, he'd married and played in local jazz bands. Most musicians have long and sometimes painful evolutions. Charlie Parker arrived on the scene virtually fully formed.

Parker worked with a lot of dance hall bands, including Jay McShann, Noble Sissle, Earl "Fatha" Hines, and for a short time with Billy Eckstine's Big Band. So he was not looking for ways to stop dance hall blues from swing. In his eighteen years as a musician, Parker's discography is incredible. In the beginning, his music was designed for the Saturday Nite Function. But Parker wanted more. He was always experimenting. From his own words:

> I remember one night I was jamming in a chili house on Seventh Avenue between 139th and 140th. It was December 1939. Now I'd been bored with the stereotyped changes that were being used all the time, and I kept thinking there's bound to be something else. Well, that night, I was working over "Cherokee," and as I did, I found that by using the higher intervals of a chord as a melody line and backing them with appropriately related change, I could play the thing I'd been hearing. I came alive.

Charlie Parker had found a way to make dance hall blues swing at even more breakneck speed. In 1945 Dizzy Gillespie and Charlie Parker began the highly respected breakneck speed recordings "Groovin' High," "Billie's Bounce," "Now's the Time," and "Ko-Ko." He recorded six brilliant albums back-to-back in 1945 and 1946. "His rendition of 'Lover Man' was one of the most stripped bare, anguished jazz performances of all times," according to Ron David in *Jazz for Beginners*.

Woodie King, Jr.

Charlie Parker was a genius. Hundreds of musicians attest to his genius. Most musicians will tell you that his music best exemplifies the improvisational, the creative, and the innovative characteristics of jazz. However, he was a heroin addict. He was the paradigm of the jazzman as victim. According to Albert Murray, in *Stomping the Blues*, "Ornithological references appear again and again in the titles of recordings by Charlie Parker whose nickname was Bird as in yardbird (his jive term for chicken). Parker's complete works include 'Yardbird Suite,' 'Blue Bird,' 'Bird Feathers,' 'Bird of Paradise,' 'Chasin' the Bird,' 'Carving the Bird,' 'Bird Gets the Worm,' and 'Ornithology.' But still and all, the chances are that no real-life bird ever actually flew like Charlie the yardbird. As magnificent as the most beautiful birds look against the sky, they mostly flap and glide—whereas Parker cut figures with dance-beat elegance."

Indeed Charlie Parker extended on, elaborated on, refined, and transcended blues music as it had existed up until that time. In doing so, he influenced a whole generation of jazz musicians. Arguing about who is the greatest jazz musician is a pointless exercise, but the name of Charlie Parker is mentioned often by musicians and jazz music lovers.

Breaking the Rules —
Education Ethics
and Ethnicity

Many use the word "culture" to refer to both the physical and the intangible: the values, shared meanings, social norms, customs, rituals, symbols, arts and artifacts, ways of perceiving the world, lifestyles, behaviors and ways by which people participate in organized society. However, some of us are more interested in "high culture," what's considered to be the best of art, literature, music, architecture, philosophy and the other expressive symbolic modes of Americana. We also respect the popular culture of music, films, popular art, fashions, etc. These young men and women who represent this new multicultural society are creating a new culture. You see it in the fashions; you hear it in the music. It's called Hip-Hop culture. And, without a doubt, this culture and this economy are now bound together.

A new generation of ethnically diverse children with no history and tradition of art or theatre as we've come to know it are challenging us, making us be more creative. How are we supposed to implement these goals and rules which are designed to make youngsters better adults? Great plays on Broadway are passé; great plays on television are things of the past! Anything and everything can be purchased or rented at the video store. New competition for the child's attention include the horrible fare on television and the vivid theatricality of street life. Television ought to be helping shape the minds of young people. Adults in the streets should be watching to make sure teachings are adhered to.

Words like "multiculturalism," "Ebonics," "multi-ethnic," "cultural diversity," and "affirmative action" are warning signs that we're no longer living in an "English only" world. To embrace the meaning of these words, we must accept who we are. Yes, it has a lot to do with identity. Who am I?, as shaped from awareness through adolescence. And, if we're Black teachers or students in a white institution either we must adjust to the rules of that institution or the institution must adjust to our rules. If we're not clear on what we want, "cultural diversity," "Ebonics," "multi-culturalism" will only further confuse an already cloudy set of issues.

Educational institutions basically exist by a set of rules perpetuated by the institution's history. The rules are carried out by mostly white teachers whose identity has been shaped from awareness to adolescence the same as Blacks. However, the two identities are as different as night and day. One is a Snoop Dogg-Tupac-R. Kelly-rap world; the other is a Holden Caufield, Andy Hardy, Rolling Stones world. So, the challenge is: how will white theatre educators "Break the Rules" when they're so well educated to know and follow the rules?

In the past thirty-five years America has become an information-based society. Ways in which to communicate information are, after all, what we're talking about here. The information-based society changed the rules. As stated in *A Nation at Risk: The Imperative for Educational Reform* (a report with recommendations for Goals 2000 Initiative, wherein by the year 2000 the U.S. will have used the findings and recommendations to attain excellence in education), "learning is the indispensable investment required for success in the information age." The report goes on to state, "All, regardless of race or class or economic status, are entitled to a fair chance and to *the tools for developing their individual powers of mind and spirit* to the utmost." Computer hardware doesn't require the nuances of one's racial, cultural, ethnicity, gender, or language. It must be reduced to *bytes*. In television, film, and theatre we're given stereotypes of people of color, especially Black people. Why is this? Because people of color are used in theatre written by white people to humanize the white people. If we're looking for more efficient ways to work with students of color we must not get into the stereotypes of their ethnicity. We must not *label* a student. We must not use surface information provided by computer hardware. The students of color must be trained early to understand what a computer can and cannot transmit.

The search for self-fulfillment causes us to find easier ways in which to identify "others." These problems are evident in predominantly white institutions where theatre educators are also predominantly white. In institutions where we are teaching our ethnic-specific youth to be *employees* rather than *employers* we're teaching them to integrate into a system that's basically Eurocentric. A system they believe hates them.

I'm not sure the young Denzel Washington, Laurence Fishburne, Snoop Doggy Dogg, Ntozake Shange, Morgan Freeman, Danny Glover, Will Smith, Debbie Allen, John Legizamo, Tupac Shakur, Jimmy Smits, etc., wanted into that system. These people were considered outcasts, difficult. Most of them remember a special teacher who encouraged them. Young minority artists must be made to feel comfortable with their identity before they can create the identity of non-minority characters. They must know the contributions of their own ethnicity before they can comfortably embrace the ethnicity of another people. One cannot be culturally diverse if one isn't knowledgeable of one's own culture.

As a result of my being rejected by white theatres in Detroit, I had no alternative but to explore Black theatre. One piece of information led me to another piece of information. That's part of the quest for information, a.k.a. the quest for knowledge. My four years in Detroit Public Library's Azelia Hackley Collection made me thirst for more information on Black people's contribution to theatre. Kurt Meyers, the librarian, became my theatre educator. He was as anxious to get me new information as I was to receive it. He broke rules. Back in those days the Public Library remained open until 9 P.M. every night. I marveled in the library!

We didn't have theatre educators like we have today. However, one teacher—there's always one—introduced me to Detroit Art Institute. Mr. John Finger instructed me in my painting. He'd often give me books, photographs, and drawings by Black artists. He broke the rules.

In the search for answers to who I am, I moved from blues, rhythm & blues, jazz to do-wop music. All of this music was in an entirely Black setting. All of this music was created out of a love for self, relatives, and those we loved. Some of the better art comes out of creating characters we love.

The Impact of Race

In my last year of high school I was told that the only drama school in the area didn't accept Blacks. I couldn't accept that. At 17 years of age I was bold enough to call and get an appointment. I met Mrs. Theresa Way Merrill, who'd been a leading actress with the Jessie Bonstelle Company, who was 67 years old and wheelchair bound, and Mrs. Celia Turner, her daughter, about 30, who taught acting and ran the school. They talked to me for about two hours. We talked about Jessie Bonstelle, Alfred Lunt and Lynn Fontanne, Basil Rathbone, Tennessee Williams. They broke the rules and gave me a four-year scholarship.

The four institutions I've been instrumental in developing are Concept-East Theatre in Detroit, Mobilization for Youth Cultural Arts Program in New York, New Federal Theatre in New York, and National Black Touring Circuit in New York. With Concept-East we took an old bar and made a theatre and art gallery that attracted Black and white artists for fifteen years. I found eleven friends who contributed $100 each. In New York's Lower East Side is a multi-ethnic, culturally diverse population of young artists who contributed the forty-five teenagers of MFY's cultural arts program.

In its first seven years New Federal Theatre was a multi-ethnic theatre training program of the historic Henry Street Settlement. By multi-ethnic I mean I had a Black theatre section directed by Dick Anthony Williams; a Hispanic workshop run by Carlos Pinza; a Jewish theatre workshop run by Moshe Yasser and Stanley Brechner; and an Asian theatre program directed by an Asian director. Within budget constraints each unit existed under the artistic leadership of the immediate directors. I'm sure my sensitivity to other cultures emanates from my comfort in my own culture.

Recalling my own experience in founding Concept-East Theatre in Detroit in 1960, I was so overwhelmed with the need to inform Black audiences about the contributions of Ira Aldridge, Bert Williams, Paul Robeson, Langston Hughes, Zora Neale Hurston, Rose McClendon and institutions like the African Grove Theatre and the American Negro Theatre that I totally forgot about money — you can't run a theatre and forget to charge admission. However, my own identity was tied in totally to the identities and contributions of these Black artists and Black institutions.

Theatre educators might better unravel classroom dilemmas if they used the writings of culturally diverse authors. And I don't mean using these writers only during Black History Month. I mean using plays with ethnic content and ethnic characters.

To be a good actor, a good playwright, a good director we must first be very secure in who we are. That's extremely difficult if we're Black. Blacks are faced with what W. E. B. DuBois called *the dilemma of double conscious-ness* — being Black and being American. If you're white you must confront the contradictions of being Eurocentric. How can you help a child be any-thing but what you are? Colleges and universities prepare us to be Eurocentric. The children we work with are more than two generations removed. They're Black and they're American and they don't relate. We're not prepared to deal with that!

Most theatre educators are professional artists in their own right. Still others are perfectly satisfied in realizing fulfillment through their students. By being a professional they recognize talent immediately. I have an actress friend who's teaching this summer in the Bronx section of New York. It's one of the rough schools. Yet, in the short time she's been there, she's discovered two students and she's called all over New York to place them on summer jobs within arts institutions. Yes, she happily informed me she'd found placement for them! It wasn't a requirement of her job to do this, yet she did it. Professors and teachers are constantly in touch with me, informing me of a student whose work is so good that I must see them on arrival in New York. Because these theatre educators are so well regarded in the profession, their students are seen and they're often employed. What is it that these theatre educators who are also professional artists are able to do? The common denominator that cuts through it all is the cultural and ethnic background of the student as it relates to characters he's defining as actor, director, or playwright. Above all else, the artist must be very comfortable with his own identity. Therefore, master theatre educators in cultural diversity should be involved in designing teacher preparation programs and in supervising new theatre educators.

How can a theatre educator prepare a student? Our quest for knowl-edge didn't end when we graduated. The universities should have given us basic skills, and most of all it gave us the ability to think clearly. We must continue to refuel our minds. We're constantly searching for self-fulfillment even though all the rules have changed. The better artists take the human condition, recreate and reshape it in a beautiful and artistic art, a beautifully realized, culturally diverse character, a brilliantly executed piece of choreography, a dance, a culturally diverse play... the unique way in which this art is given back is called *vision*. I believe the better theatre educators are also artists and visionaries. They take what a student brings and uses it to help shape that student into a piece of art.

"Cultural diversity" means absolutely nothing if the student doesn't have a sense of his own culture. Breaking the rules is extremely difficult when your education and Eurocentric institutions exist on rules.

On Producing James Brown in Liberia

My wife drove me to Kennedy Airport. She and I had coffee after check-in. We laughed a lot because our African brothers were so definite about things they knew nothing about, especially how simple it was to bring James Brown to Africa.

Five hours time change in Monrovia—I'm not sure how to calculate it. Plane departed at 5:35 P.M. and arrived in Dakar at 5:35 A.M. One hour and a half layover due to communications from Monrovia—I slept a lot, wrote beginnings of a short story that had been on my mind for about a year. Plane departed Dakar at 7:00 A.M., arrived in Monrovia at 8:35 A.M. I was met on arrival by an efficient brother, asking if I was Mr. King. Three others joined him from Rudolph Sherman's office, then Oliver Bright, efficient as ever, smiling, took us to his lounging area to wait for customs check, then to his Mercedes for a 34-mile ride to his home. Met his wife who was preparing for a trip to NYC (Boston): Violette is her name— beautiful daughter, Wyanie (4 yrs) reminds me of Patty's daughter in Detroit. Ate fried plantains, meat with sweet potato leaves, rice, and ice cream. Left for meeting with Minister Townsand in Capitol building.

From there to Ministry of Justice—met Hugh Masakela in Mr. Sherman's office—subtly trying to convince them of certain needs for groups he'd have for Liberation Committees on Thursday & Friday. He wasn't being understood. Sherman showed two articles from local newspapers on James Brown's appearance. Talked about plane going to

Amsterdam, Holland to pick up Brown. New problem, really no problem—Brown must be returned to Brussels rather than Kuwait.

Left there and went to E. J. Roye Hall, looking for Masakela & Music group—saw preparation for play, *Letters of Stephen Biko*. Promised I'd see it, however, headache...stopped on my way back home at several locations, looking for proper sound equipment—one man in particular, Mr. Mitchell of Studio One, (more about him later) was unique in his ability to say no. I was the only one who believed him. Apparently this is an old custom in Monrovia, everything requested is *no*. Promised Oliver Bright he could get some of equipment following morning at 9:00 A.M. if he brought in an engineer.

Towards evening, returning to Bright's home, we stopped and had soda at Millie Buchannan's—she had been a King before her marriage to a Buchannan. Also once modeled in New York until her return home in 1971 or 1972. Met her daughter (14) and one son (9, 10 or 11). She has another son, one-year-old.

Then to Bright's home. Headache, bothering me. Took my Shaklee vitamins. We all sat in living room and talked, drank coffee, ate fruit... didn't feel up to seeing Biko play. Went to sleep after talking with Wyanie.

Up at 8:30 A.M. (3:30 in NYC). Bright had received a telex from Amsterdam. His people couldn't find James Brown. He'd called the Hilton Hotel in Amsterdam and cancelled his reservations. They knew he was in Europe. They had to wait until 3 P.M. (American time) before calling Larry Myers, of Universal Attractions in NYC to find out the whereabouts of Brown.

Mr. Sherman and Mr. Huff arrived for 9:00 A.M. meeting with Mr. Mitchell at his *Studio One*. First thought, we had to have breakfast: coffee, melon, sea crab (very much like shrimp), boiled plantains, and grapefruit juice.

We arrived at Mr. Mitchell's *Studio One*. He was feeding his pet deer, about five of them. Since he lived next door to soccer fields, we watched men building the stage for James Brown. Bright and Sherman were angry with some of the workers because they hadn't secured the wall with glass so that people could not climb over it. Today was a holiday and they couldn't get cement.

We went into Mr. Mitchell's *Studio One*. It seemed it belonged to a group of people. Mitchell was in charge. Huff counted microphones and cable. He had everything in the studio. Discovered also an FM radio transmitter. Plans for a radio station were cut short because the government didn't allow commercial stations. Discovered a twelve-track recording studio — not in use over ten months — about $750,000 worth of equipment in all. Mitchell is a self-made man, probably from Jamaica. He's a millionaire and he and his son are whiskey distillers, scotch and vodka. He showed us his factory. It's well equipped with new German timers, distillers, etc. Mitchell gave us a lecture on Marcus Garvey before we left. It was his belief that Garvey had a better idea on how to raise money than the Liberation Committee. With 400 million Black people in the world, if half put in one dollar, South Africa would have the money to buy all the things necessary for freedom. Garvey, he said, was tricked by the U.S. government for mail fraud — a law no American knew about because it was never published.

Back at Oliver Bright's home, his wife was in preparation for her trip to NYC. Bright was to take her to the airport. On his way home, he radios his office to check on flight to NYC. They inform him with surety, there would be no trip to NYC from Roberts Field. He just smiled. He is also told that some hoodlum crossed the border into Monrovia. Also, a fight between a soldier and a policeman...all under his command...

Wednesday afternoon, we decided we must visit the Stadium. I watched the workmen put up the stage. They assured us it would be ready. People from all over Monrovia were preparing for this occasion. Hugh Masakela, the well known South African trumpet player, rehearsing Tubman's Voodoo Drummers and another group of female dancers. Masakela was working very hard because this was a benefit for his brothers fighting in South Africa against the Apartheid government. Oliver Bright's presence helped solve the problem of chairs. Where would two thousand chairs come from? It seemed, you see, in all of Monrovia, chairs had suddenly become scarce. The carpenter on the job told us he could make benches if he had lumber cut by 7:00 A.M. the following morning. Bright assured him he'd have the lumber. All around us local musicians rehearsed under the direction of Hugh Masakela. About two hundred adults and youngsters watched the stage being built.

We also had to call the Embassy in Amsterdam because the plane (Air

The Impact of Race

Liberia Jet) could not find James Brown. We did find out he had called to cancel his hotel reservations at the Clipper-Hilton. We began to worry. I suggested we call Universal Attractions in New York. Larry Myers, Brown's booker, was not in but we were assured that Brown was on his way to Amsterdam. Perhaps our people arrived before Brown. However, we had a new problem, James Brown wouldn't be going to Kuwait. He'd be going to Brussels. He'd leave Liberia the next night of December 2, 1978. You must remember we begged James Brown's people to let him perform two or three nights. They'd said he was booked solid except for November 30, 1978. Now they were telling us a day before his first performance, that he could stay in Monrovia three days.

Thursday morning, I woke up early. The Air Liberia Jet carrying Brown would arrive at 9:38 A.M. My driver and I arrived at the smaller city airport at 9:15 A.M. Some of the crowd had already gathered. My limousine was driven on the field. I was asked to wait in the Presidential lounge. It would be where the press conference would be held upon Brown's arrival. By 9:45 A.M. the plane hadn't arrived but the control tower had been radioed; it would arrive at 10:00 A.M. By now almost five thousand people had gathered to meet and see James Brown. When the plane hit the runway, a cheer from the crowd went up. Girls with hair in corn rolls, little girls carrying flowers, old people in new clothes, all aglow. The huge DC 10 jet rolled to a halt. Now all of this was Black controlled; Black policemen & soldiers knew they could not control all of these people—some of them their own brothers & sisters. All watched as Oliver Bright and I ran up the stairs of the plane to bring James Brown into view. People cried and laughed and screamed, "Soul Brother…Soul Bother #1…" Brown waved and signed autographs. He was home again.

Along the highway into the city, people waved at him and his limousine. Several times he stopped and shook hands with old and young. It's said that no other man except the President of the United States has caused such a reaction.

I kept thinking, *I made this happen*. I brought James Brown to Africa to do a concert for the benefit of our brothers and sisters in South Africa. It's at times like this that one can be proud of his profession.

We made sure James Brown was settled into the guesthouse. The crowd of two thousand or more waited outside the gates and on the fence to get a look at this living legend. Several times he walked around the veranda and waved to the crowd. At 45, he is the living symbol of what a poor boy can achieve. All those people at the airport, waiting along the road, and now outside his guesthouse are poor boys.

Bright and I went back to the soccer field, the stage was nearly complete. All of the equipment was there. Masakela was on the job. Mr. Holmes, Brown's manager, looked at the stage and was impressed by its size. He suggested that we build a riser for the dancer (who happened to be Brown's wife) and set up a 5:00 P.M. call for his stage manager to work with Huff in setting up the sound. We then went to the Ministry of Justice to set up the itinerary. It seemed that Brown had been told he'd be received by the President. However, the President had been out of the city for two days and would not return until Saturday. Therefore, Brown would have to be flown to the President's farm on Saturday. Who would meet Brown today? Minister Townsand, since he was acting on the President's behalf for these three days. Mr. Holmes set the itinerary with us and then we drove back to Oliver's house for lunch.

That same evening, James Brown performed before about seven thousand screaming fans. They knew many of his songs. His back-up was a girl dancer, a three-girl trio, three horns, two percussions, two men on electric organ and guitar. Brown literally had people dancing all over the soccer field. He sang "This Is a Man's World," "If I Ruled the World," "Sex Machine," "Papa's Got a Brand New Bag," etc. He performed for ninety minutes. He danced until sweat poured from his brow. He did the split, the twirl, the mike split, the bump with his girl dancer, they did a little pony time, and finally told the people to get on the good foot. And, yeah, they were up joining him bring the evening to a close. The crowd then ran towards him at the dressing rooms built below the stage. The police and soldiers tried to stop the people but in a city like Monrovia where everyone is practically family, what can one do? I feared they'd tear down the stage. Some held James Brown's albums above their heads, some simply screamed his name, and many more just followed the frenzy. People were hit on the legs with police sticks until they retreated. A wall that held people who'd purchased two-dollar tickets collapsed. No one was hurt because it was only ten feet high anyway.

When I got to Brown's dressing room he'd changed from his flashy performing clothes to his conservative street wear. He was all in place as if he'd recently visited a friend. I asked him if he was ready to make the mad dash to his car. He wasn't even worried—he'd been through this so many times before. He waded through the crowd to the car and we all got in. The Mercedes moved slowly through the huge crowd. I'd estimate it at about three thousand. The car moved out of the gate onto the street and sped away with the crowd running after it.

Back at the guesthouse, Brown was in good spirits. Oliver Bright was upset. It seemed Brown expected another expense check. He'd been informed via cable from his NYC agent, Larry Myers, that another check was due for this second performance. Everyone was in shock. Bright had sent a plane at great expense to pick up Brown; the plane would deliver Brown to Brussels, also at equal expense. Maybe even New York because it seemed that was where Brown wanted to go. Bright and Holmes got on the telephone to clear up the problem; however, it was 7:00 P.M. in New York because it was midnight in Monrovia.

To Brown and me this expense item was minor. We were after something much larger. We wanted to book the African countries with first-class American Artists. The first, of course, being James Brown. We wanted ten cities in ten countries. Lagos, Nigeria; Monrovia, Liberia; Dakara, Senegal; Accra, Ghana; Duvala, Cameroons; Zaire (Kinshasa); Nairobi, Kenya; Freetown, Sierra Leone; Somalia; Lusaka, Zambia; Dar-es-Salaam, Tanzania; Conakry, Guinea.

From Monrovia, we wanted to start a major recording company with studios equipped to handle local artists as well as major stars. An FM radio station would be part of this operation. We'd call it *African*. We'd manufacture the records in Africa because the oil used would be cheaper, so would the rubber.

On Friday, December 1, 1978, the day of the final performance, James Brown was honored at Hotel Dukos. Minister Townsand, and another Minister of Defense, I think, bestowed Brown with honorary citizenship in Liberia. I sat at the table with Deputy Minister of Foreign Affairs Jarrett and Minister Someo Jones. Mr. Jones had attended the University of Michigan. We talked a great deal about Detroit. It seemed he'd lived two blocks from my house. My wife lived on Kirby between Hastings and St. Antoine. Mr. Jones lived on Canfield between John R and Brush. It was the heart of the ghetto. Now he was a Minister in Liberia. He recalled all the Detroit Nite Clubs: 20 Grand, Cobo Hall, Phelp's Lounge, etc. These were the years between 1958-1962. Now almost twenty years later, we sat down at a table almost five thousand miles away and remembered. In addition to Minister Jarrett, Arthur Dixon and Tony Cook sat with us. Both are drummers in James Brown's band. Arthur Dixon is also from Detroit, now living in Seattle. He attended Eastern High School in Detroit. He too lived on the East Side. His family is, as is my family, still in Detroit.

Oliver Bright and I tried to get better sound equipment. He talked to his friend Maj. Barclay, about the use of Army equipment. It was agreed upon. However, when we got to where it was stored, the man in charge, a Mr. Jones, was out to dinner. No one else had a key. It was 5:30 P.M. and we needed the equipment to set up. Bright and an Army jeep sped through the streets to Jones' house. He was not there. It was then decided that the lock had to be broken. Almost immediately upon breaking it, Jones appeared. Huff, the soundman, looked at the equipment. It was as bad as the equipment already on stage.

That night at the final show Brown arrived one hour late. The crowd outside the soccer field was so unruly the officials thought they'd wait until the last minute to bring him.

Several groups performed as openers. A Karate expert let anyone from the audience hit him in the stomach as hard as they wanted, a group sang a rock blues homage to Liberia, and the leading singer of Liberia, Tecumsie Roberts, backed by Liberia Dreamers, with hip variations on Black Americans, performed with expert knowledge of his audience. They loved him.

Meanwhile, outside the field, Oliver Bright personally handled the tickets because the night before many people had gotten in without paying. I walked around the field several times. At this point perhaps ten thousand had gathered, and people were still coming. On stage the sound was terrible. The group of girl singers, Margie, Mary, and Florence had to stop several times. The James Brown band had to constantly instruct Huff and his technicians. At 9:30 P.M. Brown's automobile appeared on the field. The band was playing and the conductor instructed the band to continue. The crowd cheered, the motorcycle policemen let their sirens blare out the music. I don't know what was on their minds. A few minutes later, James

Brown performed. He didn't leave the stage for two hours. The equipment went out several times. Only once, however, did Brown stop performing and fortunately it was for only a few seconds. The show was far superior to the previous night in terms of artistry. However, technically it was a disaster. The audience didn't care. They'd come to see James Brown, Soul Brother #1. And there he was, live on stage before their very eyes.

The following morning, Hugh Masakela came to pick me up. He was going to introduce me to the important people. Masakela is a noted South African musician. We drive and he lectures me on the possibilities in Africa. He told me how hard he worked to make all of this happen; of course, he had done nothing in my view. I must admit he was working from Monrovia, I worked from New York. He told me the electricians were his musicians. (So that's why the show was technically bad!) He took me to look at Millie Buchannan's paintings. She was not home. We went to E. J. Roye Hall to make a plan for rental of facilities in June & July 1979. His friend wasn't there. He then drove to the home of the man who books the hall; he wasn't home either. We visited Philemon Hou's home. Hou is an actor, writer, and director from South Africa. He promised to send me material (in New York). I'd seen him perform on Broadway in 1964 in a South African play called *Sponono*. He was also a friend of Mariam Makeba's. He thought he could talk to Mariam about Cyperian Ekewensi's *Jaguanana*. I wanted her to play the lead in the motion picture version of the novel.

Masakela is also working on a Black musical version of *Romeo & Juliet* with an American playwright in Ohio by the name of Clarence Young III. Then he told me about ideas for a gathering place for artists he'd build at Gertulue Floral Park, run by Gertrude Brewer (she wasn't home either). A lot of building would have to be done: Box seats for the important people would be built in the trees. The stage would be over the swimming pool according to Masakela and over the balcony according to Hou. They both spoke at the same time. I could tell that these two fine artists should not get into the business of the arts.

When we returned to Bright's house, we promised to contact each other before the first of the year.

In less than a year, Major Doe overthrew the government. Most of the people in the government were lined up on the beach and shot.

On tour in Africa:
"Zora Neale Hurston"

My first real look at Ghanaians was at the Amsterdam Airport Schiphol in Amsterdam, Holland. Schiphol is the Netherland's principal airport and claims to be congestion free. Not true! Congestion at the flight gate into Accra was so bad the flight was an hour late taking off. European KLM flight attendants as well as those processing entrance visas into Accra were European whites. Ghanaians tried to show impartiality and friendliness; however, the treatment was somewhat crude. The second impression was where were all of these people coming from, especially through Amsterdam?

The cultural differences were also apparent. At Gate F7 into Accra, Ghana, 95 percent of the passengers were Africans, spoke a different language, wore a different kind of dress, and had many crying children. The cultural differences also extended into hair styles for the women that substantially assimilated African Americans perms, weaves, etc. The little children played with American and European created toys, Gameboy, Nintendo, toy guns, toy airplanes, etc. The adult African men were dressed in American or European clothes, especially American/European suits, hats, and shoes.

Business and other matters, like passport check and passing through the metal detectors, slowed to a crawl.

Another irony of the embarkation into Accra from Amsterdam was an apparent lack of Americans visiting Panafest '94. I did see one performing group. I want to believe they were from the Caribbean.

The Impact of Race

The airline trip into Accra again pointed out the difficulty of European whites in a power position. The KLM Flight 589 was totally full, not an empty seat. Nineteen out of twenty aboard were Africans. The Africans laughed, joked, and in short, had a good time during the six-hour trip. The stewardesses were white. They were impatient with the Africans. Although a great deal of money had gone into KLM's coffers and I'm sure they appreciated it, they had no control over their employees' feelings towards Africans.

The typical protocol of airline and passenger relations was not evident on this leg of the trip. Passengers put bags in the aisles, ignored "fasten seat belt" signs, stood up when they felt like it, asked for more than one serving of food; the toilets were constantly in use; and parents let their children play and run free. The European flight crew seemed beside themselves.

On arrival at Accra's Kotoka International Airport our group was met by a Panafest '94 host who guided us to baggage claim. I witnessed confusion in baggage claim beyond any I've seen anywhere in the world. One small conveyor in a 50-square-foot area carried luggage for almost one thousand passengers. Each passenger had from three to ten pieces of baggage. Three employees tried to help those thousand passengers retrieve all their luggage. Chaos! Confusion! Anger! At several crucial points some European and American passengers reached boiling points and started crying; some feared their luggage was missing. I noticed most of the Africans took it all as very normal procedure. Some fed their crying children and made a festive event of all of it. A few African women with hair weaves and perms talked on cell phones. After about two hours we were able to retrieve our baggage. With the help of our Panafest '94 host we exited the Accra Airport. Another five to six thousand people waited outside the exit making it very difficult to get to the waiting vehicle that would take us to our hotel. Even though it was past midnight these people — many relatives with names printed on white paper, some beggars and some hangers-on — were cheering and waving their papers.

Weeks before leaving America we'd paid Panafest '94 for our hotel accommodations, registration fee to Panafest '94, and meals. We'd wired the money into a special account. We'd been assured of lodging at the Maple Leaf Hotel in Accra. Thus, it was a shock when one of our Panafest '94 hosts informed us we'd be driven to another hotel because the Maple

Leaf Hotel was overbooked! We'd have to check out early the following day to go to the Maple Leaf Hotel! Our driver and our host would then drive us to Cape Coast Castle where our first performance of *Zora Neale Hurston* would take place.

Saturday morning, December 10, 1994, we were up and ready for the two-and-a-half-hour ride to Cape Coast Castle. However, our Panafest '94 host announced we'd have to spend the night in Cape Coast because the performances would end past midnight. Now we hurriedly had to take overnight essentials. Our Panafest '94 host assured us not to worry: the Secretariat had excellent facilities for us; that our first stop in Cape Coast would be to meet the Secretariat and hear from him directly how he'd secured the overnight accommodations.

Driving in Ghana traffic is unbelievably difficult. Thousands congest the roadways. The ride from Accra to Cape Coast gave me another view of Ghanaian people. An indelible impression of thousands of poor women working along the highway with their babies and children. They sell peeled oranges, plantains, peppers, coconuts, cola nuts, bread and assorted odds and ends. Many of the women, though poor, wear brightly colored African fabric wrap dress. Some have babies wrapped on their backs as they move about with large tubs of goods balanced on their heads. The Ghanaian men are seen sporadically in these settings. They're part of a marketplace of wood framed shops that would sprout up every ten or fifteen miles along the highway. These shops specialize. For example, one might sell sandals, another dashikis, another cane sugar, still another African carved masks. As we arrived in Cape Coast, thousands of Ghanaian shops lined each side of the streets. Nearly five thousand people worked in or owned these shops. Children ran along the side of our van trying to sell everything from ice water in plastic bags to polished seashells. Ghana, though independent since 1957, is a poor country and still developing.

At Panafest '94 headquarters in Cape Coast, we waited one hour for the Secretariat. We were informed he wouldn't be able to meet us but he'd found excellent accommodations at Cape Coast University. They were dorms! Nowhere near the $60 (U.S.) we'd paid for lodging. So, back to Panafest '94 headquarters we went, since something obviously had gone wrong. The Secretariat's assistant made copies of my receipts for payments. After another hour we were informed we'd be staying in a private house.

The Impact of Race

The drive to the private house to put our bags away and back to have dinner took another hour. It was 7:30 P.M. and our play *Zora Neale Hurston* had had no tech rehearsal. Not one of us had seen the stage!

The 8:00 P.M. performance was shared by L'Acadco Dance Theater of Jamaica and The Sierra Leone Dance Troupe. *Zora Neale Hurston* by Laurence Holder, starring Elizabeth Van Dyke and Joseph Edwards, directed by Wynn Handman, played before a packed house of Africans, Europeans, and Americans in an outdoor theatre situated in the middle of Cape Coast Castle's courtyards. We were directly above the dungeons where over 300 years earlier millions of Africans were held in chains before being sent across The Middle Passage into slavery.

The two actors, Elizabeth Van Dyke and Joseph Edwards, with the Atlantic Ocean's waves crashing against the rocks adjacent to the castle, gave inspired performances. Afterward, both spoke of some inner being driving them; something akin to a spirit moving them; speaking through them. Both actors were drenched with sweat.

Without going into it, I will say that the same spirit infused L'Acadco Dance Theatre and The Sierra Leone Dance Troupe.

Sunday, December 11, 1994, we toured Cape Coast Castle. The experience is very difficult to relate on paper. First, some history on Cape Coast Castle and Slave Dungeons. It's an historic castle, once owned by the British. It was used in the 18th century as one of the centers for slave transport to the Caribbean and the United States.

Our group descended into the male slave dungeon holding sections. These three dungeons are about 15 feet by 15 feet; the height is about 25 feet with two air holes about one foot in diameter situated at the top of the room. No imagination can possibly convey how three or four hundred men could be packed into these spaces. With the help of our guide we examined step by step the slave dungeons, slave chains, cannon guns, cannon balls, as well as holding areas with no air for rebellious slaves.

The female slave dungeons are made of two sections; they too housed as many as three or four hundred female slaves at a given time.

In each dungeon, male and female, shackles adorned the walls, showing how each slave was shackled after being captured. In each dungeon an archway led to an exit facing the sea, where slaves were carried on small boats out to large transport slave ships.

In the motion picture *Sankofa* by Haile Gerima, filmed in the Castle's slave dungeons, an American woman is transported "back" to about 1825. She "becomes" a female slave forced to endure the sufferings of our ancestors. As our group explored each area of the slave dungeon some of us were overcome with emotion and had to exit.

Cape Coast Castle and Slave Dungeons as well as Elmina held captured slaves. In the early 15th century, European populations were expanding. They needed labor. From the mid 15th century, the Portuguese began exporting slaves from West Africa to Lisbon, Seville, and other centers of Christian Europe. Regularly, slaves were purchased by the Portuguese and exported once every six weeks to Elmina, Ghana, to be sold. These slaves were captured by the tribe who happened to be in power at the time. For example, if the chief happened to be a Fante, then Ashantis or Ga were captured.

The physical remains of the earliest Ghanaians have disappeared. Many of the cultural artifacts remain, especially stone tools. During the period 300,000 to 2000 B.C. the first pioneers of Ghanaian technology developed a great variety of basic skills — chopping, flaking, chipping, scraping — for the purpose of making instruments for hunting, trapping, meat-processing, and vegetable gathering and processing. During this period Ghana's stone age ancestors lived as nomads, living in rock shelters and temporary camps.

During the period 10,000-3,000 B.C. the expanding local population was forced to devise new technologies to create a viable economy. The people developed skills for the production of fine-bladed tools for use as knives, spears, and arrows. They produced bone needles for sewing animal skins into clothing. About 4000 B.C. they began to manufacture clay vessels.

Ghana was once known as the Gold Coast. Gold has been mined in Ghana since ancient times. Caravans made the treacherous journey across the Sahara desert to North Africa. The first European trader came in search of gold as early as 1470. Gold, the "king" of metals, has been used in Ghana for centuries for sculpture, currency, and jewelry.

Ghana has become world renowned for manufacturing the textured cloth known as "kente." Prime ministers, heads of state, ambassadors, and Americans from all walks of life feel privileged to wear kente as an adornment.

The Impact of Race

Ghana represents Africa's first in everything in the post-war wave of decolonization. Although during its many, many coups Ghana hit the bottom, it has been climbing back through help and loans from the International Monetary Fund programs.

In this century, Ghana has been fortunate to have had the service of two exceptional leaders. One led the way to independence and the other arrested the all too common regional tendency toward corruption. Osagyefo Dr. Kwame Nkrumah's struggle for the independence of Ghana inspired many nationalist movements across the continent. Flight Lt. Jerry Rawlings is the other leader. He gained his position of power in a 1981 coup. He's remained in power since, and in spite of numerous attempted revolts, has retained his reputation as a man of integrity.

On March 6, 1957, Ghana became the first African colony south of the Sahara to gain its independence. Ghana became a Republic on July 1, 1960. The name "Ghana" was taken from the ancient Sudan empire which flourished in West Africa between the fourth and tenth centuries A.D. The land area of the country is 92,000 square miles; within this area live approximately 15,000,000 people. Ghana is bordered on the West, North and East by the countries of Ivory Coast, Burkina Faso (Upper Volta), and Togo, respectively.

In Southern Ghana (West and South of the Volta River) and in South-East Ivory Coast are a large number of similar cultural groups to which the generic term "Akan" is applied. The groups are homogeneous both in terms of language and culture; included are the Fante, Asante, Brong, Twi (Twifo), Wasa, Denkyira, Sehwi, Assin, Adansi, Akyem (Akim), Akwapin, and Akwamu. The most powerful and most well-known are the Ashanti (Asante) people. The next largest "Akan" group is the Fante.

Ghana's economy is based primarily on hoe agriculture and cultivation of cocoa as an export crop. Yams and coco-yams are the main crops. Other crops are maize, cassava, peanuts, pepper, and tomatoes. Fishing is most important to the Fante, whose large fishing force fish along the entire Guinea Coast. Ghanaians live in an area rich in gold, diamonds, and bauxite. The mines housing these presently employ a large number of men.

All Akan people raise sheep, goats, and chickens along with some pigs, guinea fowl, duck, and pigeons. There are regular and highly developed markets. Division of labor is such that most petty trade is carried out by women. Men are responsible for hunting, fishing, and clearing land.

The Akan people speak a number of mutually intelligible dialects of Akan, such as Fante, Asante-Twi, and Akwapim Twi.

The Akan groups with Ghanaians are characterized by matrilineal descent, inheritance and succession. The Fanti and Ashanti have exogamous patrilineage also, making a double descent system. There is polygamy. In some quarters preference is given to cross-cousin marriage, insuring that, in spite of the matrilineal system of inheritance, the daughter of a man benefits from his property. Lineage in the system of kinship pervades Africa; not just in Ghana.

On Monday, December 12, 1994 our group visited the Shrine and Mausoleum of Osagyefo Dr. Kwama Nkrumah. Nkrumah was trained in America. He first attended Lincoln University. He associated with Black Americans of the Forties and early Fifties. Many credit Lorraine Hansberry for basing the character of Asagai in her play *A Raisin in the Sun* on Nkrumah. At the Shrine and Mausoleum was a statue of Nkrumah surrounded on each side by seven statues of leaders blowing trumpets of freedom. Inside a first portal is his final burial place. At the foot of the burial place is a photograph of the leaders in traditional dress, wearing a piece of kente outer garment.

Further inside is the Nkrumah Museum where hundreds of photographs record his history. Photos with leaders from the entire third world, the United States of America, Russia, and Europe; from John F. Kennedy to Gammal Abdul Nassar. After leading Ghana to independence in 1957 and a Republic in 1960, Dr. Kwame Nkrumah was overthrown in a CIA inspired coup while he was on a peace mission to Hanoi in 1966. He died while still in exile in 1972.

We spent that Monday afternoon at The Art Center. The Center is a very large market and sells everything: art carvings of all sizes (including huge), jewelry, kente, ivory, handmade musical instruments, and wall carvings, as well as American sodas like Pepsi and Sprite. Most of the purchases are made by Americans and Europeans. The negotiating is particularly fierce. We'd been warned to let our Panafest '94 host handle our negotiating otherwise we'd be cheated. They were absolutely right!

They see a foreigner and the real price doubles. A member of our group was quoted a cost of 225,000 cedis for two masks. Our host intervened and he got five masks for the same 225,000 cedis.

The Drama Studio, University of Ghana, in the Legon Region is where we performed the final performance of *Zora Neale Hurston*. The performance was on Wednesday, December 14, 1994. The University of Ghana is situated in a region known as Legon. If we compared the distance from Accra to Legon it would be similar to the distance from Manhattan to the Bronx. The University was built by Osagyefo Kwame Nkrumah. It has a student body of approximately ten thousand. Degrees are granted in Political Science, the Arts, Psychology, and Philosophy. The Drama Studio is in an intimate 150-seat outdoor theatre. It has two dressing rooms on either side of the stage; a scene shop is situated directly behind the stage. The stage itself is proscenium, approximately 25 by 20 feet. As a matter of fact, the stage is so intimate our production of *Zora Neale Hurston* soared. The actors felt it was a better performance than the one at Cape Coast Castle. The enthusiastic audience of about sixty people cheered the performance. The audience consisted of Africans, Americans, and Europeans. Since it was our last performance at Panafest '94, Joseph Edwards, one of the actors, thanked the Ghanaian people for being so kind.

As our autovan crept through crowded streets like Oku Street, Kokonte Street, 28th February Road, Ese Foo Street, Adenkum Street, we found it virtually impossible to find an African restaurant open past midnight. However, as late as 2 A.M. vender stalls and kiosks remained open. They had lights resembling candles on each stall—thousands of stalls and kiosks all along the roads, streets, and highways.

December 15, 1994. We visited the W. E. B. DuBois Museum on Pan African Culture. Dr. DuBois died in Ghana at the age of 95 in 1963. In his lifetime he wrote forty-two books, including the seminal study, *The Soul of Black Folks*. The museum houses many of Dr. DuBois' artifacts, including the cap and gown he wore as the first Black graduate from Harvard University. His burial ground is surrounded with wreaths from the likes of Maya Angelou, Stevie Wonder, the Jamaican rapper Shabba Rank, and others. Immediately adjacent to his final resting place are the ashes of his wife, Shirley Graham DuBois.

On our final day we said goodbye to many of the Africans and the African Americans we'd met who would remain at Panafest '94 until its conclusion — some of the friendliest African people in the world.

At the Berlin Wall

Ten days after the restrictions between East and West Berlin were removed, I arrived in Berlin. Theatre work tends to set up unusual bedfellows. My meetings with Gotz Friedrich, Director of Deutsche Opera Theatre, had been changed to Sunday, November 20, 1989 at 5:30 P.M. Thus, giving me and my American producer, Al Nellum, plenty of time to see Berlin or see the wall. A taxi driver who spoke no English — and, of course, neither Al nor I spoke nor understood an ounce of German — left both of us to speculate whether we Blacks could ever be international. We couldn't even tell the driver to turn the heat on in the Mercedes Benz taxi. Laughter, then silence as I speculate on the irony of how the Germans had turned the Mercedes Benz, America's status symbol of success, into a taxi cab. What the driver did understand was: Berlin Wall and Checkpoint Charlie. Upon our arrival at the West Berlin side of the wall were thousands of people. Already set up (in just nine days) were hundreds of vendors selling souvenirs, food, coffee, and booklets describing the wall.

The wall was constructed August 13, 1961. First it was a barbed wire structure built in an almost overnight act. The wall, a more solid structure, followed immediately. The irony of it all: The East Berlin Communist Regime built the structure; jailing themselves. Now graffiti adorns at least 25 kilometers of the West Berlin side of the wall: *Deutschland Liberta Boycott My Name Is Bundesprepublik*. The graffiti blazes in hundreds of colors, i.e., large single letters, statements, distorted and abstract faces; all spray painted like a long line of New York subway trains. Between the West Berlin and East Berlin wall is a 100 foot empty space, running the length of the two walls, appropriately called "No Man's Land." If anyone set foot in this area he was shot on sight. The wall went up and the United States (and the West) did nothing to stop it. With financial support from America, West Berlin survived brilliantly; under democracy (Capitalism) it moved out ahead of its East Berlin (Socialist) brothers and sisters.

Now, twenty-eight years later, on this cold Sunday morning about twenty-five thousand people gathered at the Brandenburg gate where President Kennedy, flanked by Adenaur, Willy Brandt, and Raine Barzel, delivered his now famous (but then abstract) *Ich bin Ein Berliner* speech. Now, visitors and cameras witnessed and recorded the end of the wall and what it represented.

Of the estimated twenty-five thousand, Blacks numbered about a dozen. Many weren't expatriates as expected but Blacks from African countries or journalists; about six were Black Americans. Why were we here? In my case as well Al's, it was an accident of history. Along this West Berlin side, as far as the eyes could see, people touched the wall. Small children with little picks and little axes pretended to chip pieces of the wall as parents snapped photographs; adults with large picks and large axes tried to chip. But the wall is built solid. Policemen apologized for having to ask people not to chip the wall.

I asked a German if I could use his hammer to break a piece of the wall. He waved me away; either not understanding or not willing to share his hammer. I placed both hands, with open palms, on the wall exactly as I once placed both hands on the cave wall in Goree, Ghana. I cried then; I tried not to but caught in the emotion of the moment, I cried at this wall here in Berlin, West Germany. A lot of East and West Berliners were hugging and crying. At both the Brandenburg Gate and Checkpoint Charlie (where Soviet and U.S. tanks had confronted each other) thousands walked through freely, *Vous Sortez du Secteur Americain* (you are leaving the American Sector). *I am witness; I was there.* This feeling; this look on the faces of East and West Berliners were reflections of faces I'd witnessed during the Civil Rights Movement. I saw it on the faces of those of us who heard Martin Luther King, Jr. speak in Detroit at the foot of Woodward Avenue in 1963 and again at the foot of the Lincoln Memorial in Washington, D.C. in 1963's poor people March on Washington. I've seen their faces in photographs after the decision in *Brown v. Board of Education*. I've seen their faces...

Woodie King, Jr.

The irony of it all; this accident of history which brought Al Nellum and myself to West Berlin, which caused the National Endowment for the Arts to recapitulate at this particular time, was/is one of the many results of Dr. Martin Luther King, Jr.'s work finding further definition around the world twenty-one years after his death. Al Nellum, Hans Flury, Peter-Josephs Hargitay are in London producing *King: The Musical* and I am co-producing it. The other director is the expatriate East German, Gotz Friedrich, now Director of Deutsche Opera Theatre in Berlin. The teachings and words of Dr. Martin Luther King, Jr., had impelled East-Berliner Friedrich to seek refuge in the West in 1966.

The African-American
Theatre of Tomorrow

Not long ago there was an historic anniversary in Black theatre well worth celebrating, and remembering. For seventy-five years, in Cleveland, an institution named Karamu dedicated itself to the proposition that individual success and social responsibility are inextricably connected. It remains a social agency reaching out to help solve problems within its community. At the same time it grabs those talented individual artists and guides them towards careers in theatre, film, and television. The list of those individuals who've passed through is long and impressive.

Karamu is *the* grand parent of the Black Theatre. It existed all by itself when our minds carried the possibility of something as remote as *A Negro in the American Theatre*. In 1947 when Edith Isaac wrote her historical book *The Negro in the American Theatre*, one third of it was about Karamu. It's an institution that has been presenting plays with Black artists in leading roles since its inception. Those who passed through have gone on to some of the highest positions of leadership in the American Theatre, Hollywood Television, and the motion picture industry. Karamu also sent those-who-passed-through into leadership positions in business, education and social science. Karamu is the Boy Scouts.

If we don't celebrate our past, our history, we cannot really understand or appreciate our future. If we cannot see or understand Karamu's contribution to the place we call Cleveland, Ohio, and to our country, we all are blind and in serious trouble.

It was to institutions like Karamu that we looked in the past for that leadership; we most certainly are going to look to Karamu in the future. But what will the African-American theatre of tomorrow be? And what will it be about?

Certainly *not* about the language of the plays; certainly no longer about the fear of seeing a group of Black people gathered in one place. I think it was very basic in the Sixties: *Blacks wanted to control and run our own institutions.* This new Black Theatre was to be by Black people, for Black people, and controlled by Black people.

Black Theatre reinvented itself in 1959. It was that year that *A Raisin in the Sun* opened on Broadway. *A Raisin in the Sun* was the first play to appear on Broadway by a Black female author, Lorraine Hansberry; it was also the first drama to be directed by a Black director, Lloyd Richards. Although many Black plays had been presented in New York as well as around the USA, *A Raisin in the Sun* ushered in the New Black Theatre Movement.

This movement occurred at a time of civil unrest on university campuses across America. Media coverage of civil unrest captured our imagination on the news each night. The Black voices of Malcolm X, Martin Luther King, Jr., James Baldwin, Adam Clayton Powell, Jr., Stokely Carmichael, H. Rap Brown, and student unrest gave voice to the outrage we felt in the Black community. That outrage flamed the Black cultural community. The reinvention of the Black Theatre came as a direct result of the same issues that were blowing in the wind for freedom; the same issues that caused the Watts riot of 1964; the Harlem riot of 1965; the Detroit riot of 1967; and the Newark riot of 1969.

Those responsible for this reinvention know that many of our Black artists were "let-in-the-door" so to speak. The whole proliferation of the so-called Blaxploitation films, the many books published and "Rediscovered" by white publishing houses, and without question all the Black comedies and huge Afros on television during the Seventies.

Were those images more than surface? They certainly weren't lasting because they weren't created by us. They were created by white institutions. It was an error of that revolution that we accepted those tokens rather than the institutions we fought and died for.

A few Black institutions did emerge! Inner City Cultural Center in Los Angeles; Negro Ensemble Company; New Lafayette Theatre; ETA Theatre in Chicago; New Federal Theatre in New York City.

Woodie King, Jr.

Since the Thirties, Black Artists' energy has made substantial contributions to the American Theatre and film. Racism, of course, aborted so many of our contributions. Despite our fervor and our passion and our pride we're unable to build and support enough Black institutions. Yet, we learned one very important lesson: As long as we love ourselves and our brothers and sisters, we won't stereotype the Black lifestyles. This love tends to prohibit stereotypes in our writings and in our performance. We believe if there'd been no Black Art Movement we wouldn't have the vast number of performing artists now working in the theatre; the vast number of popular Black plays: *Ceremonies in Dark Old Men*, *The River Niger*, *First Breeze of Summer*, *What the Winesellers Buy*, *Black Girl*, *The Sty of the Blind Pig*, *In the Wine Time*, *The Taking of Miss Janie*, *for colored girls...*, *A Soldier's Play*, and, finally, August Wilson.

These plays and the many Black artists involved led to the breakthrough in filmmaking by Spike Lee, Robert Townsend, Mario Van Peebles, Bill Duke, Kevin Hooks, Gilbert Moses. I think it's obvious that these filmmakers needed a discerning Black audience to corroborate the work of the writers and the filmmakers. We believe Black institutions provide a gathering place for young artists as well as the Black audiences to grow. Let's face it, if the Hollywood system didn't believe an audience existed, the films wouldn't be financed.

In the Sixties and Seventies, Black filmmakers and film looked diligently toward our inclusion in television and film. Look at the work of pioneer filmmaker Bill Greaves, St. Clair Borne via "Black Journal" (later called "The Tony Brown Journal"), Melvin Van Peebles, Stan Lathan, Charles Lane, Bob Gardner, Ayoka Chenzara, the late Kathy Collins, Charlie Barnett, Hailie Gerima, Ossie Davis, etc. However, no Black filmmaking institution emerged. With a great deal of passion and pride, Blackness was forced into the consciousness of America. Many universities accepted Black studies and Black student unions as a viable part of university life. Black playwrights and filmmakers created work with no white characters.

With this new passion and fervor (found really in the Black Power movement of the Sixties) Black artists were more daring with their artistic instruments. Some of the artists came out of the woodshed with brilliant creations. Some actors really believed that the American way of progressing

97

for Black artists is the same as for white actors/artists. Off-Broadway hit, television career, and a career in motion pictures. However, it was discovered by Black artists as diverse in their thinking as Hattie McDaniels, Sidney Poitier, James Earl Jones, James Edwards, Dorothy Dandridge, Ruby Dee and Ossie Davis, Louis Gossett, Jr., Diana Sands, Diahann Carroll, William Marshall, and Harry Belafonte that that's the way white institutions protect and promulgate the work of white artists. Elijah Muhammad, Malcolm X, Marcus Garvey, and Booker T. Washington told us in countless ways that no matter what the individual success of Black artists that success didn't translate into the building of Black institutions.

Ruby Dee and Ossie Davis were the only Black performing artists who rethought it all and toured their work directly into the Black community.

For future progress of African American Theatre, Black Theatre leaders must have the passion and fervor like those artists of the Sixties and Seventies.

They have always paved the way in Black theatre at Karamu. However, tomorrow's artists must work even harder. Black artists are in competition with artists from around the world. With the white theatre always rewarding and recognizing their own, how does a Black artist judge his or her own ability? They reward each other with Tony awards, Emmy awards, and Academy Awards in recognition of their contribution and leadership. In competing, the Black artists must ask themselves:

> Do I love my Black self?
> What can I contribute to Black Theatre?
> What am I doing to better prepare myself professionally?

Black Theatre is a growth industry. It's an industry that has innovative writers, actors, directors, singers, and dancers. Further, the literature of Black America is so ready for film it's a very good industry to *work* in. More than ever the television industry with its insatiable appetite for product must eventually look to well-trained Black artists.

But the Black artist will only *work* in this white institution known as film and television.

What must an institution like Karamu prepare artists for? A theatre environment where there's room at the top for institution builders, leaders. Acting opens one to so many possibilities.

Many of those who passed through Karamu returned to the institution. Look at Margaret Ford Taylor.

One can come out of a Karamu and move wherever one wishes because one gets a quick education about life there. In the years spent there, one gains a certain amount of experience, confidence; a certain awareness on how things get done. It's no different in Hollywood or New York or Europe or any resident professional theatre across America.

African American Theatre of tomorrow must exist as a result of one's knowledge of the past. We must be aware of the pioneers and their contribution. We shouldn't be doing all this work to integrate into a system that hates us. We cannot drain Karamu; we must put something back. It's an institution that loves us.

It's very difficult to work in film and television, perpetuating a system we really hate for the sake of a job. We must bring the beauty of our Black culture to the bargaining table. A beauty, by the way, we learned to better understand at Karamu. When you find that to be impossible you should build your own institution.

We must not exist simply as a reaction to white values. We must remember that some whites and many Blacks don't believe in *anything*. Thus, they're open to being programmed—by media and hype—into believing in whatever the system demands. Therefore, our skin color alone isn't enough to bind us together.

Seventy-five years ago, the people who founded Karamu believed in something. That belief grew into a strong living institution.

Beyond New York — Touring and the LORT

Since the Nineties, minority and rural sections of this country have been neglected by the middle class. The areas had long been neglected by the upper class, but the Nineties ushered in an overall benign neglect of mainstream funding for better housing, social services, education, and the cultural life of minorities.

Those of us who work in these areas of the arts known as Black, Latino, Asian, multiculturalism, are now questioning our very existence. Corporations and Foundations stopped supporting non-glamorous "minority" art after the riots of the Sixties. I call that The Art That Talks— theatre, film, poetry. That art isn't abstract and always speaks in an artistic literature about minorities in America.

Since 1976 National Black Touring Circuit, Inc., has been touring "The Art That Talks" to minority and rural communities as well as colleges and universities throughout America. NBTC tries to produce and present plays about Malcolm X, Bert Williams and George Walker, Billie Holiday, Harriet Tubman, Zora Neale Hurston, Lorraine Hansberry, Ira Alridge, Muhammad Ali, etc. We also present theatrical works of historical events: *Do Lord Remember Me* by James de Jongh; *Celebration* by Shauneille Perry; *God's Trombones* by James Weldon Johnson; *Jessie Owens* and *The Game* by Garland Thompson; A Photo Exhibition on Black Theatre by the renowned photographer Bert Andrews.

Black Theatre touring companies are a relatively new phenomenon. There are so few listed in the Association of Art Presenters catalogue one would think they didn't exist. Periodically a play with Black actors will tour under the auspices of a white touring company; in other cases Black theatres will tour one of their productions. But there's no company devoted exclusively to touring Black theatre productions. Yet touring Black theatre productions are very appropriate for these times. First and foremost the artistic and historical context that frame the material bring a new dialogue that wouldn't otherwise by possible. The institutions booking these productions are only occasionally Black controlled.

In white institutions Black theatre productions open a dialogue long missing in the surrounding community. The programming in the white institutions doesn't take into consideration the changing Black audiences within the community. Many of these institutions book in arts performances that don't relate to anyone in the community. Many book performance artists such as Pina Bausch, Karen Finley, Tim Miller, or Robert Wilson.

There are certain performance artists who "just happen to be Black" — artists who deny the aesthetics of their Blackness. They generally present only "surface" Blackness. Real Black art would cause the institution as well as the artist to rethink old concepts. Indeed, reevaluating self. Traditional white institutions will bring only one Black production into their space one time per year. These institutions have no intention to change their policy of cultural exclusion.

Black institutions (or Black controlled institutions) are somewhat different. Many are so seriously underfunded they look for anything Black that can be booked into the institution and often get productions that turn Black audiences off. We must remember our Black audiences can always go across town to a white controlled institution and see highly professional non-Black theatre.

What are some of the major problems in touring Black Theatre? Well, again, one big problem is theatre *talks*. If it's Black and talks, white audiences aren't inclined to listen. This audience wants to move away from real Black subjects. Why? The artist must *talk* about and *explore* issues that are pertinent to his own existence — issues such as racism, sexism, classism. Only when these issues no longer exist will there be no need to explore them. On the other hand, Black audiences crave a theatre production that *talks* about issues.

Starting in the mid-Eighties, a culturally accepted form of self-criticism within Black arts circles (especially circles that worked within white institutions) was overwhelmingly endorsed by white institutions. These artists and their productions toured constantly. I have an acquaintance who works in Hollywood. When he sits down in a roomful of white executives pitching an idea he eventually gets these nonsense statements into his conversation:

> "Not all slaves were unhappy... I'd like to explore that in my
>   next script."
> "I must admit I really like some of Stepin Fetchit's work."
> "I would not want to live in Harlem myself."
> "I went to hear this blues singer (jazz group) and it was
>   mostly whites."

My friend never deals with the economic reality of the cost of attending a jazz/blues club or even with the treatment Blacks receive once there. Or that when the jazz/blues group appears in small Black clubs within the Black community they're usually packed to capacity. My friend usually gets the job. But none of his finished scripts ever get made. It's very important for Blacks to understand that to produce high quality work we must love ourselves, otherwise it will be reflected in our work.

Many of us who are Black started out in theatre working to be included. During the Forties, Fifties and Sixties, we knocked on the doors of white institutions soliciting inclusion. Most of us were denied; yet we kept knocking. Why, we asked? Many of us graduated from major white universities, others came through Black colleges and studied under legendary professors of theatre. Since we were constantly denied inclusion, what were we going to do with this training, this desire, this need to be a part of this American Theatre? Some of us who are Black went out and started institutions. Other Blacks who were playwrights, directors, designers, actors, technicians rushed to be a part of these institutions. With very little money but overwhelming talent these institutions produced Pulitzer Prize-winning playwrights, Academy Award-winning actors, skilled directors and technicians. Hundreds of whites work in these Black institutions.

And unlike most of the LORT (Legion of Regional Theatres) playhouses you'll find as many whites as Blacks as audience members. Some whites are on The Board of Directors of these institutions.

Lloyd Richards, for instance, the man who replaced Robert Brustein as head of Yale School of Drama and Director of Yale Repertory Theatre, went in and made successful what previous directors did not; could not or would not. He included Blacks: brilliant actor's like Courtney Vance, Angela Bassett, Charles Dutton, Delroy Lindo, etc; brought in Athol Fugard, worked closely with Lee Blessing, discovered the Drama Critics Circle and Pulitzer Prize winner August Wilson.

What's to be done? Create a new non-profit 501C3 institution at $5 or $6 million per year? Or enhance the budgets of ten of the oldest Black theatres across the United States? It seems to me foundations and other funding sources could get a bigger bang for their bucks if they enhanced New Federal Theatre in New York, National Black Theatre in New York, Billie Holiday Theatre in Brooklyn, Jomandi in Atlanta, St. Louis Black Repertory Theatre in St. Louis, Ensemble Theatre in Houston, Lorraine Hansberry Theatre in San Francisco, ETA Theatre in Chicago, Penumbra in Minneapolis, and The New Freedom Theatre in Philadelphia.

All of these theatres are over a quarter century old; some celebrated their 30th anniversary in the year 2000. For each of these theatres to be included in the membership of the League of Resident Theatre would cost them an additional $750,000 per year. That would enable the theatres to increase fees to playwrights, directors, actors, designers, and staff. It would further help these institutions set up subscription drives and development offices. Marketing and promotion would be on a par with other LORT theatres. Full-time production managers and company managers could be hired to oversee productions and deal with the artists. Only $750,000 in foundation, corporate, and donor support per theatre! Or a total of $7.5 million to enhance the budget of ten Black theatres. It sounds so much better when we hear: of the seventy-six LORT theatres, eleven are Black; rather than only one!

Celebrating Black Women

The Winona Lee Fletcher Award for Artistic Excellence in Black Theatre, initiated at the Black Theatre Network's (BTN) conference in the summer of 1995, represented recognition, for the first time, of African-American women's contributions to Black theatre.

The conference, which was held in conjunction with the Women in Theatre (WTP) subcommittee of the Association of Theatre in Higher Education (ATHE), took place from July 23 through July 27 at the Bismarck Hotel in Chicago, Illinois. The theme was "Breaking Barriers: Celebrating Women Making Theatre." The six Black women honored were Abena Joan Brown, Vinnette Carroll, Vivian Robinson, Ntozake Shange, Barbara Ann Teer, and Margaret Wilkerson.

Dr. Winona Lee Fletcher, after whom the awards were named, is a pioneer in education. She was educated at Johnson C. Smith University (AB, Magna Cum Laude); University of Iowa (M.A.); and Indiana University-Bloomington (Ph.D.). Between 1951 and 1978, she married the late Professor Joseph G. Fletcher, mothered one daughter, Betty, and directed, costumed, designed, produced and sometimes acted in well over fifty productions at Kentucky State University. In 1978, she moved permanently to Indiana University at Bloomington, where she became a professor of theatre and Afro-American studies and the Associate Dean of the College of Arts and Sciences.

During the Fifties and Sixties, Dr. Fletcher became active in the National Association of Dramatic and Speech Arts and served as executive secretary. She was also a member of the editorial boards of *Encore* and *Players* magazine. Additionally, Fletcher served on the board of directors of the American Theatre Association (ATA), and chaired their Black Theatre Program from 1974 to 1977. In 1979, the ATA bestowed one of its highest honors on Fletcher by naming her to the College of Fellows "in recognition of continuous and outstanding meritorious service to educational theatre of the nation. In 1979, she also became president of the University and College Theatre Association. The first Black Theatre Network Lifetime Membership Award was presented to her in 1991. In 1993, she received ATHE's Career Achievement Award for Theatre Education. Dr. Fletcher retired after giving forty-five years of service to theatre education.

The Winona Lee Fletcher Award for Artistic Excellence was designed by Mark Randelle King. The medallion featured on the award resembles those worn by kings and queens of Africa who embodied the artistic creativity given to them by the god Oshun. They were awarded as follows: Barbara Ann Teer for Institution building; Abena Joan Brown for Producing; Vinnette Carroll for Directing; Ntozake Shange for Writing for the Theatre; Vivian Robinson for Audience Development and Margaret Wilkerson for Scholarship. In addition to being honored, Barbara Ann Teer served as BTN's 1994 National Chairwoman as well.

Barbara Ann Teer

Teer was born in East St. Louis, Illinois. She graduated magma cum laude from the University of Illinois with a degree in dance. Afterwards, she went to Europe and studied with some of the masters in dance in West Berlin, Paris, London and Switzerland. Arriving in New York in the mid-Fifties, she danced with the Alwin Nikolais Dance Company. She made her Broadway debut in 1961 in the musical *Kwamina* which was choreographed by the legendary Agnes DeMille. Barbara Ann Teer was dance captain. However, after a knee injury, Teer began studying acting with Sanford Meisner, Paul Mann, and Lloyd Richards. Her acting credits include William Inge's *Where's Daddy*, Langston Hughes' *Prodigal Son*, Rochelle Owens' *Home Movies*, Douglas Turner Ward's *Day of Absence*, Theodore Fliker's *Living Premise*, and Ron Milner's *Who's Got His Own*.

Barbara Ann Teer went on to become the founder and driving force behind Harlem's National Black Theatre, Inc. (NBT), which got its start in a rickety loft in 1968. Under Teer's leadership, The National Black Theatre performed throughout the United States, in Trinidad, Guyana, Japan and

Western Nigeria, where her official adoption by the King of Oshogbo made her a legitimate Yoruba princess.

In 1983, after forming an advisory committee of New York's most masterful construction managers and developers, Teer purchased an entire city block of property in Harlem and diligently worked to develop a new theatre entity in the Harlem community: The National Black Institute of Communication and Theatre Arts. In 1992, the Institute moved into its $12 million arts complex on Fifth Avenue at 125th Street. According to Teer, it's the first revenue-generating African-American theatre arts complex in the country. Its tenants, who rent close to 20,000 feet of space in the new complex, already include a supermarket, a comedy club, a mosque, an art gallery, and a restaurant. Without question, Barbara Ann Teer is a devoted warrior in the struggle for the institutionalization of Black theatre.

Barbara Ann Teer is a forceful, charismatic personality, clearly more comfortable in a leadership role than any other. Along with the status comes high visibility as well as the slings and arrows that recognition often invites. Yet, among some of her former and current students, there's an almost worshipful attitude towards her.

Teer married the late actor Geoffrey Cambridge but they divorced in the early Seventies. She has two children from a later union with Adeyimi Lithcott and resides in a stately, elegantly furnished brownstone on 137th Street in Harlem. She was awarded an honorary doctorate of human letters from the University of Rochester in New York.

Abena Joan Brown

The next honoree is a very close friend and associate of mine. I've directed three award-winning productions of Abena Joan Brown's. She's a new breed of producer but like Barbara Ann Teer, she's very much about institutionalization of Black Theatre. In 1987, when I directed the world premiere of Ron Milner's *Checkmates*, her ETA (Ebony Talent Associates) theatre was an old warehouse. When I returned in the 1989-90 season to direct Rob Penny's *Good Black Don't Crack*, the warehouse was renovated into a $6 million state-of-the-art performing facility. By 1992, when I returned to direct Nubia Kai's *Harvest the Frost*, ETA had a subscription of 85 percent capacity.

Beginning as a dancer, Abena Joan Brown gained widespread experience as an actress, company manager, director and producer. Today, she's an internationally acclaimed arts administrator. At ETA Creative Arts Foundation, Brown is responsible for the overall operation of the organization. In addition, she produces five mainstage productions, two plays for children, and a reading series consisting of eight plays per year. She has produced over one hundred productions.

In the early Nineties, however, Brown grew weary of the plays she was receiving in the mail from playwrights and their agents. She created a paradigm for playwright searches called the Playwright Discovery/ Development Initiative (PDI); went out and raised the necessary funding; and brought together a panel of theatre professionals consisting of Vantile Whitfield, Rob Penny, Ron Milner, Paul Carter Harrison, Christine Houston, Kamiti Janice Porter, Euseni Eugene Perkins, and myself, among several others. The panel meets twice per year, and tries to guide promising playwrights into a Black aesthetic. If the playwright adheres to the aesthetic, ETA produces the play. In the 1993-94 season, for instance, ETA produced four plays from the Playwrights Discovery Initiative.

According to Brown, ETA is Chicago's first and only Afrocentric professional training and performance center. *Chicago* magazine has named her among one of the "50 Brightest Stars in Chicago Theatre." Today's *Chicago Woman* cited Brown as one of "100 women shaping Chicago's future," and *Dollars and Sense* magazine listed her as one of "America's Top 100 Business and Professional Women." Abena Joan Brown certainly filled the criteria for recognition by the BTN conference of "Breaking Barriers."

Vinnette Carroll

Within two weeks of my arrival in New York in 1964, Langston Hughes took me to see two productions. One was *Jericho, Jim Crow*; the other, *The Prodigal Son*, directed by Vinnette Carroll. I was so impressed that, later, Langston tried to set up a meeting. However, it wasn't until six or seven years later, after Vinnette Carroll was appointed director of the New York State Council on the Arts' Ghetto Arts Program, that we officially met. At that meeting, Carroll made it clear she knew of my work and assured me the newly formed New Federal Theatre would be funded by her program.

At the BTN conference, in an emotional introduction by Professor Joan

Lewis of Clark College, in Atlanta, Vinnette Carroll was lauded for her work with young people. Carroll was instilling values in today's young artists the same as she'd tried to do over thirty years earlier when she taught at New York's High School of Performing Arts. She points out, "You cannot be a virgin in the morning and a prostitute at night."

As founder and Artistic Director of the Urban Arts Corps Theatre in New York and the Vinnette Carroll Theatre in Fort Lauderdale, Florida, Carroll was instrumental in the careers of many of today's leading performers. At the Urban Arts Corps, she directed over fifty productions before moving to Fort Lauderdale to teach and to form the theatre in her name.

Vinnette Carroll directed for companies throughout the world, including the San Francisco Opera, The Mark Taper Forum in Los Angeles, The Dallas Theatre Center, The Theatre des Champs-Elysees in Paris, and the Spoleto Festival of Two Worlds in Italy. She received many directorial awards, including The Drama Critics Circle Award, the New York Outer Circle Award, the Ebony Magazine Black Achievement Award, and three Tony Award nominations. Her television directorial credits include *When Hell Freezes Over I'll Skate* for PBS Great Performances series, and *Beyond the Blues*, for which she received an Emmy Award. Using the music and lyrics of her long-time collaborator Micki Grant, she also conceived and directed the Broadway hits *Don't Bother Me I Can't Cope* and *Your Arms Too Short to Box With God*.

A member of the Society of Stage Directors and Choreographers and the Dramatist's Guild, Vinnette Carroll's work was usually marked by exuberant vitality. She was an extraordinary director-actor-teacher whose theatre pieces combine music, dance, and spoken words into a seamless tapestry which is a whole new form of musical theatre.

Vinnette Carroll died in 2002.

Vivian Robinson

Mikell Pinkney introduced the next honoree, observing not only that AUDELCO was then twenty-two years old, but, on a personal level, how winning an AUDELCO Award had been important for his career when he was artistic director of the Billie Holiday Theatre.

It was in 1966, after the death of her husband, that Vivian Robinson began working for *The New York Amsterdam News* as a clerk-typist. She was later promoted to advertising manager. In 1967, she was given tickets to see Marlene Dietrich's one-woman show on Broadway at the Lunt-Fontaine Theatre. She enjoyed it so much that she wrote a paragraph about the show for *The Amsterdam News*. That paragraph marked the beginning of a series of theatre and dance reviews she'd write regularly until 1980. She credits her aunt, Lucille Smith, for providing her with her undying love for theatre.

In her acceptance speech, Robinson talked about how she formed AUDELCO. In the early Seventies as she attended theatres, she noted very few Blacks attended. She began to form theatre parties to correct this situation. These theatre parties developed into an organization and on April 1, 1973, the Audience Development Committee, Inc., better known as AUDELCO, was founded.

Supported by theatregoers who were part of the AUDELCO Theatre Parties, Vivian Robinson felt the need, additionally, to do something to encourage and honor Black artists. When Douglas Turner Ward was nominated for a Tony Award as "Best Supporting Actor" for his leading role in the Broadway production of Joseph Walker's *The River Niger*, Vivian Robinson and the "AUDELCO ladies" went into action and began the Annual AUDELCO Black Theatre Recognition Awards.

Vivian Robinson has received numerous awards and honors, including Media Woman of the Year by the Media Women of New York, The Mayor's Award for Outstanding Contribution to the Theatre in New York, The Destiny Service Award (Harlem Week Committee of the Uptown Chamber of Commerce), and the Monarch Awards. She also served as President of the Board of the Black Fashion Museum and as board members of New Federal Theatre, The Uptown Chamber of Commerce, and the Arts and Cultural Committee of Community Planning Board Number Ten.

Vivian Robinson died in 1996.

Ntozake Shange

Born Paulette Williams, Shange was raised in St. Louis and Trenton, New Jersey. She graduated with honors from Barnard College and went on to earn an M.A. in American Studies at the University of Southern California.

Despite having written over a dozen plays, seven novels, and hundreds of poems, Ntozake Shange is best known for her choreopoem, *for colored girls who have considered suicide/when the rainbow is enuf.* Recently it received an outstanding production at Lehman College in the Bronx. It was originally produced in New York at The New Federal Theatre by myself and Joseph Papp. It was directed by Oz Scott. It moved from New Federal Theatre in 1976 to Joseph Papp's New York Shakespeare Festival Public Theatre where it played for three months. Joseph Papp and I then moved the play to the Booth Theatre on Broadway, making Shange the second African-American female writer to be represented on Broadway, preceded only by the achievement of Lorraine Hansberry nearly twenty years earlier. After the Broadway run, where it was hugely popular, *for colored girls...* toured the United States. In the 1978-79 season, I produced one tour to Australia, another to London, and a final one to the West Coast (Los Angeles and San Francisco).

Ntozake Shange's more recent plays in the choreopoem tradition continue to use music, lighting, dance, and poetry to examine the experience of Black women. Her quest to discover and project a theatrical aesthetic which is distinctively African-American, fully emotional and intellectual at once, has led the way for contemporary dramatists and creators such as Laurie Carlos, George C. Wolfe, and Suzan-Lori Parks.

Margaret Wilkerson

Introduced by Kathy Ervin, Dr. Wilkerson was honored for her achievements in Black Theatre Scholarship. She's presently professor and chair of the Afro-American Studies Department, and director of the Center for the Study, Education, and Advancement of Women at the University of California at Berkeley. Her teaching focuses on undergraduate and graduate level courses in African-American theatre history, literature and biography.

Dr. Margaret Wilkeson grew up in Los Angeles, as one of three daughters born to George and Gladys Buford. In 1959, she graduated from the University of Redlands with a degree in history. Further studies led to an

M.A. and a Ph.D. in Dramatic Arts from the University of California at Berkeley. In 1961, she married Stan Wilkerson.

She has written extensively on Black theatre and on the role of women in the Black Theatre. She has served as editor and co-editor on several issues of noted journals such as *Black Scholar* and *The Nation*, served on literary advisory boards for such publications as *Theatre Journal* and *African-American Literary Forum*, and in 1990, was nominated as one of six finalists for the National Magazine Awards in the category of Special Issues. Wilkerson has adapted plays, written plays, and performed in plays. She has won the Fletcher Award for outstanding scholarship, and she has written countless reviews of plays and books. Her list of published articles and essays is too lengthy to recount. Her edited anthology, *9 Plays by Black Women* (1986) has now become an invaluable resource for the study of African-American female dramatists. In 1980, she received an honorary doctorate of humane letters from the University of Redlands. She has received over twenty-five awards and honors for her theatre scholarship.

The recognition of these extraordinary women in theatre with the Winona Lee Fletcher Awards was only a part of the BTN conference, which also had a variety of panels and workshops. These panels included: Black Theatre and the Future; Female Artistic Directors; Black Community Theatre; Sexuality in Black Theatre; Actor's Equity and the Black Theatre; Black Theatre in Chicago; and Women with Different Theatre Strokes. Various workshops included an Acting-Directing Workshop led by Glenda Dickerson and Clinton Turner Davis; an Acting Audition Workshop with a critique panel headed by myself, Kathryn Evevin, Clinton Turner Davis, and Lorna Littleway; a Performance Workshop with critiques by Ntozake Shange, Lorna Littleway, Stephen Gerald, and Kathryn Ervin; a special inspirational workshop conducted by Barbara Ann Teer; and an informal fireside chat with Vinnette Carroll.

Dr. Lundeanna Thomas, the fifth president of BTN, wrote her dissertation on Barbara Ann Teer's National Black Theatre. Thomas was also very successful in getting complete involvement of ATHE's Women in Theatre (WTP). Originated to study and examine the "status of women" in academic and professional theatre; to develop women dramatists; and to promote women's work at ATHE, twenty years later, WTP was still networking and setting up preconferences prior to the main ATHE conference. WTP has taken a strong lead in directing attention to feminism and feminist critique of culture and representation. It has also examined the ramifications and influences of racism, homophobia, sexism, and the interconnections of these oppressive forces withing the field of theatre.

About thirty WTP members, who were white, attended the BTN conference. These women supported the BTN conference by registering and by buying tickets to the Winona Lee Fletcher Awards Dinner. Also, as a part of WTP, with their vice-president, Dr. Esther Beth Sullivan moderating Clinton Turner Davis of the Non-Traditional Casting Project gave the rousing keynote address "Breaking Barriers." Glenda Dickerson followed by highlighting neglected Black women pioneers to the Black cause.

"Breaking Barriers: Celebrating Women Making Theatre" was a continuation of WTP's commitment to breaking institutional and prejudicial barriers that exist for men and women of the theatre. The coming together of BTN and WTP under this theme was the beginning of a unique forum to address coalition building, as well as a means to focus on critical, historical, and performance work by women of color whose accomplishments were so elegantly celebrated that evening.

Playwrights

The Restructuring of Lorraine Hansberry's "A Raisin in the Sun"

A DIRECTOR'S VIEW OF THE CLASSIC, FALL 1994

In mid-July 1994, Kenny Leon, the artistic director of the Alliance Theatre in Atlanta called and asked me to direct Lorraine Hansberry's *A Raisin in the Sun*. It was to begin rehearsals in mid-September and open mid-October 1994. Lloyd Richards, the distinguished internationally renowned director of the original Broadway production, had been set to direct. However, a television production of August Wilson's *The Piano Lesson* was set to film in Pittsburgh at the same time with Mr. Richards directing and since it's impossible to be in two places at the same time, Lloyd dropped *A Raisin in the Sun*.

Kenny Leon is one of four Black artistic directors of white-controlled resident professional theatres in America. The other three are George C. Wolfe at the New York Shakespeare Festival, Tazewell Thompson at Syracuse Stage, and Tim Bond at the Group in Seattle. Kenny Leon is a fine actor and director. He's worked as a director all over the U.S., including The Long Wharf, The Indiana Rep, The Huntington and The Oregon Shakespeare Festival.

There were several givens with this production of *A Raisin in the Sun*. One, Kenny Leon and his wife, Carol Mitchell-Leon, would be playing Walter Lee and Ruth, respectively. Two, put the Walter Lee/Travis scene back in the play. Three, the costume designer, Susan Mickey, had already been signed for the season. Four, please use as many actors from Atlanta as possible.

Jay Binder Casting handled the casting for the Alliance Theatre in New York City and Jody Feldman at the Alliance Theatre handled casting in Atlanta. I had lengthy conversations with both. It was decided that I had to see two highly visible Atlanta actresses for the role of Lena Younger. Both had played the role successfully in critically acclaimed Atlanta productions. I was very interested in the Chicago actress, Audrey Morgan, for the role of Lena. She was still in her 40's and therefore had the stamina for the role. (Claudia McNeal was 39 when she played the role on Broadway.) Audrey Morgan had played the role for me when I directed a GEVA Theatre production in Rochester, New York.

Strangely, the casting people kept asking me what version I intended to use.

On August 5, 1994, during the National Black Arts Festival in Atlanta I held auditions for *A Raisin in the Sun* at the Alliance Theatre. I auditioned Travis, George Murchinsons, Beneathas, Bobos, and Asagais. Fifteen actors auditioned; nine were excellent. The New York and Hollywood actor Taurean Blaque was then living in Atlanta. I cast him as Bobo. The Atlanta actor Gary Yates from in Los Angeles was cast as Asagai. I wanted to wait until after the New York City auditions to cast Beneatha.

During one of the casting discussions, Kenny Leon suggested Esther Rolle might still be interested. She'd been interested when Lloyd Richards was set to direct. Since I know Esther I said I'd telephone her and ask. Please note: Esther had performed the role in three successful productions: Kuntu Rep in Pittsburgh, directed by Elizabeth Van Dyke in the early Eighties; the 25th Anniversary Roundabout Theatre Production directed by Harold Scott in the mid-Eighties; and The American Playhouse television production directed by Bill Duke in the late Eighties. Also note: Esther Rolle had been in a serious automobile accident in the early Nineties and barely survived. She didn't know if she wanted to commit herself to two months in Atlanta on a play. Her agent kept telling us she wasn't available; Esther, however, kept telling us she was available; she simply didn't want to do a play. I kept appealing to her sense of friendship and said that as an actress she should test the stage again after the auto accident. Also, I told her I could get the Alliance Theatre to pay her more than their minimum AEA salary; get them to get a car and driver; and a suite rather than a hotel room — whatever the reason, probably none of the above, Esther Rolle said YES she'd come to Atlanta and play Lena Younger. As she said goodbye, she asked me — What version will we be using?

At the first production meeting on Sept. 13, 1994, sixteen artistic and technical staff members met. I was very impressed but realizing the yearly budget of $5,000,000 I came to understand exactly where the money was spent. I related to them my artistic vision and asked the set designer, and the lighting designer to do the same. I spoke of seeing *A Raisin in the Sun* on stage in Detroit in 1959. It was the first time I'd seen a Black family on stage that made me feel proud. I wanted this version to be as close to that original 1959 production as possible. I announced that I'd ignore all stage direction inserted by productions since the original. I wouldn't use the "Mrs. Johnson" character. The section with Travis and the "rat as big as a cat" wouldn't be used. We wouldn't use the Afro-wig for Beneatha. The music would be created by Dwight Andrews. Since Dwight was not at the meeting I talked about how I envisioned the music. I used Paul Bowles and Alex North as examples, with their incidental music for *Summer and Smoke* and *A Streetcar Named Desire*.

At first rehearsal I passed out the 1959 original Broadway version. *That* would be the version! The only version Samuel French, Inc. will license is the current 30th anniversary edition. However, I don't think anyone is policing the content of resident professional theatre productions.

In the Alliance Theatre's *StageBill*, the program for many of the resident professional theatres, Sidney Mahone, director of play development at Crossroads Theatre, wrote an article recalling 35 years of *A Raisin in the Sun*, entitled "Leap to Freedom." She recalled James Baldwin's essay "Sweet Lorraine"..."Never before in the entire history of the American Theatre had so much of the truth of Black people's lives been seen on stage." Mahone went on to elaborate on Hansberry being the first African-American playwright and at age 28 the youngest writer to win the Drama Critics Circle Award for the Best American play of the 1958-59 season. The play ran for 538 performances. Mahone went on to say "for artist and audiences, *A Raisin in the Sun* heralded a new era — the era of the liberated Black Theatre Movement...it pricked the conscience of America with its

The Impact of Race

prophetic vision: one African-American family translated the turmoil and the tenacious hope of an entire nation standing on the brink of momentous social change. For the first time, one Black play encompassed a broad spectrum of themes: Male/Female relationships, Feminism, Abortion, Class conflict, intergenerational struggles, the recovery of African tradition, and the political relationship between Black America and Africa...*A Raisin in the Sun* remains the best known play in Black Theatre history."

Ms. Mahone's article had been researched and written with clarity about the original Broadway production. Yet, over the years since Lorraine Hansberry's death, it has not been the 1959 version of *A Raisin in the Sun* we've been seeing. The play has been restricted. It hasn't been viewed as the classic play we've come to understand it to be. Although done with seemingly good intentions, the estate headed by the playwright's ex-husband, saw fit to restructure and allow others to restructure *A Raisin in the Sun*.

In all current publications of *A Raisin in the Sun* by Lorraine Hansberry, the copyright carries the name of Robert Nemiroff. It clearly states © 1958, 1986 by Robert Nemiroff, as an unpublished work. Further © 1959, 1987, 1988 by Robert Nemiroff.

Since Lorraine Hansberry was very much alive March 11, 1959, when *A Raisin in the Sun* opened on Broadway and indeed witnessed its publication, originally copyright 1958 as an unpublished work by Lorraine Hansberry, it seems strange it's copyrighted in her ex-husband's name.

There are areas in the 30th anniversary edition of Lorraine Hansberry's *A Raisin in the Sun* that cry for further examination. The first, and most extensive, are the stage directions. These stage directions were obviously written by the late Robert Nemiroff, executor of Lorraine Hansberry's estate. They were published as part of a series of rewrites done by Nemiroff. There are, to be exact, thirty-five pieces of reconstruction and rewrites. Why are these rewrites allowed to be included, to taint this classic?

Let's look at the first editions of *A Raisin in the Sun*. These editions were published immediately after the play appeared on Broadway. The Random House hardcover edition was published in 1959, and the Signet Classic was published in 1961. In a special *Theatre Arts* magazine publication of October 1960, Lorraine Hansberry included an essay on how she came to write different sections of *A Raisin in the Sun*. "Me Tink Me Hear

Sounds In De Night." Another article in the May 1961 *Urbanite* magazine, "Images and Essences," further explains why her characters were developed in such a positive way.

As late as November 1984, Linda Zesch wrote in *American Theatre* magazine, "Lorraine Hansberry's *A Raisin in the Sun* is firmly ensconced as an American classic and represents a watershed in American drama that stimulated the development of a whole body of new Black dramatic literature." In another piece of writing, Dr. Margaret B. Wilkerson commented, "the timelessness of the play has not diminished. Its criticisms of materialistic values are more poignant amidst the affluence and poverty of American society today." The critic for the *Washington Post* wrote that *A Raisin in the Sun* is "one of a handful of great American plays — it belongs in the inner circle along with *Death of a Salesman*, *Long Day's Journey Into Night*, and *The Glass Menagerie*."

It is indeed sad that many of those critics praising the 25th anniversary publication and the 30th anniversary revised edition of *A Raisin in the Sun* as a classic have no knowledge of the 1959 award-winning production's original text. In general, they don't read literature by Black writers nor care anything about it. But a few, the late Robert Nemiroff as well as theatre scholars, should. Nemiroff, although long divorced from Ms. Hansberry, was named executor of the estate when she died of cancer at the age of 34 in 1965. In order to keep the Hansberry name before the public and keep the estate alive, Nemiroff realized his dream as a writer through Hansberry's writings. First he adapted her writings as a theatre piece under the title *To Be Young, Gifted and Black* (1969), adapted her *Les Blanc* for Broadway (1972), adapted *A Raisin in the Sun* into the musical *Raisin* (1975), and finally tampered with *A Raisin in the Sun*.

The same books and writings by Lorraine Hansberry reappeared in the Eighties as *The Collected Last Plays* (*Les Blancs, The Drinking Gourd, What Use of Flowers?*), edited with critical background by Robert Nemiroff (1980) with the added note "this edition restores to *Les Blancs* material omitted from the original production and not included in *Les Blancs: The Collected Last Plays*." *A Raisin in the Sun* (1989), described as the "expanded 25th Anniversary Edition with a new introduction and the 101 final performances of Sidney Brustein by Robert Nemiroff." And finally, *To Be Young, Gifted and Black*, adapted with a foreword by Robert Nemiroff.

Please note that each edition says "important lines and scenes from the ORIGINAL PLAY have been restored; now, presented in its entirety for the first time ever."

At the beginning of *A Raisin in the Sun* in the so-called production notes, "Walter and Ruth's room is lit through a scrim. Somewhere in the apartment is a photo of big Walter, whose spirit suffuses the play."

Clearly this was not in the original 1959 text written by Lorraine Hansberry, nor the elaborate stage directions, telling the actress who plays Lena Younger how to play the beats in the last scene of Act One:

> The breaks in this spech as Mama waits for Walter to speak are crucial. It must not be a continuous tirade which, in effect, drives him to defiance by denying him his chance to speak for himself. Mama gives him the space. It is the situation itself, not she, that stills his tongue.

Not one word of this is written by Ms. Hansberry. Again, in Act I, Scene One, where Beneatha's hair has been cut to an Afro style. That was not in the original text. The rewrites to accommodate the hairstyle are false and badly written, even the stage directions. In the original production the shock was in Beneatha's wearing of the African robes and the embracing of African ideals and concepts. It was shocking in 1959 for anyone Black to accept Africans outside the Tarzan concept.

Another addition to the original text I feel shouldn't have been added: in the so-called Signet 30th anniversary edition (itself a revision of the 25th anniversary edition), Act II, Scene Two, the addition of the character of the next door neighbor, Mrs. Johnson. Still another, Act I, Scene Two, where Travis and some other neighborhood children, including the janitor of the building, kill a large rat "As big as a cat, Honest!" And, finally, the cutting and revising of the Beneatha and Asagai scene in Act Three. No serious scholar of the American Theatre in general and Black contributor to the American Theatre in particular could view these tamperings and not speak out. It's a sacrilege to her memory that this tampering was allowed.

How did these changes affect characters and scenes in *A Raisin in the Sun*? Look at Lena Younger (Mama). Many think this character is based on Lorraine Hansberry's real mother. The play after all is dedicated "To

Mama: in gratitude for the dream." But in *To Be Young, Gifted and Black*, Hansberry describes her mother as "extremely delicate, feminine, vain, the kind of woman only the South can thrust on the world." Certainly not the Lena Younger of *A Raisin in the Sun*. The Lena of *A Raisin in the Sun* is a large heavyset martriarch; not Lorraine's mother. The Lena of *A Raisin in the Sun* is a theatrical invention to balance the strong Black male, Walter Lee Younger. *A Raisin in the Sun* is first and foremost a play about Walter Lee Younger and his struggle to be a man in the changing world of the Fifties. The fact is it was put together by a group of whites and Blacks bound together by relationships and marriages as well as by the politics of the radical left. So to view the play in the Eighties and Nineties, where the focus is now on a strong matriarch as head of the house instead of a major focus on Walter Lee, is disconcerting.

I hope scholars will re-examine all of Hansberry's writings. I'd hate to find this to be a common occurrence within the estate of Eugene O'Neill, Clifford Odets, George Bernard Shaw, William Inge, Tennessee Williams, and Langston Hughes.

Lorraine Hansberry's Chilren — Black Artists and "A Raisin in the Sun"

Not long after *for colored girls who have considered suicide/when the rainbow is enuf* opened, when the Black musicals on Broadway were regarded as Black theatre, I decided—out of anger—to make a documentary film on Black theatre. The film had to begin at some point that was identifiable to the current generation of theatergoers and theatre artists. The reasonable and logical way to do this, I surmised, would be to let each of the participants interviewed decide his or her starting point.

What exactly do the following people/artists have in common: Lonne Elder, Lloyd Richards, Douglas Turner Ward, Ossie Davis, Ruby Dee, Robert Hooks, Rosalind Cash, Ernestine McClendon, Ivan Dixon, Diana Sands, Shauneille Perry, Ron Milner, and most of the young writers and performers currently working in the American theatre? The answer, without question, is Lorraine Hansberry's *A Raisin in the Sun*. Hence, the title of my film, "The Black Theatre Movement: *A Raisin in the Sun* to the Present."

How to describe the effect *A Raisin in the Sun* had on most of us when it opened in 1959! From my standpoint as a resident of Detroit who'd only recently become interested in theatre and had no guide whatsoever, *A Raisin in the Sun* opened doors within my consciousness that I never knew existed. There I was in Detroit's Cass Theatre, a young man who'd never seen anywhere a Black man (Walter Lee) express all the things I felt but never had the courage to express—and in a theatre full of Black and white people, no less! I remember being introduced by someone to Ron Milner in the lobby. We both uttered something like, "This is it, man." And I remember waiting at the stage door for *any* of the actors and finally cornering Robert Hooks (then known as Bobby Dean Hooks). As we walked the ten or twelve blocks to his hotel, he listened patiently to my enthusiastic outpourings—he didn't talk much in those days. I remember showing him an article from *Theatre Arts* magazine and telling him how desperately I wanted to work in the professional theatre. My deep feelings came from the effect *A Raisin in the Sun* had had on me. Hooks laughed and said my feelings weren't unique. When he'd seen the play in Philadelphia, it had made him pack his bags and head for New York. Furthermore, in all of the cities the play had toured, young actors and actresses had been moved. The power of the play had made us all aware of our uniqueness as Black and had encouraged us to pursue our dreams. Indeed, the play had confirmed that our dreams were possible.

Sixteen years later, I interviewed over sixty people while filming my documentary on Black theatre. Over forty of these people said that, at one time or another, they'd been influenced or aided, or both, by Lorraine Hansberry and her work. Consider, for example, the case of Lloyd Richards, director of the original *Raisin*, whose acceptance on the national theatre scene dates from that production. After *Raisin*, Richards directed many plays on Broadway and in university and regional theatres. None, however, had such wide exposure and impact as did Hansberry's work. He went on to serve as artistic director of the O'Neill Theatre Center in Waterford, Connecticut, and as president of the Theatre Development Fund. Currently, he heads Yale University's prestigious drama department. The very nature of *Raisin* and its overall message to all people made it possible for those who participated in its presentation to be embraced by both white and Black.

Whatever he may feel, the role of Walter Lee Younger came at a time in Sidney Poitier's career when Black acceptance was extremely impor-tant—and elusive. His performance was a landmark and still must be considered one of the finest stage performances of an American actor. The same is to be said for the work of Claudia McNeil, Diana Sands, Ruby Dee and Glynn Turman. *A Raisin in the Sun* also made it possible for its author,

Lorraine Hansberry, to speak out and be heard on issues of race where no other Black woman had been so treated. (Witness her famous meeting with Robert Kennedy, her articles and essays on Black aspirations, etc.) The effect all this had on the current crop of Black artists is tremendous, as evidenced in part by the female playwrights who have succeeded Hansberry—Adrienne Kennedy, J.e. Franklin, Ntozake Shange and many others. To mention all of the artists whose careers were enhanced by their encounters with Hansberry and *A Raisin in the Sun* would read like a *Who's Who* in the Black theatre.

Early in my career, I performed in *Raisin in the Sun* when a summer stock company came to Detroit's Northland Playhouse. I felt I'd come full circle when, in 1978, I had the opportunity to direct the play with a talented cast headed by Minnie Gentry and Reuben Greene. (Evidence of the play's enduring effectiveness is that it was just as well received in 1978 as it had been in that small Detroit theatre years earlier, when an overwhelmingly white audience gave it a standing ovation.) *Raisin* and I met again in January 1979, in New York City when I produced the work at my New Federal Theatre—featuring, once again, the sterling Minnie Gentry. In the role of Walter Lee Younger was Glynn Turman. Significantly, Lorraine Hansberry had, twenty years earlier, personally escorted Turman (then her neighbor in Greenwich Village) to the audition that won him the role of 12-year-old Travis in the original Broadway production of *Raisin*. That Turman matured to star in the revival as an artist of award stature testifies, not only to his dedication and great ability, but also to the vision of Lorraine Hansberry.

Baraka at the Millennium

When the Sixties arrived, Leroi Jones became Amiri Baraka. His play *Dutchman* won the OBIE Award as "Best American Play" of the 1963-64 season. Three of his one act plays, "The Baptism," "The Toilet," and "The Slave" had a successful run. He, along with Edward Albee, Jack Gelber, Jack Richardson, and Arthur Kopit, were major Off-Broadway playwrights.

Leroi Jones had fame, if not fortune; his plays were controversial and successful. The language of Baraka's Theatre is found in a truth; a recognition; in a collected memory, i.e., as a visit into the holding dungeons at Cape Coast Castle and Goree Island; the hole of a slave ship; a long subway ride late at night in New York of the Sixties; a toilet in an inner city's decaying industrial complex called "School"; a song by "The Supremes" or a chant "Nation Time." These images are as much "language" as are words in a poet's theatre.

In 1965, Leroi Jones moved to Harlem and set up the Black Arts Repertory Theatre School:

> Our Theater will show victims so that their brothers in the audience will be better able to understand that they are the brothers of victims, and that their brothers in the audience will be better able to understand that they are Blood brothers of victims, and they themselves are Blood brothers.

Newsweek magazine stated: "Leroi Jones writes and harangues himself out of the company of civilized men and forfeits all claim to serious attention."

Jones/Baraka responded: "My ideas revolve around the rotting and destruction of America, so I can't really expect anyone who is part of that to accept my ideals."

Money to Haryou-Act, the anti-poverty program which had been administering Black Arts Repertory Theatre's funds, was cut. Newspaper headlines proclaimed Jones/Baraka racist, separatist, militant. Black poet/ playwright uses federal funds to wage his war of hate against America.

The Black Arts Repertory Theatre was forced to close. Suddenly (and I mean suddenly) a lot of Negroes who didn't even believe in Black Art/Black Theatre were in charge and administrators of it. However, as a result of white America's backlash against Jones/Baraka, Black artists across America and Africa began to set up Black cultural institutions, using his manifesto, "The Revolutionary Theatre":

> The Revolutionary Theatre should force change; it should be change. *All their faces turned into the light and you work on them Black nigger magic*, and *cleanse them at having seen the ugliness. And if the beautiful see themselves, they will love themselves.* We are preaching virtue again but by that to mean *now*, towards what seems the most constructive use of the word.

In 1966 Jones/Baraka left Harlem for Newark. *Home!* He started Spirit House:

> A Black community theatre owned by the people of the community... We have a permanent ensemble of actors (called the Spirit House Movers): Yusef Iman, Jaribu, Mchocezi, Katibu, Salimo, Mubarak Mahmud, etc.

Then, The Newark riot of 1967; like Watts, Detroit and Harlem. They went after Baraka! Who else could they, would they go after in Newark?

Baraka is older; like a vintage wine, as he ages he becomes better, more precious, and even mellow. Baraka still tells us we're Africans; yet our theatre is a reflection of European Theatre. The language in his plays, the focus of his music criticisms, and his volumes of essays remind us we're Africans in a European culture.

What is it about Baraka's Language that calls us to attention? I believe it's his understanding of the African continuum as well as how it plays on the collective memory.

I first produced *The Toilet/The Slave* in my theatre, Concept-East in Detroit, in 1996. Immediately thereafter, the theatre was closed down by the City Marshall for "Distributing Obscenity." In 1969 I produced *Slaveship* with Chelsea Theatre in the U.S. and Paris; *Great Goodness of Life: A Coon Show* as part of "A Black Quartet." In 1973, *A Recent Killing*; 1975 *Sidnee Poet Heroical*; 1979/80 *Baraka 50's, 60's and 70's*, starring Amiri Baraka; in the Eighties I produced *Boy and Tarzan Meet Again In a Clearing*; in the Nineties *Black History Music*; in 2000 *Remembering Weselves: A Black Renaissance in Harlem, Skin Trouble*;

We who respect Baraka and work with him cannot always follow him, we can only drink in his ideas; get crazy if we take in too much too fast.

A young friend, an actor/writer who met Baraka when he was Leroi Jones in the Village in the mid-Fifties, followed him through jazz joints and small presses into cafes reading his poetry. Baraka wrote plays and went to Cuba. My friend tried to write plays, tried to understand Castro. Baraka moved to Harlem denouncing many of the whites he had associated with up to that time. The actor/writer followed Baraka more confused than ever.

Baraka returned to Newark. *Home!* He founded the Committee for a Unified Newark, a nationalist organization. My friend followed Baraka to Newark and became a nationalist. In the Seventies, Baraka announced he'd embraced Marxism. In the next two decades in Newark, Baraka went political and almost singlehandedly got two mayors elected.

My friend, older now, re-examined his life and realized he'd been growing with Baraka; fermenting and evolving.

Come by Bullins

In 1968, Ed Bullins arrived in New York City from San Francisco with about a dozen plays in his trunk. I'd read some of his articles in *Negro Digest*; and he'd sent me some of his plays. He'd made a commitment to playwrighting; a commitment to explore the lives of Black people. His arrival signaled a change in Black theatre direction.

I met Ed Bullins soon after. I don't remember exactly how we ended up that evening at my apartment on Riverside Drive. I'd read *In the Wine Time, Clara's Ole Man*, and *Goin a Buffalo*. We talked late into the night. Ed said very little but he drank a lot of wine. We laughed a lot. He didn't mention his new position at the newly formed New Lafayette Theatre. The bottom line was/is I loved his plays and was totally committed to his writings.

I introduced his work to Wynn Handman at American Place Theatre that same week; American Place Theatre presented Bullins' one-acts *Electronic Nigger and Others*, including "A Son Comes Home," "Clara's Ole Man," and "Electronic Nigger." In the following years they presented his full-length plays *The Pig Pen* and *House Party*, and did a rehearsed reading of *Goin a Buffalo*. Robert Macbeth's New Lafayette Theatre produced the landmark production of Bullins' *In the Wine Time*. That production with Sonny Jim Gaines, Gary Bolling, Bette Howard, George Miles, Kris Keiser, Bill Lathan, and the other New Lafayette players was the most brilliantly produced and directed work in the Bullins canon. Robert Macbeth directed In the Wine Time with awesome detail.

I've produced (or directed) seven of Ed Bullins' plays: "The Gentleman Caller" (1968, produced); *In New England Winters* (1971, produced); *The*

The Impact of Race

Taking of Miss Janie (1974, produced with Joseph Papp); *The Fabulous Miss Marie* (1975, produced); *Phyllis Wheatly* (1976, produced with Steve Tennen); *Daddy* (1977, produced with Joseph Papp and directed); *Salaam, Huey Salaam* (1991, directed). Why did I produce and direct these plays? Why am I drawn to the plays of Ed Bullins? Without question his plays reaffirm details in Black life as I've come to understand it. The language and violence in his early plays, especially in *Clara's Ole Man* as well as the plays in the 20th century cycle, are so precise I could not ignore them.

In 1968, seven months after Bullins' arrival in New York City, I produced *A Black Quartet* (four one act plays by Baraka, Bullins, Caldwell, and Milner). Bullins' "The Gentleman Caller" was included. This piece is an avant-garde play in the tradition of Albee, Pinter, and Beckett. However, it's very Black in terms of language. Bullins' exploration of new forms within the Black theatre structure resonates throughout all of his plays. Bullins is, first of all, a master craftsman.

The language and the concise Blackness of Bullins' *In New England Winters* combined to take Black theatre to a level of beauty not found in the American theatre; certainly not found in Eugene O'Neill or Tennessee Williams. New Federal Theatre's 1971 production directed by Dick Anthony Williams combined the violence, the language, and the characterizations of Black life. The violence of America was further explored in my production of *The Taking of Miss Janie* (1974); that production was directed by Gilbert Moses. *Miss Janie* was co-produced by Joseph Papp, moving from New Federal Theatre to Lincoln Center for the Performing Arts. It won three Obie Awards as well as the Drama Critic Circle Award as best new American Play of the Season. My production of *Daddy* (1977) explored this violence within the context of redemption, and a kind of re-examination of priorities. Bullins seemed to be analyzing himself as an artist and as a father. Language and character are so clear in *The Fabulous Miss Marie* (1975) one leaves the theatre realizing how accurately Bullins captures the new Black middle class. *The Fabulous Miss Marie* and *In New England Winters* can take their places among the finest plays written for the Black theatre. As stated earlier Bullins is a craftsman (though often he downplays this aspect of his work). He's also an astute historian; never ever confuse his personal quietness for lack of knowledge. I listened to him early in his career destroy a theatre historian in a radio discussion on Black theatre. To understand the language and characters within Black culture as well as Bullins understands we must assume *he was a witness; he's been there*!

A recent anthology of plays by Ed Bullins on historical characters, edited by Dr. Ethyl Pitt Walker, gave the Black theatre much needed new work. Even though I produced one of Bullins' historical plays (*Phyllis Wheatly*, 1977) I was surprised to learn from Dr. Walker the vast number of these types of plays he'd written. One forgets, Ed Bullins is a playwright; a playwright writes plays.

Ed Bullins' plays are included in many of my anthologies. His work has always been integral to the Black theatre movement. Bullins has given the Black theatre anthologies, criticism, and scholarship, exploring its theories, its practices, and its aesthetics.

I often think of Bullins when I recall a speech given by Eleanor Traylor. She was speaking about James Baldwin though she could just as easily have been speaking of Ed Bullins. Baldwin had written hundreds of articles, eight non-fiction books, ten novels, hundreds of speeches, had expatriated to Europe in the early Fifties, and created a body of work on Black America any new writer must *come by* to be in the same league. Baldwin quoted the Bible wherein the Lord said in order to get into heaven, *You must come by me*! I am reminded of the vast body of work by Bullins— and warn any new playwright, *You must come by Bullins*!

Remembering
Langston Hughes

It must have been two or three years after high school or at least two or three years before college—there was a five-year gap for me—that I found Langston Hughes. I didn't find him in high school or college. In the high school I attended, especially the American literature classes, Black writers were foreign, Black poets were nonexistent. In my college they were ignored. During the Fifties, when I came of age, discovering, searching, groping for identification, teachers often turned me on to Lowell, Vachel Lindsay, O'Neill, Faulkner, Penn Warren, Twain, James, Hart Crane, and, of course, Hemingway. They were described as "true American writers" because they were white, born here, or wrote here. However, Langston Hughes was "American" because in his poetry and prose there's a deep abiding love for this country as well as for the Black man in this country.

I found Langston Hughes during my intense study of the Black theatre. (I discovered theatre in the five-year gap, too.) Dr. Alan Locke discussed Black writers in his collection *Thirteen Plays for the Negro Theatre*. It's one of the earliest published anthologies of plays about Black lifestyles. (I wish I could find that book!) He mentioned how Langston's plays had received praise at the Karamu Theatre in Cleveland. Reading Langston led me to other Black writers, Black institutions. He led me to Richard Wright, *Crisis* magazine, James Baldwin, Ralph Ellison, W. C. Handy, *Mercury* magazine...even Carl van Vechten. From articles and books I found that he was a poet, short story writer, translator and adapter. I exhausted myself in the library reading Langston Hughes: "Soul Gone Home" at least ten times; "A Good Job Gone," fifteen times; "Early Autumn," one of the most beautiful short stories in American letters, two or three dozen times. Poems: "Weary Blues," "A House in Toas" to "I've Known Rivers," "Montage of a Dream Deferred"...

So, I was aware of him long before I met him. Similarly, I am aware of Jesus, of Pushkin; if only I could have met them!

It was 1961. The newspaper, the *Negro* newspaper, announced that Mr. Langston Hughes would be coming to Detroit. He'd be escorted from the airport by police motorcade downtown to the City-County Building. Our new mayor, Mayor Cavanaugh, would then present him with the key to Detroit.

On the afternoon of the following day, after he'd received the key, a writer friend, Ronald Milner, called me. He'd met Langston, they'd talked and *he* had impressed Langston. My friend wanted me to go with him that very afternoon and meet Langston Hughes.

"Are you available, man?" he asked.

Langston was staying at the Park-Sheraton in the art center section of Detroit, equidistant from everything: downtown, westside, eastside.

It seemed that all my "Artsy-Craftsy" friends knew him, yet before the Negro press announced his arrival I assumed they didn't know him because they never mentioned him or his work. However, he was a celebrity among Black people—the factory workers, the car washers, the day workers, domestics, bartenders. They knew *one* of his plays or *some* of *Simple* they had read in the *Chicago Defender*; and they seem to remember Langston Hughes from that one piece of writing.

Margaret Danner, the poet, and a dear friend to Detroit artists and writers, had introduced Ronald to Langston. So naturally respect and aspiration for Langston grew because I knew then that the man had to be real. One can determine the effect of a man by the ones who love him, so it was with Langston Hughes before I met him.

At about that time, we were involved in something in Detroit called for nothing better, Black Discovery. We'd built our own theatre called Concept-East, Margaret Danner had opened The Boone House for poets, Henry King had opened the Contemporary Art Gallery, and both Tony Brown and Richard Henry (Brother Imari) started publishing little magazines. We had a lot of things to talk to Langston about. Would he listen?

Woodie King, Jr.

Had the new mayor and the middle-class Negro doctors and lawyers cornered him on this Detroit visit?

The first thing he did on my arrival at the hotel was to offer me a drink. I refused. (I don't drink!) *What? A writer and director? Don't drink?* Then he smiled. The cigarette with the ashes, not falling, sort of blocking some of the smile. How can I describe that smile? Have you ever studied the Mona Lisa? Draw in a cigarette with ashes. Langston's smile would create the same effect. He told us how swinging the suite was: *Man, I wish I had one of these permanently. This is something, isn't it? Wow! Hey, they gave me the key to the city.* (He started looking for the key but evidently had misplaced it.) *Brought me in by motorcade! I wish I had the money they spent on me!*

And we all broke up laughing. He was real.

Later that evening he spoke for Arthur Coar, Director for the Association for the Study of Negro Life and History, the organization that Carter Woodson founded in the Twenties and also one of the first men to hire Langston.

He and I talked again that night. I told him how much I liked his short story, "Early Autumn." He told me if I came to New York to look him up. And I think he watched me as I talked of the conditions of the Blacks in theatre. I do remember he gave Ronald a copy of his plays, *Don't You Want to Be Free!* and *Soul Gone Home.* And we tried to get a cast together and do a reading of his poetry and the two plays. But he left two days later before we could get the actors. Parting, he said something like, *it's kinda hard to get colored people together, but once you got them...well...* And he did that smile, preoccupied with his packing.

In early 1964, when I moved to New York, I called Langston after enduring about a week of the cruelties of Manhattan existence.

Hi, Woodie, he said, *come on over. How is Ron? Did he finish that big book?*

He lived in Harlem on 127th Street in one of those beautiful brownstones. I had trouble finding the house. I searched around and finally I asked a policeman, "Yeah, the poet, he lives in the next block, East 127th." He had his offices on the third floor. They was filled with books by Black writers—fiction and non-fiction from Blacks the world over. Most of the books had personal identification because Langston had helped in getting them published or had written the introduction or had helped the writer when the writer was beginning. The first thing he said, "I read that story, 'Beautiful and Black Our Dreams,' in *Negro Digest*. It's good." I didn't know how to respond. I do remember there was a long pause. He didn't fill the pause. He made me fill it. I started explaining the story, gaining confidence as I talked. Suddenly, I realized that we were talking man to man, not student to teacher or student to Great Artist. We talked about the works of other writers, particularly Ron Milner (That Big, Big Book— "Is it really going to be 1,500 pages?"), Malraux, Ellison, Sandburg, Whitman, Wright, and Dostoevsky. I found he never talked about his work. Instead he gave me copies of his work, including the autobiography, *The Big Sea*, autographing it in large bold green ink strokes, "Especially for Woody King—with a hearty welcome to New York. Sincerely, Langston Hughes, Harlem, U.S.A., April, 1964."

On my leaving, he invited me down to the Greenwich Mews Theatre's Sanctuary to see his play *Jericho-Jim Crow*. In that brief visit, Langston Hughes, as he must have done with many other Black artists, opened himself and thus accepted me and listened to me. I don't think I'd talked to any artist as I talked to him. Yet the meeting was brief, less than two hours. But this is a long time for a busy writer.

Within the next year, we met often. He invited me to other plays, recommended me for parts. I even read for his play, *Prodigal Son*.

In October of 1965, I invited him to Ron Milner's *Who Got His Own?* at American Place Theatre. I was directing it as a work in progress. He was eager to see Milner's play. He liked its construction but he felt, "that boy, Tim Jr. is awfully mad, they better not put a white character on stage talking about Negroes that way, they'll get picketed."

Our next meeting was in Cleveland at Karamu Playhouse's Golden Anniversary. I'd been invited out by their theatre department. I didn't know Langston would be there but I did know they'd be doing his play, *Simply Heavenly*. As fate would have it we all stayed in the same hotel and since it was some distance from the playhouse, we shared a cab (Langston, Malcolm Boyd, Fred O'Neal, Sidney Lanier).

"It's something of an event to have Langston back," Rowena Jelliffee remarked on the opening panel. "Langston Hughes was Karamu's first playwright away back when it supported the Gilpin Players." His play, *Little Ham*, received wide acclaim at the Karamu Playhouse. On the panel discussion that included the above-mentioned participants, he didn't put anyone down. He praised LeRoi Jones as one of the finest young writers in the theatre. He felt LeRoi Jones was equal to the best of the 20th-century poets. At this point, LeRoi was catching hell from the white people because of his Black Arts Repertory Theatre.

While we were in Cleveland talking about theatre, New York was in the midst of the now famous Blackout. Most of the New Yorkers decided to remain an extra day in Cleveland until it was over. Thus, I had an opportunity to continue the previous dialogue with Langston about poetry and the blues. He knew of my interest in the blues, we had certainly talked about it enough; so much I thought he was bored with it. I told him what I wanted to do: take his first book of poetry, *The Weary Blues*, adapt it to the stage, using his prose and poetry from that first book to his last, set it in Harlem and add W. C. Handy's blues as an integral part since he and Handy were saying the same things. He liked the idea, the possibilities. He even gave me a few more copies of his work. The idea would be to follow a young Black American from a storefront church through the Harlem streets and finally to the foreign soil of some distant land. An American soldier protecting his country from...His death.

The Cleveland visit brought Langston and I even closer, if only for a fleeting moment. Now I'd be able to adapt his work with his consent and his help. For two months I worked off and on him. We agreed that no corrections would be made until I finished a first draft.

In March of 1966, I gave him a third and final draft of *The Weary Blues*. He made large bold corrections and additions in typical green ink and returned it to me in April. I went to his home again to pick it up.

"You did it," he said.

"Yes, it took a lot of research," I said. "Man, you got work in Schomburg nobody ever heard of since 1934. I wanted to use something from the old *Mercury* and *Opportunity*."

"I didn't want you to use any of the piece that was dated; that's the only thing I was afraid of," he added. "People find the skeletons in your closets, they don't understand, they get uptight."

I knew exactly what he meant. I had been tempted to adapt a huge full-length play. Between the Countee Cullen Library and Schomburg collection I compiled enough material for a dozen full-length plays. When

I started cutting material from "The Scottsboro Boys" as it appeared in *Theatre News*, a piece that was good and fitted *Weary* but outdated, I knew I had found a spine for the play. Agit-prop theatre of the Thirties didn't fit the theme we'd set for *The Weary Blues*.

He gave me his corrected copy of *The Weary Blues*, with it was seven new poems he felt should be included, plus a new play, *Mother and Child*. (I directed it at St. Clements Church, The American Place Theatre, about a month later while he was in Dakar.) He'd marked the script appropriately, large green arrows indicated where the new additions should be placed. Then it was off to Dakar for the World Festival of Negro Art for Langston.

He sent me a postcard. Then, in August, he called to let me know he was back in New York for a minute. "What's happening with *Weary Blues*?"

"Good news!" We have a production at the Lincoln Center Museum and Library series sponsored by Equity Library Theatre."

The Weary Blues opened at the Lincoln Center in October of 1966 for a limited engagement. It was packed every night. Langston was there almost every performance. He'd give a little chuckle every night because I had Mississippi John Hurt's *got the blues and can't be satisfied* at full volume to put the audience in the right mood before the play. He brought a lot of Black guests. He also helped cast the play by securing the services of Miss Theresa Merritt.

I remember after the performance, the actor Robert Hooks invited us to his apartment for drinks. It was a lively evening. And as I remember it, Langston only stayed a minute. But he did want to come by to tell all the young performers how much he enjoyed the play and the direction we'd taken his prose and poetry. He was especially pleased with Eleo Pomare's beautiful dance of a Junkie and Norman Bush's Preacher and Cliff Frazier's Hustler. It was a strange evening. After he left, we spent the remainder of the evening quoting and reciting his poetry. You see, Langston's leaving never meant that he was gone. He always left something for the Black people.

He was always busy. He had a lot of things going, works not yet completed, publishers after overdue manuscripts. I always dreaded the thought of dropping in on him. I'd often wait until Ronald Milner came into New

York so that we could both spring ideas which always meant a long and rewarding evening for me. In December of 1966, his secretary, novelist Lindsey Patterson, called and told me Mr. Hughes was busy but he wanted to get a book of short stories for Little, Brown and Company. Did I have anything? Of course! I sent him the story that he liked from *Negro Digest*, "Beautiful Light and Black Our Dreams." He liked it and published it in the anthology, *Best Short Stories by Negro Writers*.

I ran into him a month later, January of 1967, in a small Village restaurant, after a performance of *Day of Absence* and *Happy Ending*. It was one of those cold evenings, threatening rain. I don't remember exactly what we talked about. I do know I'd given Langston's private telephone number to a friend who was starting a magazine and I was afraid he'd not approve. He *was* mad about it. I told him I'd tried to reach him by phone to tell him he'd get this call but his researcher, Raoul Abdul, told me he was out. He was with friends in the restaurant, so we didn't talk much. I thought he'd never talk to me again. I told him I'd call him, he told me he'd be away until the middle of February but would call me when he returned.

He did call.

He wanted me to adapt his collection on Jesse B. Simple to the stage. Are you interested? Drop by this evening, old boy. We have a producer for the fall season.

I remember standing in his library saying for lack of anything better *man...man!* He knew I knew the work because of the earlier research on *The Weary Blues*. He wanted to give me original material, from the first *Chicago Defender* article to the final *New York Post* article. In addition, he wanted to know if I could do it by June because the producers, Stella Holt and Francis Drucker, would have to read it. He also told me they had Alvin Ailey set to direct it. I remember telling him it'd be ready by the middle of May.

After reading the material again, I told him what I wanted the character to cover, the time of action, and of course the place, Harlem, U.S.A. We both got excited talking about what should be done with Simple: It would be set in the night since the Black ghetto usually came alive after dark. Simple would be allowed to move freely in the chaos of existence. He'd desperately search for some order in this chaos; always explaining, searching, hoping, in Langston Hughes' dialogue, Langston Hughes' poetry. Showing how, "White folk is the cause of a lot of inconvenience in my life," how they steal pieces of him, how his moral and religious faith in others saves him from total destruction.

I finished the play, *Simple's Blues*, on April 3, 1967. Langston called me April 13, 1967 from the Hotel Wellington. At the time, he was working on a project for Harry Belafonte. He moved into the Wellington because he could get away from the phone. It also gave him a chance to read the play immediately. He liked the play but he felt it had too many characters. It would cost over $15,000; the producer had only $20,000 for the two plays, *Ask Your Mama* and *Simple's Blues*.

We had some cheese dip. He and Raoul Abdul had wine with theirs and ordered me Coke. I mentioned something about he should eat better. We laughed; felt we had a hit if Stella Holt found the extra money or if I found a way to "cut some of those people out." I understood what he was indirectly telling me and went to work on rewrites. I finished them on May 6, 1967. Called Langston immediately. He was in the hospital. He died May 22, 1967.

Top: Gerald Schoenfeld and King at Shubert Alley. Bottom Left: Ruby Dee in *My One Good Nerve*. Bottom Right: Williams and Van Dyke in *Home*.

Top: George Bass and Woodie. Middle: Laurence Holder at the North Carolina Black Theatre Festival. Bottom: Estelle Rolle at the *Raisin* premiere.

Top: Olu Dara, Woodie, and
August Wilson at City
College. Middle: Woodie
and Gerald Schoenfeld at
the 30th anniversary of the
New Federal Theatre.
Bottom: Abena Joan Brown.

Top: The Company of *Survival*.
Middle: *Checkmates* with
Paul Winfield and Ruby Dee.
Bottom: Amiri Baraka and
Woodie at a rehearsal of *The
Motion of History*.
Facing Page:
Top Left: Woodie King and
Ed Bullins. Top Right: Ron
Milner and Woodie in 1960.
Bottom: Woodie and China
Clark at the *Shooting Star*
reception.

Top: Ron Trice and Louise Stubbs in *What the Winesellers Buy*. Bottom: Denzel Washington with Kirk Kirksey in *When the Chickens Come Home to Roost*.

Top: Herbert Rice and
Loretta Greene in *What the
Winesellers Buy*. Bottom:
Louise Stubbs and Kishasha
in *Black Girl*.

Top: Shauneille Perry. Bottom: Woodie
King and Vinette Carroll.

For Shauneille Perry

Shauneille Perry: genial, cultured, sensitive — a first impression but beneath it is a strong, tough survivor of this work we all know as BLACK THEATRE. I consider her a friend and a colleague. She's a teacher, talented director, outstanding playwright, and one of the best actresses in this country. She was a member of the Howard Players under Owen Dodson; acted at Atlanta University Theatre and Lincoln University under Thomas Pawley. She appeared in New York off Broadway in the plays *Clandestine on the Morning Line, The Goose, Octoroon* (big hit), *Gilbau*, and the film *Desperate Characters* with Shirley MacLaine.

"Got tired of acting, it was too slow; too much business," Shauneille says.

Keeping busy, being active, she wrote plays, teleplays, articles, radio soaps, short stories; along with her husband Don Rider raised three daughters Lorraine, Natalie, and Gail.

Her writings, whether fiction or non-fiction, are also cultured, sensitive, and precise...including an unparalled love of Black people. This love of who we are as a people was an integral part of Shauneille Perry's upbringing. She's the daughter of the late Graham and Pearl Perry. He, a civil rights lawyer and rights activist and one of the first Black assistant attorney generals of Illinois; she, one of the first Black court reporters in Chicago. Shauneille's uncles were William Leo Hansberry, a pioneer African Scholar and Carl A. Hansberry, a Chicago Realtor and father of Lorraine Hansberry (Shauneille's cousin). Lorraine Hansberry, of course, is author of the landmark Black theatre hit, *A Raisin in the Sun*.

The Impact of Race

Race pride born out of Africa's contributions to civilization is/was a part of Shauneille Perry's life.

Race pride and Africa's contributions are deeply rooted and integral in her teachings. She usually holds professorships in both Black Studies and in Theatre. She was an Associate Professor in Theatre at Lehman College. She's also taught at Borough of Manhattan Community College, Queens College, City College, Hunter College, Dillard University, North Carolina A&T, and the Fieldston School.

I met her thirty years ago when she came to direct J.e. Franklin's *Black Girl* for New Federal Theatre. Since *Black Girl* she's directed fifteen other productions at NFT; the most recent assignment, writing and directing the 1999 version of Will Marion Cook's 1903 Black musical *In Dahomey*, starring Shirley Verrett. In a long career that includes directing assignments at NEC (*Sty of the Blind Pig*), American Place Theatre (*Music Magic*), Roger Furman Theatre (*Strivens Row*), Bermuda Black Theatre, Black Spectrum Theatre, UBU Repertory Theatre, Hudson Guild, Ensemble Studio, and Richard Allen Center, Shauneille Perry has carved a special and unique niche in Black theatre in this country and in the Caribbean.

Gwendolyn Brooks

In 1964, after I'd been in New York City for several months, exploring, searching, the Group Theatre Workshop under the direction of Robert Hooks and Barbara Ann Teer presented an evening of theatre based on Gwendolyn Brooks' poem "We Real Cool." "We Real Cool" is an eight-line poem defining a period of time in the life of growing Black youth. It was an evening of theatre created by Barbara Ann Teer.

I was overwhelmed by poetry as theatre. I read *Anne Allen* and *Maud Martha*. I didn't understand *Anne Allen*. So, I read other work by Mrs. Brooks. Again she captured Black people so well in *A Street in Bronzeville* and the incredible *The Sundays of Satin Leg Smith* (which Hollywood totally misunderstood in the Black films of the early Seventies). In the center of Gwendolyn Brooks' poetry is drama. The director Vantile Whitfield designed an evening of theatre using her poetry. It was called *Among It All She Stands Like a Fine Brownstone*. It premiered in the early Seventies at the D.C. Black Repertory Theatre.

I found through Gwendolyn Brooks a direction to my kind of theatre: the poetry in drama, i.e., poetry as theatre. I explored it as a producer of *Great Goodness of Life: A Coon Show* by Amiri Baraka, the record albums for Motown, *Black Spirits, Forerunners, Nationtime*, and the Original Last Poets in the film *Right On!* In 1976, I was able to present Ntozake Shange's *for colored girls who have considered suicide/when the rainbow is enuf.*

Poetry is urgent...*now!* Drama should be urgent, *now*. The only plays that have this urgency are the ones coming out of South Africa. These plays surge with vitality because the cry for freedom in South Africa has been so *now*, so *unconditional*. Gwendolyn Brooks' poetry is urgent; it is *now*.

Gwendolyn Brooks died in 2000 but remains a national treasure. Her contribution to the world of poetry and literature is almost unprecedented in the history of Black poetry. On her 80th birthday, she was, I believe, the eldest living Black Pulitzer Prize winner. She was awarded dozens of literacy prizes and awards. And we, who came of age during the Black Arts Movements of the Sixties, remember how she embraced the young Black owned publishing company, Third World Press. When she let Third World Press publish her poetry, she encouraged other Black poets to follow her. This began a relationship with Third World Press that endured.

National treasures are likened to U.S. and national landmarks. We preserve them. We religiously revisit them. Often we make sure others are reminded to do the same. We remember cherished times spent with them. So it is with me. *Annie Allen* and *Maud Martha* are two books I've wanted to recreate into theatre. I have no idea how to do that. Yet, very recently, a young Polish Jewish artist has undertaken the arduous task of creating a performance arts, site-specific, theatre piece of *Anne Allen*. My memory is still holding onto that beautiful theatrical recreation of her Poem "We Real Cool" in 1964 and Vantile Whitfield's *Among It All She Stands Like a Fine Brownstone*. One of her poems that I often revisit is "The Sundays of Satin Leg Smith." Here's a poem wherein Gwendolyn Brooks captures all the character nuances of Black males displaced in the urban North, not as Hollywood stereotypes, but as loving family members recalling different aspects of relatives.

Gwendolyn Brooks' love of Black people is reflected in all of her poems. Her poems aren't unlike the poetry of Langston Hughes, Georgia Douglas Jackson, Claude McKay, Sterling Brown, Robert Hayden, Amiri Baraka, Haki Madhubuti, and Nikki Giovanni. Their poetry, like U.S. landmarks, ought to be revisited as a patriotic duty.

Miss P. J. Gibson

P. J. Gibson is a major voice in Black theatre in particular and American theatre in general. I write that with a huge smile, one that hides an "I told you so," spoken as far back as the Eighties. That's when I first produced P. J. Gibson's *Long Time Since Yesterday*, directed by Bette Howard. The play was so well received that my theatre produced it again the following season. In 1990, while a visiting professor at North Carolina A&T University, I directed her play *Brown Silk and Magenta Sunsets*. A sensual play, I found that this work and other Gibson plays resonate with all ages — all sexes.

Destiny's Daughters: Voices of P. J. Gibson is the collection to get if you want to get to know her and her work. It consists of five full-length plays and four one acts. All the plays, including the full lengths (*Deep Roots*; *Annie Maye's Child*; *My Mark, My Name*; *Unveilings*; *Masks, Circles: Healing the Pain*) as well as the one-acts ("The Other Side of the Passion Curtain," and The Ancestor Series: "The Taking Circle," "Blood on the Seats," and "Weeding") are very clear and very different voices of Gibson. Two of the plays: *My Mark, My Name* and *Unveilings* are classic plays from the Black theatre.

Ms. P. J. Gibson is a major American playwright; she's a feminist who's written over thirty plays, covering a wide range of subjects and voices as they relate to Black women; she's a playwright who's an associate professor, a novelist, a poet, and as such, each of her voices is focused and disciplined. *Deep Roots* explores color discrimination within a Black family immediately after the Civil War; *My Mark, My Name* is set immediately after the Revolutionary War and is based on historical documents about the First Black Regiment of Rhode Island. In *Annie Maye's Child*, a child has drowned almost a quarter century earlier, and that incident affects everyone's life in the present. This play, along with *Masks, Circles: Healing the Pain* reveals how deeply rooted Gibson is in the "art" of drama and the "craft" of playwriting. In *Annie Maye's Child*, like the Greek dramatist, Gibson explores how the past defines the present; in *Masks*, Gibson uses ritual as practiced in different forms of African drama.

Unveilings is one of my favorite pieces of writing. Even though it's a well-crafted play, I see it as film in the classic Italian neorealist world of Fellini; it could also fit very well in the grandeur and wealth explored in the films of Merchant and Ivory. The plot of this work begins on a vast family estate. An artist, the central character, a former college professor, returns to paint and live out her few remaining days, that is until disclosures and truths from her past intercede. These are themes Gibson weaves through a number of her plays.

A few words on The Ancestor Series. In *The Ancestor Series: A Trilogy*, one of the three plays, "The Taking Circle," focuses P. J. Gibson's voice through the character of Shula. Shula is the voice of the present taking us on a journey to the past. Gibson's device for this journey is an antique African chair, appropriately named the birthing chair. Shula takes us back to slavery days where Black women had to confront every kind of known abuse, including rape. Out of these rapes children were born into this vicious system. In this work Gibson explores characters who didn't participate in perpetuating the cycle of slavery. In this short shocking work titled "The Taking Circle," P. J. Gibson brilliantly claims her territory as a playwright.

Laurence Holder

Laurence Holder is a prolific playwright. His plays are varied in themes and subject. His vast body of plays includes heroes and heroines and events that virtually chronicle the history of African Americans in the Diaspora. They include Malcolm X, Elijah Muhammad, Paul Robeson, the House Un-American Activities Committee, The Harlem Renaissance, Bud Powell, Thelonious Monk, Duke Ellington, Lena Horne, Billy Strayhorn, Sugar Ray Robinson, and the list goes on and on.

Like most African American playwrights, Laurence Holder's work also covers specific areas of the African as well as the African-American experience. Mr. Holder is a brilliant "New York" playwright, yet many of the white-controlled theatres shy away from producing his work. They claim they can't "find" his plays. The African-American theatres are in constant search for copies of his plays. They've heard about them on "the drum."

Many of these theatres call me looking for Laurence Holder because I've produced two of his masterworks: *Zora Neale Hurston* and *When the Chickens Came Home to Roost*. I always tell them to locate and read Laurence Holder's first volume of plays. Included in this fine collection are *Ethel Waters, Hot Snow, They Were All Gardenias, Zora Neale Hurston*, and *M: The Mandela Saga*.

These female characters as well as these plays are favorites of New York's African-American theatre, and because Laurence Holder is a veteran playwright (he's survived the so-called test of time) with an unparalleled 125 written plays, he enjoys New York status. Without question he deserves it. If you read those five carefully researched plays you'll agree with me.

Their heroines and heroes deserve special individual attention. Mr. Holder has given each of them their own space. This volume could fall under the overall title of "Black Women Survivors in a Male-Dominated World." It would be excellent programming for a theatre to present all these plays in one season.

New York's African-American Theatre discovered the life of musicians/singers Ethel Waters, Valaida Snow, and Billie Holiday; the drama in the life of the Harlem Renaissance writer Zora Neale Hurston; and the political activist Winifred Mandela after having seen these fascinating dramatizations by Laurence Holder.

When in January 1950 Ethel Waters arrived on Broadway in Carson McCuller's *The Member of the Wedding*, and was hailed a major star, little did audiences seem to care that she'd been a major star for more than thirty years, having starred on Broadway in *Cabin in the Sky*, *Aunt Hagar's Daughter*, and several musical reviews. In *Ethel Waters*, Laurence Holder's meticulously researched and dramatic narrative, he explores exactly what is was like to be a Black female Diva in the Twenties, Thirties and Forties. Miss Waters had to struggle to control both her personal life and her career.

Hot Snow (Valaida Snow) is yet another look at a Black Female heroine; this one is bound up in the tragedy of Hitler's Germany. How did a Black woman who plays and sings Jazz come to be in one of Hitler's death camps?

Many are now familiar with Billie Holiday's music from her many fine recordings and from the Diana Ross film, *Lady Sings the Blues*. However, Laurence Holder takes us on a journey into Miss Holiday's theatricalized private life. *They Were All Gardenias* is pure Black Theatre, a Black heroine in a tragic situation, with a Black interpretation; yet universal in its execution.

I can speak very knowledgeably of *Zora Neale Hurston*. I produced the first incarnation of her story in 1981 with Phylicia Rashad playing the title role. I began touring the play in festivals, colleges, and regional theatres. To this day, it's still an attractive and well-booked production. The actress Elizabeth Van Dyke stars in and champions this touring version which was produced in New York at the American Place Theatre. Miss Hurston (1891-1960) was a novelist, folklorist, and anthropologist. Her life reached its theatrical pinnacle during the Harlem Renaissance. Laurence Holder's play focuses on this particular period of her life. At times, during the play, Mr. Holder flashes back to her years as a student at Barnard College and Columbia University, picking up during the writing periods when she was creating *Mules and Men* and her magnificent opus, the novel *Their Eyes Were Watching God.*

M: The Mandela Saga I save to last. Even though it's about the relationship between Nelson and Winnie in the years immediately before and after Nelson's release from prison, Mr. Holder focuses on Winnie. Their break is a painful one, leading to a painful divorce. Again Laurence Holder finds the drama as well as the humanity in that relationship.

The Plays of Ron Milner

The Black literature of the Forties, Fifties, and Sixties seemed totally consumed with the search for identity, especially in the writings of Richard Wright, Ann Petry, Ralph Ellison, and James Baldwin. Questions raised in the writings are: Are we Black people other than who we let white people know? As Black writers, are we identifying ourselves for the comfort of white people or the rejection of white people? Young Black writers of the Sixties wondered how they could get these answers from the radical left and liberal whites they dialogued with, especially since (from all indications) racism emanated from the color of one's skin.

Young Black writers in cities like Detroit, Cleveland and Chicago didn't depend on dialogues with white radicals; instead they found information through the rich Black culture found in the public libraries in those cities. It was already known that within the walls of these libraries one could interpret Dostoyevsky, Chekov, Ibsen, Henry James, Mark Twain, Thomas Mann, Faulkner, Hemingway, and etc. Now through research and cross-referencing the vast world of Black history was within reach.

In the Fifties, the world of Rhythm and Blues music had already been recognized in Detroit. Groups like Andre Williams and the Five Dollars, The Detroit Emeralds, The Diablos, and The Fantastic Four carved out a special niche for themselves. Blues music had been popular in Detroit since the Thirties. These musicians played the Warfield Theatre, The Flame Show Bar, The Madison Ballroom, and The Greystone Ballroom.

The Black Theatre hadn't emerged from the small community theatre that presented white plays with a Black cast. Most of the theatre talent— such as Lloyd Richards, Walter Mason, Powell Lindsey, Laurence Blaine—

155

left Detroit for greener pastures in New York. However, one group, Drama Associates, headed by David Rambeau, remained. It kept Black theatre alive through the Fifties and Sixties. Actors who could express their talents—like Alma Forest Parks, Kent Martin, David Boone, Council Cargle, Bernice Avery, and Gil Maddock—performed maybe once per year in the community.

Black Detroit vibrated with a unique rhythm in the music. However, it wasn't until Ron Milner emerged did that rhythm enter into Black plays. Milner entered theatre after completing a very long novel entitled *The Life of the Brothers Brown*. He won a Saxton Fellowship to complete the novel. Milner was 20 years old at the time and received considerable press for his accomplishment.

Milner and I met a year earlier at the old Cass Theatre. The touring production of Lorraine Hansberry's *A Raisin in the Sun*, directed by Lloyd Richards, was playing. How we decided to meet there is a memory I cannot find. Yet, flashes of the Detroit Public Library indicate it had something to do with it all. Milner was very excited about *Raisin*. He was deeply moved by the story. As a novelist, he knew the writer must be able to tell a good story.

A Raisin in the Sun had what we've come to know as the Black aesthetic; that aesthetic was integral to the entire production. The drama took place within a Black household—focusing entirely on the Black family. The characters were Black and they were real. We could identify with them. *A Raisin in the Sun* wasn't like the Black literature of the Forties and Fifties. As 19- and 20-year-old Black artists we finally found characters we could identify with; we embraced Walter Lee Younger. As a result of *A Raisin in the Sun*, Ron Milner abandoned the novel form and entered the theatre as a playwright.

Milner's first play was, *Life Agony*. I produced and directed it in 1962 at the Unstable Coffeehouse Theatre. It ran on a bill of plays, including William Saroyan's "Hello Out There" and Tennessee Williams' "Talk to Me Like the Rain..." Two years later in New York, *Life Agony* was produced by Robert Hook's Group Theatre Workshop and Public Television's Experimental Negro Theatre. Later *Life Agony* reemerged as Milner's first full-length play *Who's Got His Own*. I hand-carried the first draft into New York. The lead role would be an actor's dream come true. I gave the draft to Wynn Handman and Lloyd Richards. Wynn Handman was Artistic Director of the American Place Theatre in New York. He loved *Who's Got His Own*. In its 1965/66 season The American Place Theatre produced the play. It was also distinguished by Lloyd Richards' brilliant direction. Although *Who's Got His Own* embodies those Black rhythms I spoke of earlier, it's not a play about street life, but about a Black family struggling to find answers as well as forgiveness and redemption. *Who's Got His Own* was chosen by Robert Macbeth's New Lafayette Theatre to open its 1966/67 season. It was the first time a play was produced downtown in a white theatre and then produced uptown in Harlem, winning critical acclaim in both communities.

In 1968, Milner's long one-act, "The Warning: A Theme for Linda" was produced off-Broadway; it was part of an evening of plays produced under the title, *A Black Quartet*. The three other playwrights were Amiri Baraka, Ed Bullins and Ben Caldwell. *A Black Quartet* was a tremendous critical success. The white critical establishment "discovered" these Black playwrights. It was as if these writers hadn't been writing before *A Black Quartet*. Many of the Black and white critics embraced Milner's "The Warning: A Theme for Linda." Remember, at that time Amiri Baraka had won the 1964 Obie Award for *Dutchman*; Bullins was the outspoken award-winning playwright-in-residence at New Lafayette Theater in Harlem; Milner was coming out after the success of *Who's Got His Own*; and Ben Caldwell was one of the most produced playwrights in small Black Theatres across America. Milner was in excellent company and his writing was showcased to overwhelming success.

It wasn't difficult to produce *What the Winesellers Buy* (1973). *Winesellers* was originally produced and directed by me at New Federal Theatre. Subsequently, because of my relationship with Michael Schultz, Gordon Davidson, and Joseph Papp, *What the Winesellers Buy* was also produced at the Mark Taper Forum in Los Angeles and was the first Black play produced by Joseph Papp at Lincoln Center for the Performing Arts. But the real success of *What the Winesellers Buy* was its unparalleled box office grosses on its 28-month national tour.

What the Winesellers Buy will sweep you away by the sheer power of the theatre of Ron Milner. Milner has taken the Hasting Street of our Fifties and Sixties memory and brought it into a reality. Hasting Street existed in our youth not as a ghetto but as a home. Milner honors the people in our home. Looking back, Milner wanted us to know "What the winesellers bought one-half of so precious as what they sold." He peopled *What the Winesellers Buy* with what has become known as the Detroit Rhythm. It's a slight musical tone in the speech pattern of women; a southern tone in Black men (not unlike the tones of Smokey Robinson or James Brown). A rhythm that at first appears as if the character is tired. (But don't bet against him in a basketball game!)

Some critics called *What the Winesellers Buy* a morality play. I don't see any problems in that. We are a moral people. Traditionally, white people fear any kind of morality. Milner created a moral image in the Rico character because Rico's values are based on what the white world taught him. His statements, though hidden in Black rhythm, are based on a white value system. Without a doubt, Rico is one of the most fascinating Black characters in contemporary Black theatre. At one point Rico tells Steve, "There are only two kinds of people in this world: Those standing around trembling, waiting to be told when and how to move, and those with guts enough to jump in and tell them *When* and *How*." Pay particular attention to Jim Aaron, a strong Black man, who's a deacon in the church that Steve's mother has retreated to. Early on in *Winesellers* he tells Steve, "Wanna know what a man is, don't look at his car, his clothes, his bank account, look at his woman. Whatever he is will be right there in her. If she's a whore, then he is a whore too..."

What *What the Winesellers Buy* had was a rapport with Black audiences. The production ran for an unprecedented fifteen weeks at The Shubert Theatre in Chicago. As a matter of record, the tour from 1974 to 1975 was the highest grossing production until that time, playing to a 95 percent Black audience. Black people really love Milner's characters.

Even though *What the Winesellers Buy* was produced in the early Seventies, it's a play of the Sixties. Milner's plays challenged traditional white perceptions of Black people. White America really believed that angry Black characters on stage would incite radicalism off stage. In general, white theatres don't want these kinds of Black characters on the stages of their theatres. On close examination, the content of the plays of Ron Milner is a moral attempt, in the tradition of Tom Paine and Frederick Douglass, to change these perceptions.

Milner's plays are produced extensively in Black theatres in the United States, Africa and the Caribbean. In 1998 *Checkmates*, starring Ruby Dee, was invited to the Bermuda International Arts Festival. However, it's the two-year journey of *Checkmates* from ETA Theatre in Chicago (1986) to Broadway (1988) that's a road map on how to produce and develop a Black play.

The journey of *Checkmates* began when it was first produced at ETA Theatre in Chicago 1986; then to Jomandi Theatre in Atlanta, where Marsha Jackson starred; Inner City Cultural Center in Los Angeles where we picked up Denzel Washington and Paul Winfield; on to the Arena Stage in Washington, D.C. where we added the legendary Ruby Dee; then a production in San Francisco at the Lorraine Hansberry Theatre where it was seen by Phillip Rose, the veteran Broadway producer of *A Raisin in the Sun*. All of these theatres except for Washington's Arena Stage are Black owned and all are non-profit, tax-exempt organizations. Milner constantly worked on *Checkmates*. In 1988, Phillip Rose joined forces with James Nederlander and produced *Checkmates* on Broadway at the 46th Street Theatre.

Checkmates takes us into comedy and drama while contrasting the lives of the two Black couples, who are generations apart in age and attitudes. The play speaks specifically to the crises faced by young educated Blacks obsessed with upward mobility. In contrast, the elder couple are bonded by a life together, dedicated to the survival of each other, and prove more to compromise than to compete. Note how Milner appropriates aspects of Black culture, one old and rural (Frank and Matte), the other contemporary and urban (Syl and Laura); both help to shape Black American cultural life. Milner knows his Black history yet is an artist of the present.

Milner is a cultural anthropologist as much as a playwright. His plays are deeply rooted in the people and places of his hometown of Detroit. Black people inhabit his plays. White people don't play any great role in the stage life of Milner's characters or in his stories. Black audiences identify immediately with Milner's world. In *Urban Transition: Loose Blossoms* (1996) Milner set his story in a middle-class home in suburban Detroit. The sociologist in Milner demands that he examine the vast drug subculture in Detroit in particular and other trans-urban settings in general. We must remember Milner ran a theatre company and wrote plays in the middle of the 1967 riots. During the turbulent Sixties, he was in contact with other writers and artists in New York, Newark, Los Angeles, etc. He saw first-hand the passion which led to the riots in the inner cities after the death of Malcolm and Martin. All of that is reflected in his writings. Therefore, it's not by accident that he's examining how the drug subculture rises to the top and weaves its way into mainstream culture. *Urban Transition: Loose Blossom* is so current one can actually see it as we shop and work. Young boys, too young to drive, owning Benz's and BMWs, supporting mothers, grandmothers, and siblings; young boys who wouldn't dream of working at McDonalds for $4.35 an hour when they could earn fifty times that in an hour by making a "delivery" and picking up a "package." Milner forewarned us about these "pick-ups" and "deliveries" in *What the Winesellers Buy* back in 1973.

Ron Milner is one of America's foremost playwrights. His plays represent a major departure from the Black literature of the past. Milner's characters must negotiate space, must already know who they are or they'll be destroyed. His plays aren't about self-destruction, losers, or images beyond reality. Instead, they're deeply rooted in the reality of the Black lifestyle.

Festivals

National Black Theatre Festival — African Heritage and Kinship

Festivals are by their very nature African in origin. Originally festivals were centered around the celebration of a deity or other periodic religious occasion. Most of the activities of these festivals were fun, joyous, and merry. In most African countries, festivals and carnivals aren't international in scope but very specific to that particular country.

In 1966 the First World Black and African Festival of Arts and Cultural was held in Dakar, Senegal. Many Black Americans participated in that Festival, including the late poet/playwright Langston Hughes, the artist Romare Bearden, and some of our finest jazz musicians. Nigeria was formally invited to host the second festival in 1970 but due to the internal unrest following the military action of Aguyi Ironsi, which later sparked the Biafra War, the Festival couldn't be held. The Festival was rescheduled after the Nigerian Civil War for January/February 1977. The federal government of Nigeria, under Olusegun Obassanjo, served as Patron of The Second World Black and African Festival of Arts and Culture (FESTAC '77). Prior to FESTAC '77 Guyana hosted CARIFESTA. CARIFESTA was an overdue attempt to fill the void created when no festival occurred in Africa immediately following the Dakar festival. It was held in August 25 – September 15, 1972. Carnivals are extremely popular in the Caribbean. Festivals are a part of the lifestyle of Black people.

Some festivals commemorate the migration of a people, others are for

163

the kings to meet for discussions, mend differences, and make plans for future progress. In Africa many people in big cities travel "home" to see their leaders, honor their ancestors, and fraternize with friends. Most of the African festivals are week-long celebrations.

The First Biennial National Black Theatre Festival occurred in Winston-Salem, North Carolina in 1989. It was billed as a "national celebration and reunion of spirit." The national chairman was Dr. Maya Angelou, Reynolds Professor American Studies at Wake Forest University. Special co-chair that year was the popular television talk show host Oprah Winfrey. It was hosted by the North Carolina Black Repertory Theatre. Both the National Black Theatre Festival and The North Carolina Black Repertory Theatre are under the artistic leadership of Larry Leon Hamlin. The Festival had been an idea searching for realization for over five years. Hamlin felt, "the isolation and fragmentation of Black Theatre must come to an end, since they only serve to weaken and prevent the progress of American theatre as a whole... During this week the nation's attention will be focused on the courageous and profound efforts of Black theatre in helping to improve the quality of life not only for African-Americans but for all people."

In that first year Maya Angelou wrote a manifesto that still holds true for any National Black Theatre Festival:

> All the world might not be a stage after all, but the National Black Theatre Festival hopes this week to provide a stage upon which all the Black theatrical personages can reveal the worlds they know and even those they dare to hope for.

The Festival was Larry Leon Hamlin's dream. Mr. Hamlin is a graduate of Brown University, where he received special guidance from his late professor and founder of Rites and Reason Theatre, George Houston Bass. However, this first Festival, according to Hamlin, owed a great deal of its success to Maya Angelou. "Ms. Angelou unselfishly shared her resources; gave advice, courage, and inspiration... she obviously knew of the tremendous obstacles awaiting me."

In addition to the workshops and performing groups from across the United States, each day of the six-day long Festival features an open press conference with invited celebrities. In that first year were Ossie Davis and Ruby Dee, Oprah Winfrey, Louis Gossett, Cicely Tyson, James Earl Jones, and Roscoe Lee Browne. Each answered questions and spoke eloquently on the state of Black people in the entertainment industry. This open press conference remains a popular part of each Festival. In the six days of Festival, Winston-Salem's streets are also filled with celebrities.

In a discussion with Pearl Cleage in 1989 about the Festival, she said:

> You begin to see the problem. 'We' are a wildly diverse group of performers, directors, writers, teachers, designers, producers, and patrons. We have accepted no unifying creed or set of values, embraced no collective aesthetic, defined no common enemy and agreed upon no mutually beneficial strategies for survival. We have few, if any, institutions that are not heavily dependent on resources granted to us from outside of the communities in whom our work should be deeply rooted and to whom our work should be of definable use and value...It is madness to consider the future of Black theatre outside of the context of the future of Black America. Any attempt to do so removes us from our cultural traditions and from our historical responsibilities.

That statement seems to be what Larry Leon Hamlin wants the Festivals to address. The Board of Advisors consists of performers, educators, and business people. In a series of seminars and workshops that are now an integral part of each Festival, discussions take place on the economic impact of The Black Theatre, Who Is Our Audience?; The Aesthetics of Black Theatre as well as The Craftsmanship of Playwrights, Directors, Designers, and Performers. It's virtually impossible to participate and/or attend every workshop or performance at the Festival.

Even though the Festival is supported by traditional founders as Pearl Cleage suggests, the most enthusiastic support for the event has come from theatre companies across the country. Leon Denmark of The Negro Ensemble Company (at that time the nation's premier Black theatre company) said, "Black Theatre in America has reached a critical juncture in its organizational development. This gathering will allow us to...

develop strategies to strengthen our groups." Twenty theatre companies from across the United States participated in that first Festival. Over 20,000 people attended. The Festival spanned ten stages around Winston-Salem, featured entertainment for the entire family from some of the best Black theatre companies. The funding of $500,000 was a major problem because the Festival was asking funders for major dollars for an event that had never happened before.

The Festival served as a vehicle for Black actors, directors, producers, administrators, playwrights, designers, and other technical artists to voice their concerns. Many feel they're alone against the world, not realizing many others are experiencing the same struggles. The free series of workshops titled, "Bridging the Gaps" was planned along with the Black Theatre Network.

In 1989, National Black Touring Circuit was one of the companies invited to participate in the Festival. The company presented *I Have A Dream* adapted from the writings of the Rev. Dr. Martin Luther King by Josh Greenfield. It's a company that tours the U.S. and Europe. Among many other productions were *Don't Bother Me, I Can't Cope, Sister*; *Do Lord Remember Me*; *Club Zebra*; *Malcolm X*; *Stepping Into Tomorrow*; *Ain't No Use In Going Home*; *Jody's Got Your Gal and Gone*; as well as *Dark Cowgirls and Prairie Queens*.

The theme, "Celebration and Reunion of the Spirit," continued in the 1991 Festival. The national chairpersons were Ossie Davis and Ruby Dee. Ossie Davis stated, "Ruby and I are always ready and available to encourage talented people to produce. We're honored to co-chair the 1991 National Black Theatre Festival."

Larry Leon Hamlin said, "The Festival allowed all of the Black theatres in America to come together, to unite, to discover ways of supporting one another, of rededicating, recommitting ourselves to keeping this vehicle alive." It took Hamlin's passion, his determination and his boundless optimism to make the Festival a reality.

"This Festival to me, and perhaps to some others, is a way of coming back home again." Ossie Davis declared. "We believe that Black theatre has its own statement to make, has its own world to portray, its own passions to share with the rest of the world."

In 1991 the Festival took place August 5-10. An ambitious schedule of workshops and performances included twenty-two plays—again, from select Black theatre companies. The number of performances topped that of the 1989 Festival and the workshops doubled in quantity and scope. Those honored were Academy Award winner Denzel Washington; playwrights Lofton Mitchell and George C. Wolfe; actors Glynn Turman, Avery Brooks, Moses Gunn, Esther Rolle, Beah Richards, and Helen Martin; and film directors Bill Duke and Michael Schultz. Several one-person shows saluted Black heroes. Avery Brooks gave a brilliant performance in Philip Hayes Dean's *Paul Robeson*, Elizabeth Van Dyke was the independent Zora Neale Hurston in Laurence Holder's *Zora Neale Hurston* and Esther Rolle gave an excellent *Mary McLeod Bethune*.

The Festival also includes a series of play readings coordinated by The Frank Silvera Writer's Workshop of New York. Workshops that year were conducted by myself, Voza Rivers (Roger Furman Theatre), and Crossroads Theatre Company of New Jersey. Ossie Davis made these remarks about the workshops: "We must be just as concerned about the craft of the business, the craft of producing, the craft of the entrepreneur as we are about the artistic craft."

Ruby Dee commented on the 1991 Festival, "It was exciting to see so many artists! They were everywhere you turned. The networking opportunities were enormously valuable."

Ossie Davis added, "It was a magnificent celebration. And you know how Black people love a celebration. The Festival gave me my first sense of a national theatre, a national statement. It gave us strength."

In most African countries ancestors are honored as well as the elders. It's believed that the ancestors live as they did on Earth. The living have a sense of dependence on the ancestors; it's believed that they're constantly watching over the living and will, indeed, punish those who break customs. The elder is always respected as both the head of the "family" and the intermediary with the "spirits." Old age is held in very high esteem.

In each of the National Black Theatre Festivals, productions are selected that honor the ancestors and the Festival itself honors "living legends." The 1989 Festival selected productions such as *Can I Speak For You, Brother* adapted from the writings of Frederick Douglass, Booker T. Washington, and W. E. B. DuBois; *Malcolm X*, by August Wilson; *Do Lord Remember Me*, a play of original slave narratives by Dr. James de

Jongh; as well as *I Have a Dream*. These four plays honored our ancestors. They brought these ancestors and their contributions to over ten thousand young people attending the Festival. That same year the elders were Ossie Davis, Ruby Dee, and James Earl Jones.

As the King and Queen of Black theatre, Ossie and Ruby discussed Black theatre past and present. Again, in 1991 Ossie Davis and Ruby Dee were involved in the Festival as co-chairs. In that year productions honoring ancestors were *Paul Robeson*, *Zora Neale Hurston*, and *Mary McLeod Bethune*. Elders honored via Living Legend Award were playwright and historian Lofton Mitchell, actress/director Gertrude Jeanette, producers Ashton Springer and myself, actor/director Douglas Turner Ward (Negro Ensemble Company), veteran actress Helen Martin, actor Whitman Mayo, and Frederick O'Neal, Dick Campbell, Rosetta LeNoire, Melvin Van Peebles, Joe Seneca, and Vinette Carroll.

Elders and ancestors were highlighted again in the 1993 National Black Theatre Festival. Veteran actor Sidney Poitier co-chaired with Harry Belafonte. Brock Peters and Della Reese were special guests of the Festival. Honored ancestors were noted in productions as diverse as Bessie Smith, playwright Lorraine Hansberry portrayed by Elizabeth Van Dyke, bluesman Robert Johnson portrayed by Guy Davis, Toussaint L'Ouverture portrayed by Antonio Fargas, Theolonius Monk portrayed by Alvin Alexis, and Bud Powell portrayed by Tony Jackson. Living legends were Robert Earl Jones, The Negro Ensemble Company, Lloyd Richards, Ron Milner (Garland Anderson Award), Lonne Elder III, Pam Grier, Janet Du'Bois, Micki Grant, Robert Guillaume, Ivan Dixon, John Amos, Barbara Montgomery, William Marshall, Bill Cobbs, Clarice Taylor, Garland Lee Thompson, Dick Anthony Williams, Amiri Baraka, and Al Freeman, Jr.

Networking is a form "of meeting people." Networking gained momentum in the Eighties and became a specialty of upwardly mobile Blacks in the Nineties. At the National Black Theatre Festival networking reaches new levels from 11 P.M. to 3 A.M. each night at the bar in the Festival hotel headquarters. Hundreds of attendees mingle with Hollywood stars and professors from major universities. Business cards are constantly exchanged. At the center of it all is an "open mike." Anyone who thinks he or she can sing simply gets up and performs.

In the 1993 Festival amid the dancing and drum playing, the brightly colored African prints, the big-shouldered security guards for the TV and movie celebrities were 83 performances in twelve venues by some of the 250 Black theatre companies in attendance. In addition, as in previous Festivals, were workshops, classes, discussions, news conferences, celebrity receptions and readers' theatre performances attended by over 20,000 participants.

Sidney Poitier in accepting the Festival's Lifetime Achievement Award said, "I'm so glad that you have chosen to honor me with this award while I have most of my hair, and my stomach isn't obscuring my view of my feet." Poitier then read off a list of those who'd gone before and paved the way.

Harry Belafonte opened the third biennial National Black Theatre Festival with this important statement: "I believe that this is a forum to give us an opportunity to sit down for a couple of days to see where we are and talk about what we can do about it. Certainly theatre, which is the least problematic in terms of control, gives us the great opportunity to be able to express who and what we are as a people and what the world looks like from our point of view. However, the greater truth and reality is that we are here and we do see each other and it's 'family.'"

After the third Festival one began to notice encroaching commercialism. It became an African market for hundreds of vendors. Hotels and food shops began to raise their prices. The Festival staff found itself too small to handle the thousands of requests from theatres around the country wanting to participate. Thousands of videotapes were sent to the Festival and many were lost. Without question the Festival had grown beyond even Larry Leon Hamlin's imagination.

The 1995 National Black Theatre Festival was held July 31 through August 5. It was larger in quantity and scope. It called itself "an international celebration and reunion of spirit." Billy Dee Williams, a longtime stage actor and now Hollywood star, was Chairman of the Festival. Elders and Living Legends were Vinie Burrows, Ed Cambridge, Vivian Robinson, Nick & Edna Stewart, and Joseph A. Walker. Ruby Dee, Ossie Davis, Della Reese, Leslie Uggams, Carmen De Lavallade, and Geoffrey Holder were specifically designated "elders."

For the first time in this Festival, Black theatres from around the world came together in an International Colloquium/Workshop, entitled, "The Black Theatre: A Stage Beyond National Boundaries." This was a very important workshop because the dialogue was among Black theatre artists, poets, playwrights, and scholars from South Africa, America, Brazil, Republic of Benin, Cuba, England, Ghana, the Caribbean and Nigeria.

The opening event of the 1995 Festival was New Federal Theatre's 20th Anniversary Production of Ntozake Shange's *for colored girls who have considered suicide/when the rainbow is enuf.* This production was also directed by Ms. Shange. It was the first time a production that didn't originate out of the North Carolina Black Repertory Theatre opened the Festival. As stated earlier, Larry Leon Hamlin, the Artistic Director of both the Festival and the North Carolina Black Repertory Theatre, is very concerned about history and tradition. When he saw the opportunity to make a profound statement about Black women represented in Black Theatre he grabbed the opportunity to open the Festival with this award-winning, controversial choregraphy.

Two other important events were Susan Sherman's translation of *Shango de Ima* produced by New York's Nuyorican Poets' Café and Trevor Rhone's *Two Can Play* produced by Trevor Rhone Productions in Jamaica. *Shango de Ima* originally written in Spanish by the Cuban playwright Pepe Carillo was brilliantly directed by Rome Neal. It captures the humor and sensuality of the coming of age of *Shango de Ima. Two Can Play*, written and directed by Trevor Rhone, captures the humor and passion of a married couple in a Caribbean country in revolutionary struggle. *Shango* and *Two Can Play* illustrate the growth of the Black Theatre Festival as it embraces Blacks in the Diaspora.

The Impact of Race
on Two Cultural Festivals
in Atlanta

National Black Arts Festival (NBAF) and the Atlanta Committee for the Olympic Games (ACOG) bookended each other in 1996. From June 28 through July 7, Atlanta, Georgia came alive with dance, music, visual arts, film, Black art and literature. All of these disciplines were fueled by some of the finest Black artists in America. One week after the close of the National Black Arts Festival, Atlanta hosted the Olympic Games. As an integral part of the Olympics, Atlanta also hosted the 1996 Olympic Arts Festival. It too presented professional theatre, dance, music, visual arts, and literature. The two events were as different as night and day, as black and white. National Black Arts Festival events were attended by a predominantly Black audience; the Olympic Arts Festival events were attended by an international, predominantly white audience.

In each of my twenty-three days in Atlanta, I attended a play or a literary forum plus the four events that I personally produced. After the last performance of each evening, artists and old friends convened at Festival headquarters; there at Festival headquarters we argued or drank into the early morning. These days and evenings were both exhilarating and exhausting.

This was NBAF's fourth festival; it's held every two years. Its artistic director was the stage and television star Avery Brooks. Prior to becoming artistic director, Brooks was a consultant to the Festival. His performance in Philip Hayes Dean's *Robeson* was an astounding success in the first NBAF in 1990. At that time the overall director was Stephanie Hughley, a former company manager with the Negro Ensemble Company. However, it was the Commissioner of Fulton County, Michael Lomax, who waged a two-year campaign to raise the funds for the Festival. As a result, many Atlantans felt Lomax would be elected mayor of Atlanta in the 1992 election. He was not elected. Stephanie Hughley crossed over into the position of director of the 1996 Olympic Arts Festival, pledging to use some of the Atlanta Committee for the Olympic Arts Festival funds to support NBAF events. However, one year prior to the actual events, Ms. Hughley abandoned ship to become a director at the multi-million-dollar New Jersey Center for the Performing Arts. NBAF was left with no funding from the 1996 Olympic Arts Festival and in a few cases it had to compete with it for cultural events. Avery Brooks was a director of a $3 million festival. However, he ran it from the Hollywood set of *Deep Space Nine*.

National Black Arts Festival pulled together approximately 450 events, 1,500 artists including twenty literature panels and seven theatre productions. The literary panels explored issues of Black identity. Each panel had a highly visible moderator. The theatre productions were selected because the casts were small and because the subject of the plays were Black heroes (or sheroes). A few of the literature panels or literary personalities were: "An Evening With Dr. Maya Angelou"; "The Spiritual Vitality of African Diasporic Literature: Honoring Bessie Head"; "The Blood of the Lamb: James Baldwin and African American Religion and Spirituality"; "An Evening With Gwendolyn Brooks"; "Editing the Century: Honoring Hoyt W. Fuller"; "My Dungeon Shook: The Language of Resistance in African American Literary Traditions"; "A Conversation With Margaret Walker Alexander"; "A Conversation With Katherine Dunham"; and a panel on which I participated titled "Institution Builders." Amiri Baraka, the poet/playwright/activist, participated either as moderator or panelist on many of the panels.

The seven plays selected were: *Having Our Say*, adapted by Emily Mann; *Lady Day at Emerson's Bar & Grill* by Lanie Robertson; *A Huey P. Newton Story*, written and performed by Roger Guenoveur Smith; *Zora Neale Hurston* by Laurence Holder; *The Ghosts of Summer* by Marion McClinton; *The Confessions of Stepin Fetchit* by Matt Robinson; and two other theatre pieces I didn't see. All the plays except *Having Our Say* were performed at the 14th Street Playhouse. *Having Our Say* was performed at the Alliance Theatre.

The first literary panel I attended was in the Crown Room of Festival headquarters, The Sheraton Colony Square Hotel. This was a large room on the top floor of this newly renovated hotel. One question on the minds of the radicals at the Festival: *Why should a major festival reaching out to Black people be held in a white-owned hotel in a city known for its large Black population?* Since the panel consisted of Amiri Baraka, Haki Madhubuti, Sonia Sanchez, Mari Evans, and moderated by Joyce Ann Joyce, this question was bound to resurface over and over. This panel was entitled, "My Dungeon Shook: The Language of Resistance in African American Literary Traditions." Baraka's paper was on language as culture. "The people and the culture are the repository of culture," Baraka said, "all our language speaks as resistance." He went on to explain how Africans were always socialized around the arts. "We (Black people) are the oldest artists in the world. Slave masters took the drums away because we (Black people) were 'rapping' to each other. Rapping is as old as the Africans speaking in rhythm. Our language rests in symbols, metaphor...our Duke is Duke Ellington not John Wayne, and our Divine One is Sarah Vaughn not Bette Midler. Our language must change quickly because we must change or be co-opted."

Haki Madhubuti's paper included two of his most recent poems. Both poems were inspired by mentors on the panel. Baraka and Sanchez really enjoyed the poems. Madhubuti explained how today's African American writers are able to dance with words. Language in context of the poem can change the human spirit. Madhubuti went on to talk about language in the Black community; a young Black man in the Black community is more respected for his slam-dunk than for his knowledge of Richard Wright, Franz Fanon, and Gwendolyn Brooks. "A writer who writes about his community is branded a propagandist." he added. He went on to explain that he, too, believes that language is cultural. "Our language is our name," he said. "Our language carries our history. Rap today is derivative of the poetry of the Sixties, a liberation cry for self-determination. Rappers must also understand the word 'nigger' cannot be made positive; the words 'bitch' and 'whore' are negative. Anyone can rap reality," he said. "Only an artist can create a better world."

Sonia Sanchez's paper posed the question, "What are you going to do when you get that freedom you been fighting for so long?" Ms. Sanchez reminded the room of what happened in South Africa when they got freedom. The women there are left out because they're not educated like South African men. Ms. Sanchez's point is, Black people must be prepared for freedom. However, this was only a preamble to her exploration of language. Of her several observations of Black people and the inextricable connection of oppression and language, she pointed to one very telling example. It seemed a 747 en route from New York to Los Angeles, had a Black pilot. Before takeoff the pilot door opened and some of the white passengers called the stewardess and complained; the stewardess went into the cockpit to the pilot. The Black pilot said he'd talk to the passengers. "Ladies and Gentlemen," he said, "I want to assure you everything will be all right. I am a graduate of Harvard, M.I.T. and Yale University. I also taught all the pilots in World War II. So sit back and relax and I'll get this big muthafucka off the ground in a few minutes." What Sonia Sanchez's paper emphasized is that language and Black oppression are inextricably connected. She also felt strongly that Black language is about resistance.

Another panel explored the contributions of Hoyt W. Fuller who died in 1981. For many years Fuller was editor of the illustrious literary magazine, *Black World*. The magazine introduced the writings of some of America's finest Black writers and thinkers. The panel illuminated the contributions of one of the century's most important conveyors of contemporary African American culture. The panelists were Haki Madhubuti, Eugene Redmond, Tom Dent, Robert Christman, and Charles Rowell.

Haki Madhubuti met Hoyt Fuller in 1967 in Chicago. In 1976, immediately after Fuller had been fired from the Johnson Publishing Company, Madhubuti confronted the company with a group of other Black protesters. There'd been a Jewish backlash to the magazine's articles on Palestine. Fuller was never confused with his ideas. He believed that liberation for Black people is possible. However, not to act, not to function, is an act against the liberation of Black people. Fuller never let his personal feelings get in the way of selecting writers for *Black World*. Every issue of *Black*

World is a collector's issue. The other panelists all spoke in glowing remembrance of Hoyt W. Fuller. In some cases he championed the concept of Black studies; in others he was compared to the literary giant Alain Locke. But it was his friend, Charles Rowell, who really defined the contributions of Hoyt W. Fuller.

He published a whole generation of young Black writers. It was the role he played as an editor, by shaping our sensibilities during that time. The literature affirmed us as a people. He had a Pan-African vision. That vision was positive...instructive, assertive. We should be about building Black institutions. Each issue pointed to that purpose; and is, thus, responsible for many of the writers of today. It's the example of Hoyt that informs our lives.

A panel on Ms. Toni Cade Bambara, who died in 1995, reconstructed her life through anecdotes and reminiscences. This panel was entitled, "Portrait of a Young Girl's Passage: Homage to Toni Cade Bambara." This panel included Clyde Taylor, Rosa Guy, Ntozake Shange, Ellease Sutherland, and Virginia Hamilton. All spoke glowingly of Ms. Bambara's contribution as an educator, critic, filmmaker, and writer. *Gorilla My Love*, *The Sea Birds Are Still Alive*, and *The Salt Eaters* are three books of fiction that define Toni Cade Bambara.

The second panel, "Institution Building" consisted of myself, Barbara Ann Teer, and Abena Joan Brown. Each panelist recounted how their respective institutions were built. It seems all were built on energy and a love for people. My own two New York institutions, New Federal Theatre and National Black Touring Circuit, were then twenty-seven and twenty years in business, respectively. Barbara Ann Teer is the founder and CEO of New York's National Black Theatre. Abena Joan Brown was then a co-founder of twenty-five years' standing. All panelists agreed that building an institution is like raising a family and holding that family together— extremely difficult and time consuming. In both, a lot of love is needed to get through each day. Each of the institutions were shaped by its founder and the individual history of the founder. Within a very short period of time an institution will take on the personality of the individual at the head of it. However, all agreed that institutions cannot be one-person run. The leader must open it up. Other directors or playwrights must be invited to work. That will generate a variety of ideas within the Black aesthetic.

The Impact of Race

"A Conversation With Margaret Walker Alexander," was moderated by JoAnn Gabbin. Ms. Alexander is the octogenarian grande dame of Black letters. She's in excellent health, constantly lecturing. She's the author of two seminal classics, *For My People* and *Jubilee*. She earned her first degree at the age of 20 and shortly thereafter Houghton Mifflin published *For My People*. She went on to earn her masters degree and doctorate at the University of Iowa.

She recounted meeting Langston Hughes when she was only 16; Claude McKay and W. E. B. DuBois at the age of 17; and her tumultuous relationship with Richard Wright at the age of 20 (detailed in her 1989 non-fiction book, *The Demonic Genius*). She explained how these writers and thinkers represented all the humanity of the human being. One of these writers introduced her to *Ten Days That Shook the World* and it moved her to action as a writer. She joined the W.P.A. in 1936, where her friendship with Richard Wright began.

"The humanist tradition of African American literature," she said, "did not begin with Homer. It's an epic tradition that began with The *Book of the Dead*, a pre-Homeric epic." Ms. Alexander went on to say "The writer must see the future by looking at the present...Racism, sexism, and fascism are our worst enemy. The role of the Black writer is to put it on paper."

The Festival presented 450 different events. I'm reporting on a representative sampling. Of all these events only seven were plays. The plays were presented under the title "Portrait Theatre Series." *Huey P. Newton* is a play with incidental music. It was written and performed by Roger Guenveur-Smith. I'd seen *Huey P. Newton* performed in 1995 at the National Black Theatre Festival in Winston-Salem, North Carolina. After that production it journeyed to Los Angeles and San Francisco. It's a one-character play that's exceptionally well conceived and brilliantly performed by Smith. It's the basic story of Huey P. Newton's last days. As you will remember, Newton was the controversial leader of the radical Black Panther Party of the Sixties and Seventies. Smith's research in both writing and performance is exceptional. In performance, Smith is made up into a striking resemblance of the late Huey P. Newton. The play and the performance are so close it's impossible to tell what's script and what's performance. After the four performances in Atlanta, *Huey P. Newton* was slated to play Louisville, Washington, D.C. and finally the New York Shakespeare Festival Public Theatre.

The following day I caught the matinee of Emily Mann's production of *Having Our Say* at the Alliance Theatre. I'd seen the production at McCarter and on Broadway. However, this production had two actresses I wanted to see: Lizan Mitchell and Micki Grant. They were excellent. *Having Our Say* is the Broadway play recounting the life and times of the 100-year-old Delany sisters and its inclusion in the National Black Arts Festival was something of a coup. It was a huge hit on Broadway and then again at the festival, where thousands of Black people were convening. Many had heard of the play; many were pleased that among a large array of events they could see a Broadway show.

That evening I caught the performance of *Lady Day at Emerson's Bar and Grill*, by Lanie Robertson (who isn't Black), starring Gail Nelson and her husband, Danny Holgate. Again, I think I went to see the play because Gail and Danny urged me. It wasn't a particularly exciting production. Yet, the theatre was filled to capacity. Blacks who attend the Festival try to see all the events. They're not as judgmental in Atlanta as they'd be in their own hometown.

I produced the Festival's production of *Zora Neale Hurston* by Laurence Holder, starring Elizabeth Van Dyke and Joseph Edwards, directed by Wynn Handman. Even though I've seen the production dozens of times at other Black festivals, I found myself attending three of *Zora's* four performances. At these festivals one becomes fascinated by the audiences. They're thoroughly immersed in Black culture and Black history. If the work on stage is true to its Blackness, the audience will identify with it. Coming from various sections of the country, the audiences attend the Festival to see as many events as possible and are not overly critical. Thus, *Zora Neale Hurston* was been filled to capacity each night. It also received prolonged standing ovations after each performance.

The only other production in the Portrait Theatre Series I had an opportunity to see was *The Confessions of Stepin Fetchit* by Matt Robinson, starring Roscoe Orman, directed by Bill Lathan. This one-character play was originally produced by The American Place Theatre. Roscoe Orman's performance was masterful, giving this despicable character human qualities and making audiences understand his dilemma.

The Impact of Race

One week after the conclusion of NBAF was the 1996 Olympic Arts Festival. It offered the AT&T Theatre Series, July 10 through August 3. This festival was an integral part of the Atlanta Committee for the Olympic Games (ACOG). Thirteen productions were to be presented. These productions were from a diverse collection of theatres around the world. For example, the Royal National Theatre of Great Britain presented *Dealer's Choice* by Patrick Marber; Anne Bogart's and Tadashi Suzuki's Saratoga International Theater Institute (SITI) presented *Small Lives/Big Dreams*, derived from the five major plays of Chekhov; *The Harvey Milk Show* by Dan Pruitt and Patrick Hutchinson, directed by David Bell; The Center for Puppetry Art put on six of their works; *Lizard* by Dennis Covington came from the Alabama Shakespeare Festival; *Blues for an Alabama Sky* by Pearl Cleage, directed by Kenny Leon was from the Alliance Theatre; *When the World Was Green* by Joseph Chaikin and Sam Shepard, directed by Joseph Chaikin, from Seven Stages; *The Last Night at Ballyhoo* by Alfred Uhry, directed by Ron Lagomarsino; *Blue Monk* by Robert Earl Price, starring Gilbert Lewis, directed by Ed Smith; *Ali* by Geoffrey C. Ewing and Graydon Royce; and *Hip 2: Birth of the Boom*, a musical by Thomas W. Jones, directed by Marsha Jackson, from Jomandi Productions. I saw four of the productions in the Festival. I'd seen two prior to Atlanta and felt once was sufficient.

Over on the Clark-Atlanta University Campus, I was brought in to produce four cultural events. Although these events were a part of the Olympic Arts Festival they were produced on this Black college campus within two city blocks of some of the Olympic games. Thus, security was tight. Automobiles couldn't park within ten blocks of the campus and taxis were rerouted.

The cultural events I produced were Amiri Baraka's *Black History Music*; *Dink's Blues* by Phillip Hayes Dean, directed by Dick Anthony Williams: "Ossie Davis and Ruby Dee in Conversation," moderated by Pearl Cleage; and "A Conversation With Esther Rolle." Now, look at the politics of these two venues. At the same time, if it's possible, look at the politics of the Atlanta Committee for the Olympic Games. The very site on which these games was being held is where Black and poor Atlanta residents were displaced. The site of the Olympic games became a way of ridding Atlanta of its ghetto. The politicians hoped to use this two-week event to lure foreign investors and coax white suburbanites back to the Black Majority City. As Olympic organizations stormed into town, people were getting evicted from their homes. The city razed these areas to make way for the Olympic Village. Developers uprooted up to 15,000 home-owners, tenants, small businesses, and homeless people. These people couldn't return after the games, as the Village was slated to become dorms for Georgia State University.

Clark-Atlanta University used funds from the Atlanta Committee for the Olympic Games to build a new stadium, to construct a new four-block wall, and to beautify existing structures. A small portion of the funds were set aside for cultural events from "a Black perspective." However, Black people in Atlanta were angry at being displaced and at being left out of the commerce. Blacks and other visitors were being packaged from the hotel to the Olympic games. Clark-Atlanta University wasn't part of the package. Those productions that were a part of the package were the ones in highly visible venues, i.e., the Alliance Theatre, the 14th Street Playhouse, and the Center for Puppetry Art.

Blues for an Alabama Sky was a well-written and produced production. It also had as its leading lady the brilliant Phylicia Rashad. The set by Marjorie Bradley Kellogg and the lighting by Ann C. Wrighton added immensely to the production. Very effective mood music by Dwight Andrews helped make this one of the finest productions of the Festival.

What seems to distinguish *Blues for an Alabama Sky* is Pearl Cleage's vision; it seems to be a vision indoctrinated in Black culture. Although *Blues for an Alabama Sky* is a play with fictional characters, the story is set in the Harlem community of the Twenties. Outside the immediate environment the fictional characters interface with the likes of Langston Hughes, Wallace Thurman, Rev. Adam Clayton Powell, Bruce Nugent, Josephine Baker, and Margaret Sanger. Although we never see these people, they're clearly drawn. For example, Ms. Cleage's fictional characters are getting dressed in their finery for a party Bruce Nugent is giving for Langston Hughes' return to Harlem. That party actually happened.

The journey of the protagonist through enlightenment and redemption is what *Blues for an Alabama Sky* is all about. Each of the five characters fled to Harlem to enhance his life. Two of the lives end in tragedy and three evolve. The published version of *Blues for an Alabama Sky* appeared in the July/August 1996 issue of *American Theatre Magazine*.

When the World Was Green premiered during the Festival. It was a commissioned work by The Arts Festival. The play was written by Joe Chaikin and Sam Shepard and directed by Chaikin. The setting by Christine Jones consisted of a small table and one chair, an ottoman, and a triangular box. All were painted in deck grey. Upstage in the center of the back wall was a one-foot by one-foot square window. This was a cell, a prison.

When the World Was Green is about an old man who presumably murdered his best friend. Now, a mysterious young woman comes to interview him in prison. She's either the angel of death or the daughter of the man he killed. She's there to help the old man return to the richness of the earth; to fertilize the mangoes and the greenery that emanate from the earth. The story unfolds in a series of blackouts.

This kind of collaboration between Mr. Shepard and Mr. Chaikin spawned two other major works: *Tongues* and *Savage/Love*.

The Last Night at Ballyhoo was presented at The Alliance Studio Theatre. This is the same space *Driving Miss Daisy* had a two-year run in after New York. Uhry was back on familiar territory. He and his director, Ron Lagomarsino, used every inch of space. *The Last Night at Ballyhoo* is a period piece set in the late Thirties around Christmas. It's a play that fits the definition of the "well written play." Beginning middle, and end; all symmetrical. It's the story of two Jewish girls (first cousins) who return home to Atlanta from college under different circumstances. Both are looking for love. They fall in love with the same man. Their return coincides with the 1939 Atlanta premiere of the film *Gone With the Wind*. However, the film is only a metaphor for the larger issue of anti-Semitism. The cast was excellent, headed by Valerie Curtin and Dana Ivey. Others in the cast were Stephen Largay, Terry Beaver, Jessalyn Gillsig, Mary Bacon, and Stephan Mailer. The set was by John Lee Beatty.

The last play I had an opportunity to see is *Blue Monk*, by Robert Earl Price, directed by Ed Smith. *Blue Monk* was a world premiere. It was developed by Seven Stages for the 1996 Olympic Festival. The play was a mess. However, Lewis gave a brilliant performance. How does a writer translate jazz music into a theatrical event? Jazz is based on improvisation.

Can a play in two acts, covering the life if its composer be improvised? Are there parallels between a musician's training and an actor's training? *Blue Monk* doesn't answer these questions. It's obvious the playwright loves jazz music. He knows the language of jazz musicians. Yet, all this didn't sound right coming out of the actors. The director also loves jazz music and musicians. But all of this love never penetrated past the surface of *Blue Monk*. I really question whether one can base a drama on "the haunting lyricism, evocative moods and dramatic tensions heard in the musical compositions of Thelonious Monk." The playwright attempted this by having actors play the roles of different instruments, i.e., pianist, trumpet, sax, drum, and bass. Music provokes feeling; theatre provides reason and logic. A theatergoer can feel deeply, yet if what is happening on stage makes no sense he will turn off.

The Eleventh Biennial Theatre Communication Group Conference

The Eleventh Biennial National Theatre Communications Group (TCG) conference was held on the Princeton University campus, Princeton, New Jersey, June 26-30, 1996. Its unofficial host was the McCarter Theatre, the resident professional theatre company housed on Princeton's campus. This conference, the first in twenty-two years without director Peter Zeisler, distinguished itself in being the first to have a keynote address by the award-winning Black playwright, August Wilson.

What shall I say about August Wilson? That he's a gifted playwright? That his penetrating insight into the complexities of the Black experience has won for him widespread recognition? That he's the winner of five Drama Critic Circle Awards, two Pulitzer Prizes, two Tony Awards, and over a dozen other major awards? Should I give you the names of his plays that journeyed through the non-profit Resident Professional Theatres to Broadway? Plays like *Fences*, *Ma Rainey's Black Bottom*, *Joe Turner's Come and Gone*, *The Piano Lesson*, *Seven Guitars*, and *Two Trains Running*. That he distills from the Blues, Jazz and Fine Arts pure poetry when creating the characters in an amazing body of work chronicling his view of the Black Experience in the 20th century? Characters called Hedley, Loomis, Bynum, Bono, Boy Willie Sterling, Wolf, etc. Shall I tell you his characters are storytellers; that they're African American griots (Africa's genealogical storytellers)?

The Impact of Race

I won't attempt to embellish August Wilson's accomplishments with superlatives. I will tell you that from the beginning, the life and the career of August Wilson have been of continuous growth. He was born in Pittsburgh, April 27, 1945, one of six children. He attended parochial school, Central Catholic High School, transferred into a vocational high school, and finally into a public high school. He dropped out of school (after a teacher accused him of plagiarism) and discovered the public library. Along with the library, he discovered the Civil Rights movement, and the upsurge of Black culture, and a consciousness deeply rooted in the Black aesthetics. In 1968, he founded Black Horizon Theatre in Pittsburgh. It was there at Black Horizon Theatre that I had the pleasure of first seeing August Wilson direct works by Ed Bullins, Amiri Baraka, and his associate Rob Penny. At Black Horizon Theatre, August Wilson was set designer, costume designer, director and sometime actor. August Wilson represents a rare combination of judgment, imagination, and an unparalleled commitment to truth.

As artistic and managing directors arrived in the traditional hustle and bustle of activity, it appeared a typical TCG conference. As in the past, McCarter Theatre was the headquarters. Most of the main or evening sessions were used for break-out discussions and sessions. Each day elaborate breakfasts, lunches, and dinners were offered to those who paid their $400 to attend. At each session, artistic or managing directors from different geographical parts of the country met or re-acquainted each other regarding artistic, managing, or funding. While picking up pre-registration packets one immediately noticed the new or loyal funding sources of TCG's conference, i.e., AT&T Foundation; The Pew Charitable Trusts; Dayton Hudson Foundation; The Blanche and Irving Laurie Foundation; VIACOM, Inc.; and The Canadian Consulate General, New York. However, as with most American businesses, what's beneath the surface will eventually rise to the top.

Peter Zeisler retired in 1993. John Sullivan, from San Francisco, was hired in July 1995 after an overlapping year-long search. The transition, on the surface, looked smooth as silk. Peter Zeisler's longtime Associate Director, Lindy Zesch, would keep her job with TCG; and be there to remind Sullivan of the "way we used to do it when Peter was here."

On Wednesday, following the reception and dinner, the conference attendees were welcomed by TCG Board President Ricardo Khan. That was followed by another welcome and opening remarks by John Sullivan, the Director of TCG; then the lacerating keynote address by August Wilson, titled, "The Ground On Which I Stand."

This conference was John Sullivan's debut. Over thirty other prominent theatre personalities were invited to speak, conduct a workshop or perform. George C. Wolfe brought his team from *Bring in 'Da Noise, Bring in 'Da Funk*; including Savion Glover, Jimmy Tate, Jeffrey Wright, Daryl Waters, Ann Duquesnay, Reg E. Gaines. *New York Times* Pulitzer Prize–winning critic Margo Jefferson introduced and moderated a discussion.

The following morning, playwright Wendy Wasserstein introduced and moderated a panel discussion, "Seeing Through Other Eyes"; the novelist Ann Douglas, the filmmaker Renee Tajima Peno and the visual artist Fred Wilson recounted how they were drawn into theatre or how they retracted from theatre. Since two interesting panels convened at the same time I had to move quickly across campus to McCosh Hall for "Non-Profit Mergers and Partnerships." This panel consisted of Jessica L. Andrews, Managing Director, Arizona Theatre Company; David Ira Goldstein, Artistic Director, Arizona Theatre Company; David P. Saar, Artistic Director, Childs Play; Geoffrey Shales, Managing Director, Puerto Rican Traveling Theatre; and Esther Wermouth, Director, Extension Centers, Mercy College. The panel was moderated by Nancy Sasser, President, National Arts Stabilization. At the same time, a panel on "Working With the Commercial Sector" was given. Even though it had excellent general managers from four of America's leading resident professional theatres, I couldn't make it. Several other panels worth a mention are the "Playwrights' Slam," where each of three playwrights read five-minute excerpts from new works. Eduardo Machado read from "Kissing Fidel"; Oyamo, "Pink and Say"; Diana Son, "Fishes"; and Paula Vogel from "Minneola Twins." Actor Reggie Montgomery, an Artistic Associate at Hartford Stage Company, moderated.

On this second day, the conference provided an hour and a half for twelve "Affinity Groups" to meet. Here are a few of the headings under which interested participants could gather: Urban Theatre, Small Budget Theatres, Medium Budget Theatres, Large Budget Theatre, Theatre Workers of Color, Gay/Lesbian Theatre Workers, etc.

The Impact of Race

That evening, after dinner, Miguel Algarin, Poet, founder of Nuyorican Poets Café, along with poets Bob Hollman and Adrienne Su read or performed. From there all proceeded to "the TCG Club," where deals, co-productions, employment, and other discussions occurred over drinks.

Before filling the reader with so much theatre I think it necessary to look at three of the speakers, i.e., Ricardo Khan, John Sullivan, and August Wilson. At the time of this conference Khan had been the president of TCG's Board of Directors for two years. Certainly one of the most powerful positions for any Black person working in the American Theatre. At that time his theatre was co-producing Pulitzer Prize–winning poet Rita Dove's new play with the Oregon Shakespeare. He was also directing the play. Khan reminded us of our first time coming into the theatre; the first time we had the urge to start an institution. He asked the question, "what caused us to start an institution?" He was very positive. He didn't talk about the drastic cuts in arts funding nor did he talk of the paucity of funding for Black institutions across America; not even the gigantic deficit of his own institution, Crossroads Theatre Company.

John Sullivan, the new Executive Director of TCG, thanked AT&T and Pew Charitable Trust for their continued support; he reminded us that to funders like AT&T and Pew non-profits owe a great thanks. Sullivan said, "this Eleventh Biennial National Conference is one of the largest in TCG's history." He also spoke of change, the purpose of our work, the value of our work. He said, "this conference will have many themes because so many theatres are restructuring and going through vast changes."

Sullivan didn't talk about the recent lawsuit brought against TCG by past director Peter Zeisler. It seems Sullivan fired Associate Director Lindy Zesch after making that commitment to Zeisler to keep her on the TCG payroll; nor did he mention that neither Zeisler nor Zesch had been invited to this conference. However, Sullivan did what Peter Zeisler never did—he brought in a Black artist of international reputation to make the keynote address. Sullivan's introduction and the appearance of August Wilson received a prolonged standing ovation.

August Wilson began his keynote address by first recalling his first TCG conference in 1984. He remembered the eloquent talk the late director John Hirsch gave. Then Wilson dug into his main theme. It was the Black Power movement of the Sixties that fueled his consciousness. However, he felt that the Black Power movement was dwarfed by the Civil Rights Movement of the same period. "The Black Power Movement shaped my life...my writings. I am what our people call a race man...there are some people who might say Black Americans don't have a culture..."

Wilson blasted the American Theatre community for supporting only one Black theatre out of a list of 66 LORT theatres across America. "It is not a complaint, it is an advertisement." He went on to show that there are "two distinct and parallel designs in Black theatre: one is entertainment for whites. The second defines a world where we are the spiritual center." Wilson named Black artist and playwrights who epitomize this tradition: Ron Milner, Ed Bullins, Amiri Baraka, Lonne Elder III, Richard Wesley, Barbara Ann Teer, Sonia Sanchez, etc. These are some of the artists who filled his consciousness; some of the artists who help shape August Wilson. "I am eternally grateful."

Wilson took the definition of Blacks and whites from Webster's International Dictionary and contrasted the two. Blacks were defined as a color that had no basis for even existing while white is the source, angelic and pure. He went on to recount Robert Brustein's fear that "funders are only funding socially visible minority artists, not quality." (Wilson's read: European Elitist Artist.) "Robert Brustein is short sighted...we can meet other artists at the crossroads if we know all of the barriers of racism are removed from the 66 LORT theatres." Wilson talked of meeting on common ground, sharing our differences. He gave this example: we have different ideas of what a party is...we share different ideas of culinary taste. "For example, we enjoy different parts of the pig, i.e., feet, ears, intestines as opposed to loins, shanks, etc."

One of Wilson's vitriolic attacks on resident professional theatres concerned non-traditional casting. Wilson believes Black artists are capable of expressing who we are intrinsically. He believes "color-blind casting and non-traditional casting are rejections of who we are...an all-Black version of *Death of a Salesman* is a violation of who we are. We (Blacks) are unique and we are specific. The term 'people of color' is an abstraction. Does it balance if 'people of color' stand on one side of the room and 'whites' on the other?...Is there that much spiritual value in 'whites?' We must protect our spiritual elders. For example, Michael Bolton's music influences are defined in a *New York Times* article as Mick Jagger, Rod Stewart,

Joe Cocker, and a few Black singers. That is a blatant disregard of Black contribution to blues and gospel music."

Wilson also disagreed with several long cherished Black philosophers, i.e., W. E. B. DuBois on the concept of "the talented tenth"; that Black people would be guided by an elite highly educated 10 percent of the Black population. Wilson felt it dangerous to separate one group of Black people from another. After all, he surmises, "the journey of the Black artist from the hole of the slaveship to these shores conditioned him for equality among his brethren."

Finally, Wilson spoke of "the theatre we choose to work in is European; that it's based on the Greek theatre designed by Aristotle. We choose to adjust and change it…the American theatre is based on subscription, yet that subscription keeps Blacks out of the American theatre…they (subscriptions) are the death of American theatre."

On Thursday, June 27, 1996, the playwright, Wendy Wasserstein introduced and moderated the discussion, "Seeing Theatre Through Others Eyes." Panelists were Ann Douglas; filmmaker Renee Tajimi-Pena; and visual artist Fred Wilson. They related the theatre experience from vastly different perspectives. Ms. Renee Tajimi-Pena, an Asian American, talked about her mother. Her mother had been diagnosed with a terminal illness, so Ms. Tajimi-Pena moved her to Los Angeles from Kansas. It seems her mother had lived in Kansas all her life; she spoke no English. She wanted her mother to see some theatre. She took her to see Arthur Miller's *All My Sons*. Her mother left after the first act. Her next play was *An Inspector Calls*. She couldn't understand it. Finally she went to the Bilingual Theatre Foundation production of a non-English play. She understood it! She noted that her mother preferred theatre that catered to the needs of everyday situations. Now that her mother had discovered a theatre that embraced her, she enjoyed going to the theatre.

Fred Wilson works in museums. At one time or another he has worked as a curator, a museum guard. He has worked in Pittsburgh, Houston, and New York. In each city he attended a lot of theatre (at TCG's expense). He noted that audiences are very different. In larger theatres audiences are often there to be seen; in smaller theatres they are happy to communicate about the experiences. In Pittsburgh he saw August Wilson's *Jitney*. He saw the play twice. The first time the theatre was filled with sedate subscribers.

The second time it was more of a mixed audience. Blacks actually spoke to actors on the stage. "Go head, girlfriend!" "Tell him to go to hell!"

Wendy Wasserstein interjected she'd like not to be able to anticipate the play's point of view. Ann Douglas talked about a theatre that had the power to teach the unteachable. Ms. Tajimi-Pena saw a parallel between public television and theatre—each programs for an older white audience while professing to go after younger audiences. Both public television and theatre are afraid to program for a younger audience. Both Tajimi-Pena and Wilson would embrace a theatre that traveled outside of its own environment. Wilson was disturbed by the outdated theatre lobbies, and theatre programs that didn't relate to the play on stage or the newness of the audiences. Ann Douglas concluded by pointing out how effective and exciting theatre in the Sixties, Seventies, and Eighties seemed. "It was exciting and innovative because writers like Baraka, Pinter, Albee, Shepard freely mixed politics and art."

All TCG panelists are selected because of their expertise. On the panel, "Non-Profit Mergers and Partnerships" distinguished panelists were Jessica Andrews, Managing Director, Arizona Theatre Company; David Ira Goldstein, Artistic Director, Arizona Theatre Company, David P. Saar, Artistic Director, Childs Play, Temple Arizona; Geoffrey Shlaes, Managing Director, Puerto Rican Traveling Theatre, New York City; and Esther Wermuth, Director Extension Center, Mercy College, Dobbs Ferry, New York.

Mercy College's interest in mergers was interesting. To attract local ethnic students they set up "extension centers" out in the community. At the time Mercy College had eight sites. These sites made it possible for small classes. The largest consisted of fourteen students. The college offers theatre students Associate and Bachelor degrees. Mercy College has a partnership with the Puerto Rican Traveling Theatre. Shlaes pointed out that the merger has been beneficial to both Mercy College and the Puerto Rican Traveling Theatre. It increases the earned income for the theatre. He gave an example of this potential by citing that fifty students would increase their earned income by $100,000 per year. It was during the same session that other artistic leaders from the Arizona Theatre Company spoke of merging in order to share audiences and solve cash flow problems. On the other hand, Jessica Andrews would like to see an institutional relationship rather than an artistic director's relationship. However, there are problems interrelating boards, managing directors, staff, and artistic directors.

"Strategic Organizational Direction, Vision, and Design" was an excellent talk session by Patricia Moore. Ms. Moore is a management consultant. First, she raised several questions regarding visionary leadership by focusing on several commercial companies. She listed in no particular order eighteen companies and their visions and then compared each, basing the findings on stock and investor's return. From a one-dollar investment in 1926, she asked what would that return be in 1996. A non-visionary company would get a return of $56; a visionary company would get a return of $6,530. Ms. Moore gave a brief definition of a visionary company: one that has leadership successions, usually a No. 1, No. 2, and No. 3 person in place. Thus, if the number one person dies, the number two person assumes leadership of the company. In addition the company has a guiding philosophy, a mission. This focused the company, defined its future, and promoted its progress. The company also has a tangible image. All of these are formed by the leaders' values; the leader instills these values into others in the company. "Why are we here?" It's usually beyond profit and it's usually for the betterment of mankind. This *core* philosophy must be presented to staff and to the public at all cost. Progress must be stimulated consistently.

A series of side discussions began to form. One such discussion group "Theatre People of Color" formed to clarify for white conferees August Wilson's keynote address. Another panel of Chicago theatre people formed a discussion group. In addition, "Reinventing Our Institutions," "Developing New Musicals," "Speak Out!" and, of course the after-hour "TCG Club."

In Zelda Finandler's introduction of two Alan Schneider Awards she casually dropped that Peter Zeisler, former director of TCG, hadn't been invited and that he and Lindy Zesch were in a major dispute with the current TCG administration. Ms. Finandler also gave a glowing history of the late Alan Schneider.

The 1996/97 winners of the Alan Schneider Director's Award were Mark Brokaw and Roman Paska. These two directors were given $15,000 plus an opportunity to work for six months at a major resident professional theatre. The Alan Schneider Director's Award is administered by TCG.

Prior to my exiting the conference, I had the pleasure of attending a discussion with the British actor/director/writer Simon Callow. It was moderated by Kenneth S. Brecher, the director of Sundance Institute. It was in the form of a fireside chat. Callow was extremely articulate on the differences between American actors and British actors. He spoke on the misconception on the part of American actors that British actors are so well trained and that they're so brilliant at performing Shakespeare. Callow disagreed. What he did observe is American actors aren't specific with emotional character; further, that actors should be accurate, specific, not general. Brecher asked why the English are so reluctant to accept American directors, yet British directors are accepted in American Theatre. Although his answer was somewhat vague, Callow did point to the acceptance of Harold Prince and Jerry Zaks. "How do you see American actors in British production?" Callow used the National Theatre as an example saying it would be a theatre without a style. Color blind casting in England is so different. However, he did say an actor should be able to play any role he can make an audience believe. "Acting is hard work, especially creating characters." Directing is also very hard work. "Perhaps," said Callow, "I missed the better part of my acting life when I found writing and directing."

My last day at this conference seemed anticlimactic. I knew it was time to depart after my third day. More time was spent in meetings than in the TCG planned sessions; more time still in the TCG Club in the evening.

Woza Afrika! Festival, "Sarafina!" and the Plays of Wole Soyinka

After its reopening in 1967, the Lincoln Center Theatre Company produced a festival of South African plays, *Death and the King's Horsemen* by Nobel Prize winner Wole Soyinka, and the South African musical *Sarafina!* African-American audiences had never been sought so vigorously.

Lincoln Center Theatre Company produced the South African Woza Afrika! festival in 1986. In that Festival five South African plays were produced between September 10 and October 5, 1986. The plays were *Asinamali!* (We Have No Money!) by Mbongeni Ngema; *Bopha!* by Percy Mtwa; *Children of Asazi* by Matsemela Manaka; *Gangsta* by Maishe Maponya; and *Born in the R.S.A.* by Barney Simon and The Cast.

The audiences of African-Americans at Lincoln Center were very large. At some performances the percentage of African-Americans was double that of traditional white theatergoers. These audiences were learning something about Africa, especially South Africa. All of these plays came from South Africa's Black townships.

In South Africa's Black Townships there are no theatres. Performances take place in community halls, churches, cinemas, and school classrooms, venues which don't provide facilities nor the conditions necessary for professional performances. Nevertheless, out of this environment, Black theatre companies emerged from many townships all over South Africa.

The Impact of Race

All of the African theatre companies that were a part of the Woza Africa! festival shared a common objective: to keep theatre alive and provide work for the talented actors in the townships.

Duma Ndlouv, the chief organizer of Woza Afrika! was born and raised in Soweto, Johannesburg. In 1981 he began working in the U.S.A. with The Roger Furman Theatre, a leading Black theatre in the Harlem community. Through his efforts The Roger Furman Theatre produced authentic South African works, introducing African-Americans to real African artists and African theatre.

In a foreword to the publication of *Woza Africa!* Wole Soyinka wrote, "...these (plays) contain the images of reality that flood the mind by the mere fact of contemporary South African Theatre. Such is the overwhelming presence in the world consciousness today of this irrational denial of humanity to millions, the willful abrogation of identity, the staggering scale of repression that every statement is constantly dwarfed by the images it provokes. The artistic effort to come to terms with any situation of tragic horror, borrowing from an environment whose future seems permanently overcast, presents the mind with that paradox born of the fact that the act of creating is firstly an act of affirmation, however stubbornly the material of existence denies it...much sooner than later, the last word will revert to the people, and the (poets) of the struggle will inscribe the epitaph of apartheid."

In an open discussion before an audience of six hundred while he was in New York directing *Death and the King's Horsemen*, Soyinka was asked by Dr. K. Anthony Appiah why he'd discussed apartheid and South African in his Nobel lecture. Soyinka replied, "A lot of my writing has been concerned with injustice, with inhumanity, with racism, inside and outside of my immediate environment, which is Nigeria. This was a world platform and I could not think of any more appropriate moment for voicing this particular level of my literary concerns."

Wole Soyinka was born July 13, 1934. His powerful writing of novels, plays and poetry enabled him to become the first African writer and the first Black writer of any nationality to win the Nobel Prize for Literature, in 1986. Soyinka was educated at Government College and University College in Ibadan before moving to England in 1954. He attended The University of Leeds and received a degree in English. While in London he worked at

The Royal Court Theatre. In 1960 Soyinka returned to Nigeria as a research fellow in Drama. He quickly became established as a dramatist, actor, and director of exceptional talent. In 1967 he was arrested and accused of conspiring with anti-government rebels fighting to establish an independent state called Biafra. Soyinka was imprisoned for almost two years. After his release, he lived in exile in Europe and Ghana. He returned to Nigeria in 1976 and taught classes at Ife University. Wole Soyinka is a prolific writer of drama, fiction, poetry, essays and criticism. Erika Peterson, an actress who worked with Soyinka, stated, "He has never been what anyone expected him to be. Thus with his experiences it's not likely Soyinka will take easily pigeonholed intellectual stances. His is a kind of truth that dwells in the heart of Paradox."

In 1987, Wole Soyinka's *Death and the King's Horsemen* opened at New York's Lincoln Center Theatre for the Performing Arts. The play was directed by Mr. Soyinka. It attracted the largest African-American audience until that time of any play written by an African playwright. It should be noted that *Death and the King's Horsemen* had a cast of actors comprised almost totally of African-Americans. Mr. Soyinka was extremely visible yet *Death and the King's Horsemen* closed one week earlier than its announced closing date due to a lack of white audience support.

Soyinka spoke of his reason for accepting the premature closing of *Death and the King's Horsemen*: "After the reviews came out, I agreed to the idea that the play would close a week early so as not to demoralize the actors by having empty seats. You have to be realistic. It's quite true that a review like the *Times* would keep away potential [white] audiences and I believe it's good for the show if you have a good number of people over a shorter time rather than the same number spread over several days. So, in principle, I was not against that, but what I said was I would go along with it as long as you use the period when the play's running to really fight these bastards. Adverts [advertisements] should have been taken on the pages of that very newspaper. I know that comments were taken from people in the lobby [of the theatre] and played over Black radio but this [critical] assault was not by Black radio and they [Lincoln Center Theater Company] should have used the same critical medium, of this assault. They should have taken a full-page advert and quoted from statements which were made to me during previews by members of the Board of Directors, by individuals, the Administration, and a host of others . . . the Administration itself should have written a letter to *The New York Times*! They should have taken a full-page ad. I wouldn't even mind giving up some of my royalties to pay for it. [Laughter.]"

The nature of traditional African theatre exhibits the roots of the traditional Black church in America as it mixes storytelling, music, and dance, and forces the audience to participate actively in the celebration. It's apparent from watching the artists perform that their energy comes from within, and the execution of dances and songs evidences natural ability as opposed to learned skills. The complete integration of acting, music, and dance demonstrate how African theatre involves more than one creative art form. In African theatre the interplay between actors and audience is an integral part of any performance. African performers and audiences need each other's active participation to be successful. Both African and American audiences come to the theatre for spiritual celebration as well as entertaining fulfillment, and neither group leaves satisfied unless *everyone* becomes involved.

The traditional theatre in Africa, especially Nigeria, has been able to develop uninterruptedly at its own pace and has remained unaffected by elements incompatible with it own needs and laws. According to Oyin Ogunba in his *Theatre in Africa* (1978, Ibadan University Press), "Traditional African theatre is an indigenous cultural institution, a form of Art nurtured on the African soil over the centuries and which has, therefore, developed distinctive features and whose techniques are sometimes totally different from the borrowed form now practiced by many of our contemporary artists. This definition doesn't carry a mere time categorization in the sense of something that is already dead or moribund or something which has to be periodically exhumed and displayed as a showpiece. On the contrary, a festival (performance) is an integral, dynamic part of the culture of an unalienated African, an occasion to which he responds spontaneously."

A traditional African theatre audience is an active, vocal and participating component of a performance event. Such an audience is often labeled as "noisy," especially by critics who aren't familiar with African and African-American audiences. The African and the African-American audience is an integral part of the performance and functions on three simultaneous capacities as spectators, performers, and critics.

Woodie King, Jr.

In *Death and the King's Horseman* the songs and dances, lovingly staged by Mr. Soyinka himself and accompanied by the great Nigerian musicians Yomi Obileye and Tunji Oyelana, remain vivid theatrical memories. Rather than depend on someone else's proclamation of his identity, Soyinka simply takes his cultural background for granted. One of the actors in the production remembers Soyinka trying to help the young African-American actors capture the nobility of their characters, saying to them, "You are royal; you take it for granted. It is not something that you have to prove."

Wole Soyinka gently admonished the Black actors because they were really Americans and knew very little about Africa and African people.

"We believe that there are various areas of existence, all of which interact, interlock, in a pattern of continuity. The world of the ancestor, the world of the living and the world of the unborn. The process of transition between these various worlds is a continuing one and one which is constantly mediated. For instance, the function of ritual, of sacrifice — whether it's a ram or a chicken — the function of seasonal ceremonies, is in fact allied to the ease of transition between these various worlds. So, in effect, death does not mean for such a society what it means for other societies. It's only if one has established that kind of context, through whatever symbolic means, that one can begin — distanced as you and I are from this particular kind of society — it's only by exposing that world as a hermetic, self-regulating universe of its own, that a tragedy of a character like Elesin can have absolute validity. So within that context, this is what enables him to commit himself. For him it is not Death."

Specific advertising approaches were used by Lincoln Center Theater Company to get African-American audiences. In a letter to the *Black Mask* readership Lincoln Center offered a specific discount to the *Black Mask* readership as well as an inexpensive membership.

When the Company opened *Death and the King's Horsemen*, they actively sought African-American audiences for the African play. The Company hired David Lampel of the popular Black radio station WLIB to come to the opening night party. He moved about the room with a hand-held tape recorder, spoke to Black people from the audience and recorded their comments about the production. The Theater edited the comments down to a 60-second radio commercial which was then played on the Black radio stations WLIB, WWRL, and WBLS.

The Impact of Race

In three previous New York productions of Wole Soyinka's work very few African-Americans had the opportunity to see it. The reason for this lack was due to several levels of racism. The theatres were small; they were controlled by Black producers, they didn't have the proper promotional funds to get the word out; and white critics ignored the plays and the institutions because they were Black.

The first attempt was by Belgraves-Farris Productions in the mid-Sixties with Soyinka's "The Trial of Brother Jero" and "The Strong Breed." These two one-acts were presented at the Greenwich Mews Theatre in lower Manhattan. Cynthia Belgraves, the director of both plays, promoted her productions in the Black community, especially in the Black church. The two plays opened November 9, 1967, and closed February 18, 1968, for a total of 115 performances. The Nigerian actor Afolabi Ajayi was a co-producer as well as an actor in the production. The costumes were imported from Nigeria. African-American audiences helped in keeping the plays running for three months.

According to Ken Farris, one of the producers of "The Trial of Brother Jero" and "The Strong Breed," the plays spoke directly to Black people without white people being involved. African-American audiences found the plays. At that time novice producers such as Farris-Belgraves hadn't yet found sophisticated ways to promote African plays. The composition of the audience for these two plays was 70 percent white and 30 percent African-American. The advertising in the traditional media didn't bring African-Americans into the theatre. Mr. Farris felt the African-Americans who did come to see the plays came as a result of the actress Diana Sands. He said Ms. Sands was like a silent partner on the producing team.

Even before this Off-Broadway production, Channel 13 had done an abbreviated version of "The Trial of Brother Jero." Cynthia Belgraves, one of the producers of the Off-Broadway production, played the role of Amope, the shrewish wife.

In recalling how Farris-Belgraves Productions had raised the investment for the two plays, Ken Farris wrote, "Nobody was much interested in investing in a production of an obscure African work at that time. We had raised about fifteen thousand of the twenty we needed when the Biafran-Nigerian conflict broke out. Wole was thrown in jail for saying in effect, a plague on both your houses...He was something of a folk hero then and neither side wanted to hear his views. Amnesty International came to us pleading that we begin production immediately. Their view was that publicity would prevent his demise in jail. And since we got a lot of publicity it may well have done so. As I stated, about the audience, we always had about 30 percent of our customers from the African-American community but that was largely accidental in that we had no special focus, though I think we advertised in *The Amsterdam News*. Our actors promoted the show in churches. If I had to measure the support of the African-American community it was significant. Five or six hundred customers a month could keep a play running three or four months."

Farris-Belgraves Productions optioned *The Lion and the Jewel* for Broadway. The company held onto the play for over two years. They intended to present a musical version. At that time they secured the services of Max Roach and Abby Lincoln. Max Roach would write the music and Abby Lincoln would star in the production.

On April 9, 1968, in its first season The Negro Ensemble Company opened *Kongi's Harvest* by Wole Soyinka. When asked back then: What does your audience come looking for? Artistic Director Douglas Turner Ward replied, "I find the Black audience doesn't come with any pre-conception. They probably were told that there was a play which had something to do with them and one that they could afford. Our highest ticket is $4.95. And we have some preview tickets for only one dollar. We've done everything to get the audience we want. One way is to give group rates and to do radio advertising. The Negro Ensemble Company consciously seeks participation of Black audiences. The first production of the season we had 20 to 25 percent Blacks. The last show of the first season we had 65 to 70 percent Blacks."

Mr. Ward wrote in *The New York Times* on August 14, 1966, of the kind of theatre he envisioned for African-American audiences: "A theatre concentrating primarily on themes for Negro life, but also resilient enough to incorporate and interpret the best of world drama—whatever the source. A theatre of permanence, continuity and consistency, providing the necessary home base for the Negro artist to launch a campaign to win his ignored brothers and sisters as constant witnesses to his endeavors...."

As a result of that *Times* article The Ford Foundation supported the founding of The Negro Ensemble Company. Ward recalled, "All ingredients that became The Negro Ensemble Company were contained in the two experiences that we had had without support from anybody. We had done it. We had organized a training program and a Black producer has produced a Black writer's plays utilizing fourteen actors. And we had also succeeded in gaining a Black audience. You can get to our theatre from six Black communities in the New York metropolitan area in no more than forty to forty-five minutes by either car or subway."

African-American audiences kept *Kongi's Harvest* running for forty performances. According to Judy Ann Elder, one of the original cast members of *Kongi's Harvest*, "At that time there was a resurgence of interest in things Black and in our African brothers and sisters."

In 1980 the late Hazel Bryant produced Wole Soyinka's *The Lion and the Jewel* at the International Festival for the Performing Arts at Lincoln Center. She had an organization called The Richard Allen Center for The Performing Arts. The Center had been operating out of a theatre space at 63rd Street and Broadway in the Empire Hotel. The Theatre's location was directly across the avenue from Lincoln Center. Ms. Bryant was the first African-American producer who realized festivals are very short in duration and they attract large African-American audiences. The African-American audiences and the themes of Soyinka related immediately.

The Lion and the Jewel was written in 1963 and it was first performed in London the following year. Immediately thereafter it was performed in the United States. A critic wrote, "*The Lion and the Jewel* alone is enough to establish Nigeria as the most fertile new source of English-speaking drama since Synge's *Discovery of the Western Isles* — Even this comparison does Soyinka less than justice, for he is dealing not only with rich folk material, but with the impact of the modern on tribal custom: to find any parallel you have to go back to the Elizabethans."

According to Clebert Ford who played a leading role in *The Lion and the Jewel* in New York, The Richard Allen Center production played two weeks. One week at the Richard Allen Center and one week at Lincoln Center. Because Rev. John Bryant came to New York to help his sister promote, large church groups supported the production at both locations. Mr. Ford also remembered that The Black Theatre Alliance of New York was very active at the time and supported the production as well as other Black plays that were in the Festival. At times the African-American audiences were as high as 70 percent. This production had music by Billy Taylor; costumes by Myrna Colley-Lee; direction by Mikel Pinkney; and the lead actors were Loretta Devine, Clebert Ford, Milledge Mosley, and Fran Salisbury.

The Lincoln Center Theatre Company's production of *Sarafina!* represented African theatre at its very best. From direction, writing, music, choreography, and setting *Sarafina!* touched African-American audiences. Although the Nobel Prize went to the great playwright and poet Wole Soyinka, he even acknowledged the contribution of South African artist Mbongeni Ngema.

Mbongeni Ngema, a director/writer/actor, who'd been represented in the Woza Afrika! festival had been in workshop with an unfinished musical inspired by Winnie Mandela. Ms. Mandela had suggested to Ngema a work about the courage and revolutionary endurance of township schoolchildren. Since the 1976 uprising children had been at the forefront of the Black majority's battle against apartheid.

Ngema assembled thirty young people. They lived and worked together as a family, building their story around a young girl's passionate remembrance of the history of Black South Africa's struggle. This developed into the musical *Sarafina!*

The haunting music was written by Hugh Masakela and Ngema; it was performed by Hugh Masakela.

Sarafina! opened at Lincoln Center Theatre in September 1987 to mixed reviews but wildly enthusiastic African-American audiences and an extended sold-out run. In January, 1988 the political passion of *Sarafina!* moved to Broadway to become a major hit of that season.

Letters

"Women's Wear Daily" Critiques Black Theatre
June 9, 1970

Editor
Drama Section
The New York Times

Dear Editor:

Martin Gottfried has taken it upon himself to define Black Theatre to
Blacks and whites in the garment district's tabloid *Women's Wear Daily*.
Did he ever see a Black play in a Harlem loft? The Free Southern
Theatre in cotton fields? Other than off-Broadway and Broadway, where
did his information come from?

The professional and artistic standards for Black theatre are defined by
Black people. It's white people who try and hustle off Black art, putting
on stupid plays calling it Black theatre because they threw in a few Black
actors. Know too that all the actors aren't Black; some are Negro, some
are colored, some are Black! (Do you know the difference?)

His rundown on the Negro Ensemble is so far away from rational
thinking that one would think that Gottfried is a raving maniac.
Anyone with any knowledge of Black theatre knows that NEC has one
of the best acting companies in the country. They also know that
Song of the Lusitanian Bogey, Kongis' Harvest and *Ceremonies in Dark
Old Men* are among the finest works presented off-Broadway in
the past three years. The Negro Ensemble exists because white theatres
are racist. It is the Martin Gottfrieds of the country that should be
attempting to change *that*.

American Place Theatre is another story. Fortunately or unfortunately,
we ran into each other in its beginning and we've been picking each
other's brain ever since. They picked Milner, Bullins, and Russell off me.
(Read Clayton Riley's detailed article in the *Manhattan Tribune* 3/4/70

on Woodie King, Wynn Handman and the American Place Theatre.)
By the way, what is a superior "white" play? One Black play per season
or not, Wynn Handman has never selected a play for the American
Place unless he believed in it. The same is true of Douglas Turner Ward.
To think that both men have the same frame of reference is absurd.

The all-Black *Hello Dolly* is hustling David Merrick. He could produce
an *all-negro* Andy Gump. Hungry actors, all colors, all nationalities will
beg to be in it.

Let it be known, there are as many bad white actors working today as
bad Black actors. Most white producers would like to get Black actors
who look Black, but act white, sound white and hate their Blackness.
That's the reason Black playwrights would rather have Black critics judge
their work. White people have been living three hundred years with
Black people and refuse to see them. How can a white critic who's stated
that Black actors should play white roles in white make-up judge a Black
play? Wow!

The Great White Hope isn't perceptive about Black people. James Earl
Jones did perceptive character studies off-Broadway for twelve years, long
before Howard Sackler knew Jack Johnson existed.

Whether Martin Gottfried intended it or not, his article implies Blacks
are not qualified to set their own professional and artistic standards.

Sincerely,
Woodie King, Jr.

Woodie King, Jr.

What are black artists and dramatists to do?
September 1977

Editor
New York Times Leisure Section

Gentlemen,

Regarding your two magnificent articles in the Sunday, August 28, 1977 issue: "Will Cultural Apartheid Poison the Arts in America?" and "In the Months Ahead the Arts Debate Will Center on Populism." The apartheid article by Henahan and the Populism article by Kisselgoff place a Black working in the arts in a conundrum. Should our efforts be directed towards integrating Lincoln Center or building our own institution? Integrating *The New York Times* or writing for our own Black newspaper? History has shown us that white people aren't really interested in Blacks as people or as artists. If they had been interested why would they have enslaved us? When we were stolen, our culture and our art were stolen.

Needless to say many of us would love to be a part of these mighty institutions but why should we continue to beg for this involvement? Few of these boards know anything at all about Black people. Their lives are lived on another level. Our images are projected to them via television and film — images which were lies when first invented. The subscribers are white because the art is white. The directors of many of these institutions are so into their artistic trips they wouldn't know an artist unless he acted exactly like the last white artist passing through his door.

Many of us feel Blacks can save the Arts in this country. Some say it has to do with our humanism, our belief that respect and dignity is the key to our survival. If we believe it necessary to train oneself to be white in order to be American, are we saying whites are already Americans and we Blacks are something else? We cannot say that! We believe we were brought here before many of the immigrants. We believe we were great artists before the Mayflower came to these shores. Everyone knows Black art and Black artists should have one of the theatres in Lincoln Center and The Kennedy Center. Will apartheid or populism keep this from becoming a reality?

Apartheid is a white concept as Blacks see it. Populism is a Black concept as whites see it. Kisselgoff's brilliant article might have over-shadowed apartheid by showing the origin of Martha Graham at the Neighborhood Playhouse (Henry Street Settlement) and Alwin Nikolais at the Henry Street Playhouse. *Black Girl*, *What the Winesellers Buy*, *The Taking of Miss Janie*, and *for colored girls...* also came out of Henry Street Playhouse. The conundrum: Did I make these plays happen because of an apartheid system or because Black people long for reflections of themselves in beautiful and artistic form?

Sincerely,
Woodie King, Jr.

Casting "Miss Saigon" in a Bad Light

August 1990

Dear Editor of *Backstage*:

The Miss Saigon racism saga really began in London when producer Cameron MacIntosh cast Jonathan Pryce in the role of The Engineer rather than casting an Asian actor (male or female). There's nothing uniquely Asian about Mr. Pryce's performance; he sometimes speaks in pidgin Asian and parody of an Asian pimp. This grave disregard for the civil rights of minorities is very traditional in the British theatre hierarchy (I was one of the consultants to *and* auditioned and cast most of the performers in the recent fiasco *King: The Musical* in London). The British theatre hierarchy believes its minorities should appreciate and be thankful for the position they're in. Look at the paucity of Black or Asian theatre companies there. What other productions has Mr. MacIntosh produced in Britain that had minorities in the starring role?

Mr. MacIntosh says he believes so strongly in Mr. Pryce's work, that only Mr. Pryce can play the role, that he'd forsake an American public ticket advance of $25 million — an advance, by the way, that defines *Miss Saigon* as a smash hit no matter who plays the role of the Engineer. Art and politics are inextricably connected and Americans would be extremely foolish not to recognize this as it relates to *Miss Saigon*.

As with civil rights and affirmative action programs here in America, non-traditional casting, in concept, is supposed to give minority performers an opportunity to play roles traditionally given to white performers. (White performers don't believe they're *given* roles, however. Yet, they believe if a minority performer auditions ten times for a role; that performer is *given* the role.) The non-traditional casting concept was never designed to provide opportunities for white performers to take away the few minority roles available.

It's so sad when Frank Rich equates the casting of Denzel Washington

209

and Morgan Freeman in New York Shakespeare Festival Productions with the Jonathan Pryce/*Miss Saigon* situation. The New York Shakespeare Festival has been casting Blacks, Latinos, and Asians in starring roles since its inception in 1956. *Miss Saigon* isn't *Taming of the Shrew* or *Richard III*. The fall of Saigon is recent history (1975) and Shakespeare wrote his plays 425 years ago.

Fifteen years ago, when Mr. Pryce won a Tony Award for Trevor Griffith's *Comedians*, the concept of non-traditional casting had not yet been imbedded into the fabric of the American Theatre. Unlike the Euro-centrics in the white community, minorities throughout America are hailing Equity's decision as a monumental gesture. The majority of Americans (white, Black, Asians) aren't Eurocentric and don't cling to the ideas of Euro-aestheic oppression despite Mark Howard Edelman's unbelievably naive letter to the editor (Aug. 10, 1990).

However, as controversial as the *Miss Saigon* decision may seem, Mr. MacIntosh, Mr. Jacobs, Mr. Eisenberg, Euro-americans, and all the *others* who are in line to receive a substantial share of *Miss Saigon*'s box office will work it all out before the curtain falls on 1991.

Sincerely,
Woodie King, Jr.

Woodie King, Jr.

In Response to John Simon's "Black and Blue"
February, 1997

Editors
New York Magazine

Dear Editors,

In responding to theatre critic John Simon's article "Black and Blue" published in *New York* magazine (February 17, 1997): it seems you are under the impression Black run and white run theatres are comparably funded; they are not. White millionaires support many of the 66 LORT theatres. Foundations, Corporations, Federal, City, and State funders are supporters of non-profit 501C3 institutions. The majority of these founders are white.

Item: Non-profit Black theatres find it extremely difficult to reach their audience, to sell them a ticket. The white media (like *New York* magazine) controls the distribution of information to Black people. White media decides when it will review a play in a Black institution. However, critics are at the opening night of most white theatres and the review—good or bad—appears the following day in the dailies and the following week in the weeklies, thus, bringing immediate attention to the play. An audience knows it's there!

Item: Many of August Wilson's plays were produced by a consortium of resident professional theatres. These theatres have the money to do *that*. These theatres also serve as tryouts enroute to New York's Great White Way. The Great White Way was named that after the installation of the electric light, not for the exclusive use of white people.

Item: New Federal Theatre is a non-profit organization celebrating its 27th year. If having very little money is the way to define it as *near demise*, then it has been in a state of *near demise* for its entire 27 years.

The Impact of Race

Item: The 20th-anniversary revival of our production of *Do Lord Remember Me* by James de Jongh ended a critically acclaimed five-week run at the Sylvia & Danny Kaye Playhouse, Sunday, February 16, 1997. New Federal Theatre will open its next play, a revival of Richard Wesley's *The Last Street Play* (*The Mighty Gents*) April 9, 1997.

Item: New Lafayette Theatre went out of business almost twenty-five years ago; Negro Ensemble Company ceased to function in its original way in 1987. It now operates as a non-union company. Foundations, Corporations, Federal, City, and State funders don't, in general, like to fund Black theatre because it *talks*. A Black theatre most often speaks out against oppression.

Item: Where did this term "Chitlin Circuit" come from? Are the audiences for the plays on that circuit people who eat the intestines of hogs? Is it a definition of the visible producer/playwright/director, and (often) the lead actor? In the old days it was called the Theatre Owner's Booking Association (TOBA). The association was owned by a tightly knit group of white theatre owners. It's the same today; only today they're called "Local Promoters." They are the invisible producers of the plays on the "Chitlin Circuit." They control what plays go into certain theatres in Philadelphia, Baltimore, Washington, Atlanta, etc. They don't want plays by Ed Bullins or Oyamo. They don't permit union productions of Black plays. They pay the "producer" a small weekly guarantee. The *local promoter* does everything else; the *local promoter* keeps all the profits; if there are no profits, he immediately drops the production, leaving actors, set, costumes, etc., stranded. The *local promoters'* names seldom appear in the program.

Sincerely,
Woodie King, Jr.

Woodie King, Jr.

Left Out in London

September 3, 1999

Editor
Arts and Leisure
The New York Times

To the Editor,

Having just returned (August 31, 1999) from my yearly sojourn to theatres in London, I was so surprised Benedict Nightingale's report, "The Latest From London: A London Season As Unsettling As the Weather" (Sunday, August 29, 1999) failed even to mention three critically acclaimed Black shows.

Two of the shows are currently at the Royal Shakespeare Company and one is in the same space as Martin Sherman's *Rose* (mentioned!) at Cottesloe in the Royal National Theatre. Poet Laureate of the United States and Pulitzer Prize Winner Rita Dove's *The Darker Face of the Earth* is at Cottesloe (not mentioned). At the Royal Shakespeare Company at Stratford-on-Avon can be seen Michael Attenborough's acclaimed *Othello*, starring Ray Fearon, as well as Aphra Behn's *Oroonoko*, in a new adaptation by the Nigerian playwright BiYi Bandele, directed by Greg Doran. All are critically acclaimed works.

Great theatre (including dance, music and poetry) was also the focus of about 3.5 million Black and white viewers and participants who came into London for the 20th Annual Notting Hill Carnival on Sunday, August 29th and Monday, August 30th, 1999. Two full days of integration of Blacks and whites in London. Not mentioned in Nightingale's piece.

Why this disparity?

Sincerely,
Woodie King, Jr.

Appendices

"Shades of Harlem" in Japan

With all the excitement of a new adventure, the *Shades of Harlem* company embarked on a week-long performance schedule in Osaka, Japan. The American musical hit would perform in Theatre Drama City in Osaka to a 100 percent Japanese audience, less than 10 percent of whom on any given night would be familiar with English. The twelve-member company of Black Americans (with one exception, the white drummer David Silliman) consisted of Ty Stephens, Jeree Wade, Branice McKenzie, Nina Klyvert (she brought her husband of one day, Ron Lawson), Rashamella Cumbo, Jan Johnson, Ludie Jones (celebrating her 78th Birthday), Emma Kemp, Earl May, Adam Wade (the director), and myself (the American Producer). The drummer David Silliman served also as company manager in Japan.

The excitement within the *Shades of Harlem* company manifested itself via laughter, jokes, many cameras, pamphlets, and maps on Japan and Japanese culture. David Silliman prepared packets of information, including restaurants, subway information, taxi information, etc.

The Japan Airlines flight 51 took sixteen hours. It made one stop in Tokyo, where the company changed planes. The flight from Tokyo to Osaka took about an hour. There's a twelve-hour time difference between New York and Osaka. The company arrived Monday night at 7:30 — back in New York it was only 7:30 in the morning!

The airport was full and active as we wove our way through customs.

The Impact of Race

Passports and international visa check took about a half hour. Representatives of our Osaka producers met us.

Osaka is 341 miles west of Tokyo, 26 miles southwest of Kyoto, and 212 miles east of Hiroshima. The history of Osaka dates back about 1,500 years. The magnificent Osaka castle, the city's proud monument, was built by Emperor Hideyoshi Toyotomi in the 16th century. During the Edo period, such arts as Kabuki Theater and Bunraku Theater flourished.

Osaka is now an industrial city with a population of about 2.8 million, making it the third largest city in Japan after Tokyo and Yokohama. Osaka still has a reputation throughout Japan for its fine food, its Osaka Castle, and its Bunraku puppet theatre.

Once we'd been driven to the Mitsui Urban Hotel of Toyosake Avenue in Kita-Ku we had a technical meeting for *Shades of Harlem*. We were surprised that about twenty people attended this meeting. In America a technical meeting at a Black theatre would have about seven people. The meeting consisted of the stage manager, Mr. Nakajima; the lighting staff from a company called Osaska Kyoritsu; the sound operator, Mr. Hibino; the stage design company, Nihon Stage; representatives from the Osaka Presenters, TV Osaka, Liberty Concerts; and Eri Komazake, assistant to Masakazu Shibaoka, the presenter who'd booked the show.

The translator, Ms. Kaoru Nakahara, had been hired specifically to interpret our technical needs to the non-English speaking crew. Ms. Nakahara is a young woman who works out of Tokyo. She's in the process of setting up her own company. The representative from Liberty Concerts, Ms. Masayo Kitamura, also spoke English. She'd relate our technical needs to actual cost since her company was one of the financial partners. Ms. Eri Komazake, assistant to the President of EMS Entertainment, was yet another English speaker. Ms. Komazake is a graduate of Adelphi University in Long Island, New York. She also related technical needs to cost. These three young women are part of a new Japan. They're not relegated to the home. All three are working on jobs that traditionally had been dominated by men.

The technical meeting was conducted by Adam Wade, the director of *Shades of Harlem*. Ty Stephens, the choreographer; David Silliman, the company manager; Jeree Wade, the creator; Branice McKenzie, the musical director; and myself, the American producer also attended.

The meeting lasted two hours. The set had to be adjusted because it had to be built in two days. The lights were extensive. Because *Shades of Harlem* is a musical, it needed follow spots for the show. The operator who spoke no English had to learn the show in two days of technical rehearsals. From this technical rehearsal meeting we began to see patterns in the behavior of the individuals—although they worked in the theatre, they were also representative of the people of Japan.

The people are very Americanized, yet hold onto their traditions. Many are small and not overweight. One notices immediately the business attitudes; the assimilation of American mores, including dress; so many are well dressed. Even office workers, technical people, and junior executives carry crafted leather briefcases. So many of the middle class and the young smoke. Traditional transportation within the city and some parts of the countryside is the bicycle; older people as well as the very young ride the bicycle. In the city the subway and the bullet train are so economical and so clean and safe it would be foolish for the people not to make it the main means of transportation. Finally, the automobiles, though made by the same companies that import American automobiles, are different. With the Subaru, the Nissan, and the Suzuki the differences are in the designs. For example, in America a Toyota Celica is designed differently than a Toyota Celica in Osaka. In Osaka they're very much like an American deluxe sedan. Even taxis are sedan style. Of course, steering is from the right as in most European automobiles.

Almost every member of the tech crew smoked. At the corners of many of the avenues lurk cigarette vending machines. The machines contain about fifteen different brands of cigarettes. Names like Frontier, Cabin, Seven Stars, Casters, Peace, Mild Seven, and Next are new American brands right in there with traditional American brands like Lucky Strike, Kools, and Phillip Morris. Many of the brands are light and superlight.

Many of the tech crew were surprised when we demanded they not smoke during the tech meeting. The members of the crew would take turns and leave the room for a puff. Almost as many brand names were used as there were members of the tech crew. The crew found it interesting that among our company of twelve only one person smoked. I showed them the warning on the American pack of cigarettes; no warning on their pack *that they are dangerous to your health and could kill you.* A pack from the machines can cost anywhere from 220 to 250 Yen (about $2.20 to $2.50). Television commercials for these products are abundant.

The people of Osaka aren't, in general, overweight. This despite the city's reputation for fine food. Most of the people are very much aware of the hazards of being overweight and out of shape. This is true of both men and women; old and young. (Improved health care, diet, and living conditions have extended the average life expectancy for a Japanese female born today. Japan's workingwomen constitute 40 percent of the labor force.) Of course, food portions are nowhere near the size of portions in America. This consciousness of weight is a definite contradiction to the health hazards of smoking.

The people, especially the young, are very fashion conscious. Fashion designers from around the world import their clothes into Japan. Georgio Armani. Calvin Klein, Valentino, Udomo, Nino Cerruti, and Faroni are worn not just by the store window mannequins but by the junior executives and "office ladies" as well. During the summer and sunny days, women cover their heads from the sun with umbrellas. On any avenue during a sunny day you might see hundreds of umbrellas designing the landscape.

On its completion, Osaka Castle was the largest castle in Japan. The original building was eight stories high; rising 130 feet. The castle spans over 350 years of Japanese history. Built by Hideyoshi Toyotomi in 1583, it served as a treasury, an armory, and an observatory until it was burned down in the Summer Siege of the 1615 Civil War. The castle was rebuilt by Shogun Hidetada Tokugawa in 1626. It was again destroyed in 1665, this time by lightning. The castle was again rebuilt by Shogun Tokugawa and was again burned down in 1868 during the Meiji Restoration. The existing structure of ferroconcrete was erected in 1931 with donations by Osaka citizens. The interior serves as a museum of history.

The architecture of Osaka Castle shows a ground plan made by Shogun Hideyoski Toyotomi in 1614. It's the only architectural drawing in existence; it clearly shows all the outer enclosures, i.e., the moats, stone walls, inner bailey, outer bailey, outer enclosures, and outermost citadel — thirteen ancient buildings constructed in the Edo period. Osaka castle was built and rebuilt at a time when space still existed in Osaka, Tokyo, and Kyoto.

In the new Japan, whether it's Osaka or Tokyo, that luxury of space no longer exists. According to Noriaki Okabe, associate architect of the new Kansai Airport Terminal building—which will be built out on the ocean—"Osaka today seems to be missing human space, with the exception of the Yodogawa River Area. Only thirty years ago there were many more canals which gave the city a human dimension...Osaka is very dense. There are no great open spaces. Life outside companies and buildings in Osaka isn't very human and can be frustrating. There are cultural problems with the city as a whole. (In other) cities many cinemas and cultural events start later in the evening after the workday has long been finished. In Osaka, as in most of Japan, the last show at cinemas is around 7 or 8 P.M. Osaka needs more cultural diversity and flexibility to realize the status of a great world city."

In the 17th century, in the Dotonbori Area alone there were twenty theatres. Wealthy patrons went to the theatre in boats, docking along the Dotonbori Canal. Nowadays Osaka's Bunraku tradition is still alive in the National Bunraku Theatre. Bunraku dolls can be up to five feet tall and weigh as much as sixty pounds.

The establishment of Dotonbori as an official entertainment site dates back to 1626. Long before then, however, it had been a popular center where "Kabuki" dramas, puppet shows and other types of entertainment were held, drawing large audiences.

The word "Kabuki" derives from the verb "kabuku" meaning to act or behave strangely or differently. This concept symbolized the distinctive, lively activities of citizens as the medieval age gave way to the modern age and thus can be viewed as a candid, though highly dramatized, representation of their lives.

The trip from Osaka to the old city of Kyoto took about one hour by bullet train. As the train passed through the urban landscape on its journey, one could see that very old traditions nonetheless persisted. Traditional dress took on its own character. The women wore long silk kimonos with a very large waistband. I'm told this form of dress goes back over twelve hundred years. The train passes traditional rice fields behind buildings with clothes hung from clotheslines. In these rice fields old women in wide hats still tend fields and "gardens." The contradiction is how the young race through the city on motorcycles. Some young women lounge on the front porches reading fashion magazines.

The Impact of Race

Kyoto served as Japan's capital city for more than a thousand years, from 794 to the Meiji Restoration in 1868. Kyoto's first few hundred years from about 800 to the 12th century were its grandest, a time when culture blossomed into the Heian Period. Buddhism flourished and temples were built. Toward the end of the Heian period, military clans began fighting for power. These clashes resulted in a series of civil wars, pushing Japan into the feudal era of military governments that lasted nearly 680 years, until 1868. Despite these civil wars culture flourished. Zen Buddhism was the rage.

Kyoto served as the home of the imperial court until 1868, when Emperor Meiji moved to Tokyo following the Meiji restoration. The old architecture of Kyoto is as old as the city. Outside the city of temples and shrines, in the downtown area, newer architecture abounds—including department stores, Kyoto Towers, automobile parking garages, and the train station itself. However, with 1,700 Buddhist temples and 300 Shinto shrines, the old city and its structure are as strong as ever.

The architectural splendor of the Yasaka Shrine is a wonder in itself. This shrine was built in 876 A.D. It was originally dedicated to the Shinto god of medicine, Susano-No-Mikoto, to his consort Kushi-Inadahine-No-Mikoto and their eight children to protect the citizens of Kyoto against epidemics. Within the large gate of this shrine are over a dozen compounds. Each compound has a specially designed series of living quarters and ancillary living accommodations. The temple of the Yasaka is off from the other compounds. It's the place of worship and therefore more intricate in its design. In America it would be similar to the church.

Another magnificent temple is the grand head temple of the Jodo sect of Buddhism, Chion-In. It consists of six major architectural structures. They're the scripture library, the statue hall, the main gate (this wooden gate is one of the biggest temple gates in the world, Shogun Tokugawa Hidetada ordered it built in 1619), Amida Hall, the Mausoleum, and the Grand Bell.

Today Japan, with a population less than half that of the U.S. boasts an economy almost two-thirds as large. The sudden infusion of wealth sent reverberations across Japanese society. It all really began in 1989 when the new Emperor Akihito was enthroned and a new imperial age began. The new era of PEACEFUL ACHIEVEMENT.

The salary man (white-collar worker) who works six days a week, sixteen hours a day, is the country's laborer. Advertisements on billboards ask the question. "Can you work and fight 24 hours a day, salary man?" Throughout Japan, the salary man wants more from life than to work and fight. Young Japanese workers are demanding higher pay, shorter hours, and greater benefits.

Yet the people are very traditional. They celebrate and love their country. The people are as loyal to Osaka as they are to Tokyo or Kyoto.

On Monday, June 6, 1994, Kyoto residents and tourists turned out for a major festival. It represented the midway point of a full year celebrating the 1,200th anniversary of Kyoto.

Shades of Harlem is a musical revue inspired by Harlem's Cotton Club during The Harlem Renaissance. Its primary innovation is its music. Songs like "Take the A Train," "Sweet Georgia Brown," "Satin Doll," "Stomping at the Savoy," "Cottontail," "If You've Never Been Vamped By a Brownskin, You've Never Been Vamped at All," "Black Coffee," "I Got It Bad and That Ain't Good," "My Man, Body and Soul," and "God Bless the Child." All of these songs and more are clearly arranged by musical director Frank Owens and executed by its brilliant cast, including The Renaissance Ladies dancers (80-year-old Ludie Jones and 77-year-old Juanita Boisseau). *Shades of Harlem*, because of its music, transcended language and culture. The Japanese audiences after each performance rose to give *Shades of Harlem* a standing ovation exactly as white audiences off-Broadway and Black audiences in Harlem had.

Top Left: *3 by 3* with Woodie King, Max Ferra, and Tisa Chang. Top Right: Larry Leon Hamlin, G. L. Thompson, and Woodie at Winston-Salem, N.C. Bottom: August Wilson, Kojo Ade, Marion McClinton, and Woodie King.

Top: Woodie, Count Stovall, and Al Freeman, Jr. at the premiere of *Conflict of Interest*. Middle: Walter Mosley, Melba Moore, and Woodie at Sardi's. Bottom: Woodie and Robert Townsend.

Top: Woodie and Hal Williams in 1999.
Bottom Left: Wole Soyinka and Woodie
in 2000. Bottom Right: Max Roach, the
composer of *Jazz Set*, and Woodie.

Top Left: Ntozake Shange and Woodie at *for colored girls who have considered suicide/when the rainbow is enuf.* Top Right: Dick Smith and David Rambeau at Detroit in 1995. Bottom: Lou Gossett and Woodie King.

Facing Page:

Top: Andre DeShields and Woodie. Bottom Left: Cliff Frazier. Bottom Right: Barbara Ann Teer and Woodie at the Otto Awards in 2001.

Top: Woodie and Ron Milner at Wayne St. in 1995. Middle: Filmmaking class at the "Mobilization for Youth" conference in 1968. Bottom: Melvin Van Peebles and Woodie at the AUDELCO awards. Facing Page: Top Left: Samm-Art Williams and Naydene Cassandra in *Home*. Top Right: Elizabeth Van Dyke in *Zora Neale Hurston*. Bottom: Woodie, Michael Lee King, and Woodie Geoffrey King, taken in 2001.

Top Left: Bill Harris. Top Right: Woodie and Lloyd Richards at the *Black Mask* magazine reception. Bottom: Woodie King, N. Shange, Judy Dearing, and Micki Davidson at the revival of *for colored girls who have considered suicide/when the rainbow is enuf.*

A Black Henry VIII at the Public Theatre

Why would I have so much interest in Shakespeare and classic theatre staging? First, for over twenty-five years, I've directed in the Black Theatre. It was both a pioneering effort and, at the same time, a love of recapturing Black people in a beautiful and artistic way. Yet, only on a very few occasions in all those years have I been afforded an opportunity to direct any of the classics. Over the years I began to doubt my ability to direct these plays. Although I've read most of the works of Shakespeare and also the classics, I've never directed a Shakespeare play.

My first attempt at an observership was at the Roundabout Theatre on Dion Boucicault's *London Assurance*. Todd Haimes, the artistic director, finally returned one of my many telephone calls; he informed me that *London Assurance* would be previewing in a few days and that what I *needed* was the rehearsal experience. Therefore, I ventured to the New York Shakespeare Festival Public Theatre.

The New York Shakespeare Festival was founded in 1954 by Joseph Papp. It has grown into one of the nation's pre-eminent cultural institutions. In 1962 The New York Shakespeare Festival opened its permanent summer-time home at the Delacorte Theatre in Central Park. In 1987 The New York Shakespeare Festival, under Joseph Papp's leadership, launched the Shakespeare Marathon — a commitment to produce all of William Shakespeare's plays. In 1991, when Joseph Papp died, the institution kept Papp's commitment and continued the Marathon. With this summer's production of *Henry VIII*, directed by Mary Zimmerman, the Marathon will be complete.

Henry VIII would be ideal since it was the final production in the Canon. Ironically, it was also the play that was in performance when the Globe Theatre burned to the ground. Within *Henry VIII*'s text is also contained a bit of controversy — was it written by William Shakespeare or John Fletcher or both? Certainly scholars feel very strongly that John Fletcher wrote the opening prologue.

I had a long history with Joseph Papp and the New York Shakespeare Festival. I co-produced six plays with the Festival, including *What the Winesellers Buy, Mondongo, The Taking of Miss Janie, for colored girls...*, *Daddy*, and *The Dance and the Railroad*. However, even though I've tried, I've had a different relationship with the current producer, George C. Wolfe. It's basically a historical respect George has for me and not an artistic respect. In a sense he sees me as one of "the old school" that didn't help him when he arrived in New York City from Los Angeles.

Mary Zimmerman is an artistic associate at The Goodman Theatre, where she adapted and directed the award-winning *Journey to the West* and *The Notebook of Leonardo Da Vinci*. She received a Drama Desk nomination for her direction of The Manhattan Theatre Club production of *The Arabian Nights*. She's visiting associate professor in the Department of Performance Studies at Northwestern University. She's a professional artist deeply rooted in literature; and she's a professional who also works in academe.

How will observing the rehearsal of *Henry VIII* help me as a director? This is the question I asked myself each day I attended rehearsals. Therefore, it was the director who I observed at all times. Mary Zimmerman is an assured, well prepared, yet cautious director. It's a joy watching her deal with a company of almost thirty-five people. When I arrived, *Henry VIII* wasn't yet departmentalized. Will it be departmentalized? On this first day they'd be rehearsing Act I, Scene III.

I'd anticipated the observership for about two months. It was in early March when I asked George C. Wolfe if the observership was possible. He said he'd get back to me. Meanwhile, I had to call his office and remind his secretary. The secretary told me that rehearsals would begin on or about May 9, 1997. As a precaution, I wrote George a note thanking him for the observership. It was Rosemarie Tichler who ultimately followed up and eventually worked it out with the director, Mary Zimmerman.

Rosemarie wanted to know if all I wanted to do was sit in on the rehearsals and she wanted to walk me into rehearsals and introduce me to Mary Zimmerman.

I knew of Zimmerman's fine reputation from her work in Chicago, especially her *Journey to the West*. It was also good that I'd seen Ms. Zimmerman's work in the Manhattan Theatre Club's production of her adaptation of *The Arabian Nights*. This came about when I was directing *And the World Laughs With You* at Crossroads Theatre Company. Ramon Moses (who died in 2001) was appearing in my production and was cast in Ms. Zimmerman's *Arabian Nights*.

The LuEsther Rehearsal Hall is on the third floor of New York Shakespeare Festival's headquarters at 425 Lafayette Street. The rehearsal room is about 150 feet in length and 70 in width; within these dimensions are 14 columns and 28 archways. They reduce the size of the actual rehearsal space to 105 x 35 feet.

Act I, Scene III is a scene between Lord Chamberlain, Lord Sands, and Sir Thomas Lovell. Ms. Zimmerman moved quickly into specifics of the scene. Since the actors are very good, she concentrated on movement that illuminated the scene. This, she said, was an information scene wherein information on the fashion, the women, and Britain's attitude toward France. Zimmerman knows her set and her costumes very well. When in doubt, she went to the rear wall of the rehearsal hall. There on a large table is a miniature set and on the wall are drawings of each character in costume. It was not unlike rehearsals of a contemporary play.

The language of *Henry VIII* did seem difficult to me. Yet, the actors seemed very comfortable with it. All the actors have solid reputations in classic works. Familiarity feeds into excellence.

Zimmerman doesn't waste time at her rehearsals. On the actors' breaks she listened to music the composer had Fed Exed to her. Since Scene IV the Masked Ball was next, Zimmerman knew what she wanted musically. This scene further developed the characters of Lord Sands, Lord Chamberlain, Cardinal Wolsey, Sir Thomas Lovell, Sir Henry Guildford; Anne Bullen was introduced into this scene. The other ladies and gentlemen at the Masked Ball would be introduced later.

Furthermore, Zimmerman and her choreographer explored how she'd add ten females who'd be put on the payroll two weeks into rehearsals. Here I learned that, after two weeks of rehearsing her principle actors, she'd have additional work on this scene later. What could be done with the actors present? Zimmerman used her dramaturg, John Dias, to clarify relationships and certain parts of the text.

On this particular rehearsal, Zimmerman loosened her actors with a series of questions on Shakespeare: Did Shakespeare really think he was Shakespeare? Did he think his work would last down through the ages? The cast had various opinions. Was there ever a period when Shakespeare wasn't done? The dramaturg clarified.

On this particular rehearsal, I noticed the non-traditional casting of Black and Latino performers. Reuben Santiago Hudson, a Black actor, was playing Henry VIII. Hudson had distinguished himself with roles on Broadway in *Jelly's Last Jam*, Off-Broadway in *East Texas Hot Links*, and a Tony Award in August Wilson's *Seven Guitars*.

Teagle Bougere played the very small role of Cromwell. Peter Jay Fernandez played Gardner; Julio Monge in the role of Earl of Surrey, Miguel Perez as Duke of Suffolk; Sybil Walker as Patience and the Gentlewoman; Michael Hyatt; and Rueben Jackson. According to the performers they were cast by Mary Zimmerman with the assistance of the New York Shakespeare Festival casting office.

May 14, 1997. The rehearsal will be Act II, Scene III between the characters Anne Bullen and the Old Gentlewoman. This scene explores Anne's reticence at the thought of Henry offering to marry her and making her queen. The Old Gentlewoman implores her to consider the offer. Anne's dilemma stems from the fact that Queen Katherine is such a good person.

Mary Zimmerman blocked this entire scene from the entrance of Anne Bullen and the Old Gentlewoman to the entrance of Lord Chamberlain and his Page. In the blocking, she gave actors a lot of freedom, especially Anne Bullen. She wanted that movement because of Anne Bullen's energy. The role of the Old Gentlewoman played by Bette Henrette is an excellent example of Zimmerman's casting. Henrette is so right for the role. She can play it broad or full of subtleties.

In the concluding part of this scene Lord Chamberlain delivers to Anne part of a £1,000 per year dowry from Henry VIII. Zimmerman wanted Chamberlain to be somewhat embarrassed in bringing this money. Zimmerman introduced church bells in the middle of Lord Chamberlain's speech to set up irony, contradiction.

The actors wanted to explore the divorce/separation of Henry VIII and Katherine. Henry needs the church to sanction the divorce before he marries Anne Bullen. Before he married Katherine, she'd been married to his brother. The actors felt this had significance in playing the scene. Zimmerman had the actors sit in a circle. The circle included the characters of Henry, Katherine, Cardinal Wolsey, Cardinal Campeius, Crier, Scribes, etc. After one read-through of the scene, she was open to questions. Only two questions, one from the actor playing Henry VIII on a pronunciation and one from the actress playing Katherine. Nothing at all about the divorce/separation of Henry and Katherine.

Now Zimmerman could stage the scene. She placed the furniture according to the floor plan and proceeded. She suggested that the movement of actors be organic, especially between Henry and Katherine. She's at her best when actors are working according to her plans.

May 15, 1997. Zimmerman would begin preliminary work on Scene III, the Mask Ball. This is to be worked very slowly. She announced that she's uncertain who will be where...she laid out moves for practical things like the men setting chairs and benches for the ladies. Early on she discovered she didn't have enough men to bring onto the stage the required chairs or benches. She also discovered Sir Harry Guildford wouldn't be the one to bring on a chair or serve drinks to the assembled party. I noted that these large scenes are basically about solving traffic problems. By calling on all the supernumeraries she was able to solve her immediate problems in less than two hours.

Zimmerman stayed on schedule and moved into Act II, Scene I. This scene sets up Buckingham. Again, actors had questions on matters of how rough they should be in the arrest of Buckingham. Zimmerman explained the context in which Buckingham is accused of being a traitor by Cardinal Wolsey and what the people think of Wolsey and what they think of Buckingham. Zimmerman noted the previous scenes had explained how the people felt. She noted that the people respect Buckingham. Therefore, the guards would let him stop and talk.

Zimmerman moved on to Act II, Scene II. This scene included the Dukes of Norfolk, Lord Chamberlain, and the Duke of Suffolk. This scene passes on information regarding Cardinal Wolsey's power over King Henry. The Duke of Norfolk and the Duke of Suffolk intrude on Henry's meditation...his privacy...this intrusion angers Henry. By contrast, the intrusion of Cardinal Wolsey and Cardinal Campeius pleases him. Accompanying Wolsey and Campeius is Gardner, Henry's new secretary, loyal to Wolsey. When Zimmerman staged Act II, Scene II, it all made sense.

That same day the director repeated work on Act II, Scene III between Anne Bullen and the Old Gentlewoman. Again, she talked to the two women about the characters, then plunged into the movement of the scene. Where would the movement take the characters? Would it help to clarify anything? I noted again how well she'd cast the Old Gentlewoman. On each work-through the actress brought something entirely different, fresh...

Scene IV. The divorce trial in Blackfriars. This is basically a repeat of the previous day's work. Others are now added to the scene. Zimmerman took a lot of time with Katherine on this scene. She's exceptional at making decisions on her feet. Perhaps it's her thorough understanding of the text. More than ever, I am convinced a director must be deeply immersed in the text and the subject matter of the material he or she is directing. Blocking a scene often takes care of itself, especially with good actors.

May 16, 1997. There's to be a work-through of Act I. Zimmerman announced that this "stumble through" is only to see where *she* is. It's not so much for actors as for her. However, the work-through, from my vantage point, worked exceptionally well. All of the principle actors took the time and worked on specific problems. It was exciting! All of this after only one week! After this work-through some of the actors had questions: i.e., How aware is Guard of the machinations and maneuvering of Cardinal Wolsey?

I liked the release which the Mask Ball provided after the tension of the first few scenes.

Zimmerman felt since Act I had now been shaped, perhaps we should listen to the music for the Mask Ball. She explained how the music would be utilized by the choreographer in the Mask Ball and that rehearsals would be posted in the coming weeks.

A good work-through usually puts everyone in a good mood. So it was with this one. Zimmerman talked about what she loved about good theatre; what puts her in a state of grace. It's being placed in the rare position of the audience and not knowing what comes next. She admitted she normally writes and adapts her own plays even though she has directed Shakespeare (including a critically acclaimed production of *All's Well That Ends Well*). Good Shakespeare also puts her in a state of grace.

Act III, Scene II. Zimmerman stood with actors and talked the scene through. Questions from the actors she couldn't answer she postponed until later. Herb Foster, who plays Lord Chamberlain, explained that England is Catholic but is changing to Protestant. This is heavy on the mind of the nobility. He thought he should mention this. He felt the text bears this out. Mary Zimmerman said she wouldn't have the time today to both read it through and block it. She decided to block the scene. As stated earlier, she acts very fast on her feet. Quick! Smart! Well prepared! The blocking of the scene concentrated on Cardinal Wolsey.

May 20, 1997. Act V, Scene III. The Council. Today Zimmerman must work with actor Teagle Bougere who plays Cromwell. Bougere has a sprained back. He cannot move well and one can tell he's often working while in pain. In this scene Gardiner, Lord of Winchester (Peter Jay Fernandez) is pushing the Council to arrest Cardinal Cranmer; Cromwell cautiously defends Cranmer. Zimmerman tried the scene several different ways, trying to find the correct "color" for the scene. She is ever mindful of Bougere's back.

May 24, 1997. Act I, Scene II, Page 11. On this morning Zimmerman adjusted blocking and let actors move and adjust. I'm not sure what I'm watching today. By this I mean, are the actors so good that the production directs itself? Or is Zimmerman so prepared that it only looks this simple.

It's interesting to note that the actors were thrown off when they forgot seemingly insignificant words. Is this a trait in classic theatre?

The scene of Wolsey's unveiling by Henry VIII is rehearsing today. That scene is played out by Josef Sommer as Wolsey and Reuben Santiago Hudson as Henry VIII. Hudson wanted to play this scene not so final as Zimmerman wanted. This became an exciting discussion between Hudson and Zimmerman. Hudson feels Wolsey is like a father to him. He trusts Wolsey. He feels Wolsey is true in his heart and not in his head. Zimmerman wants Hudson to play the King as if he knows Wolsey betrayed him. Zimmerman is a tough, secure director who knows what she wants. But Reuben Santiago Hudson knows the text and his through line of action *very, very, very well*. How will this discussion resolve itself?

I've noticed that several questions arise in acting and directing classics. The most obvious is, how does it relate to modern times? How is this text being focused? Should it simply be lifted off the page and placed on stage? This *Henry VIII* poses a special problem. A Black actor is playing the title role and he brings his history from birth to adulthood with the interpretation. At the same time, it's also difficult because it's a confused play.

That afternoon Zimmerman worked on the offstage coronation scene. Downstage two actresses excitedly discussed what happened at the coronation while across the rear of the stage an ensemble marched in slow motion, left to right. Zimmerman wanted this scene to overlap into the next scene. She explained how this would be done. She wanted Lord Cromwell to have a special entrance. She carefully worked out this entrance. The others would be choreographed into the scene by the choreographer, Sabrina Peck. Zimmerman suggested the actors visit the Delacorte Theatre and view the actual set.

Sunday, May 25, 1997. The Mask Ball is to be choreographed today. The Ball isn't defined in any great detail in the text. In the Zimmerman production it's to take almost five minutes. Therefore, I felt it necessary to observe even when Zimmerman wasn't in the rehearsal. Here I noted actors will try anything. Many of them had dance and movement training in college.

Zimmerman didn't attend these dance rehearsals. She let the dance expert work out problems, then appeared and approved the final product. In this instance, Zimmerman watched the final product several times and asked that it be done again.

May 27, 1997. Rehearsal starts late because of the holiday. Today, Zimmerman will continue work on the Duke of Buckingham arrest. Larry Breggman as the Duke of Buckingham is a master of the language of Shakespeare. Is she uncomfortable with Bryggman? Could she not relate to what he is doing? Once or twice she helped him articulate the language.

When she couldn't spend time on the scene she moved on. Breggman wanted to work with her on the scene. However, the dance had to be completed.

This makes the third day of rehearsal on the Mask Ball. Sabrina Peck divides the ensemble into two groupings. She designates an "A" group and a "B" group. Although movement for the dance is complicated some of the actors picked it up quickly. Zimmerman's problem becomes how to place Cardinal Wolsey, Lord Chamberlain, Lord Cromwell, etc. into the scene.

The costumes are all drawn and the drawings are in the rehearsal hall. There are twenty-six panels. The drawings give color and a sense of shape to each costume. All male costumes have hats. The hats all have plumes and these plumes are uncomfortable for Reuben Santiago Hudson. This becomes a minor problem in several rehearsals. Actors are told to use pieces of costumes for rehearsals. Pieces are brought into the rehearsal hall. These pieces, especially the dresses, are helpful in the rehearsal of the dance.

Saturday, May 31, 1997. Dance rehearsal with Reuben Santiago Hudson as Henry VIII and Marin Hinkle as Anne Bullen. Zimmerman didn't appear for the first hour of this rehearsal. Sabrina Peck worked with the stars. Both Hudson and Hinkle did a lot of talking, explaining. They didn't want to do the actual work. Hudson is very concerned that the King not get lost in all the choreography. He didn't want to lose focus of the love story between Henry and Anne. He discussed it with the choreographer in some depth. When he failed to get satisfaction, he suggested they both talk to Zimmerman when she arrived. Zimmerman did arrive about an hour later. However, Hudson didn't discuss the dance with her.

Sunday, June 1, 1997. There'll be a run through of Act I. Again, it looks great. However, Zimmerman isn't pleased with Larry Bryggman's Lord Buckingham. Again, she says it's hard to listen to. She's unable to fix the scene. But as a novice I keep trying to figure out what the scene needs.

The two stage managers are Jim Latus and Buzz Cohen. They seem to have been around NYSF for a long time. Buzz Cohen recently received praise from Andre Braugher when he received his Obie Award for last year's *Henry V*. It's been apparent how much the stage management team helps Zimmerman in the realization of *Henry VIII*. If Mary Zimmerman had a question on placement of people or props, Jim or Buzz answered it immediately. Every move by every actor is notated. An excellent stage manager is essential to a good production.

June 4, 1997. Rehearsals on *The Spirit of Peace, The Vision of Angels* scene. This is really the beginning of Katherine's death scene; along with Griffith and her Lady in Waiting, she hears of Wolsey's death. The veteran Mark Hammer plays Griffith. Julia McIlvane, a 10-year-old blond girl plays "The Spirit of Peace." Zimmerman wants Jayne Atkinson to talk to her about the line, "My eyes grow dim," and how this is Katherine's anticipation of death.

The actors in the Council wanted to discuss the scene. The questions they wanted clarity on are: Why, if Henry warned Cranmer, did they bring him before the Council? Is Henry testing the Council members? Is it a public relations ploy? Was it an issue of church and state? Michael Stuhlbarg who plays Cranmer, wanted to know if it was too late for costumes to indicate a progression to the high position of Archbishop. The scene revealed that if the church, which was represented by the Catholic Wolsey, changes to be controlled by Protestants a lot of the wealthy Council members will lose their cushy positions. Zimmerman explained how the kings kept the wealthy collection of "Lords" and "Dukes" happy. Therefore, the trial was concerned with the larger issue of the new position of Church and state.

Lunch is 1 P.M.; a tech meeting is set for 1 P.M. Tables and chairs are set in place in the center of LuEsther Hall by 1:05 P.M. The tech meeting with twenty tech people started at 1:10 P.M. Some of the people brought lunch, all brought back-up material. Mary Zimmerman was at the head of the table. The production manager conducted the technical meeting. The producer, George C. Wolfe, didn't attend.

The technical schedule determines what will be discussed. However, the most important message from this meeting was that Zimmerman would be able to move on stage the evening of June 5th. Toni Leslie James, the costume designer, announced all costumes would be available for ten out of the twelve, Sunday, June 8th. The production manager reminded all that the full dress (rehearsal) would be Tuesday, June 10th at 7 P.M.

Thursday, June 5, 1997. The cast of *Henry VIII* is finally on the Delacorte stage. It's not a good night. Temperature hovers in the 50's. It's cold! At 7:30 P.M. the stage manager asks the actors to walk around the stage, get a feel of the stage. There'd be no cue lights or monitors. Notice the exits and entrances. He asks the actors to explore backstage. At 9:15 P.M. the stage manager announces "Places," for a work through of "entrances."

Saturday, June 8, 1997. In the Delacorte. Begins with Act II, Scene II. Actors are in partial costumes. All are wearing hats. Most are miked up for sound. Mary Zimmerman is very relaxed. She walks around the center section of the Delacorte. The sound is small mikes hidden in the hair of the performers. The battery is worn around the waist, similar to a belt.

Zimmerman spent a lot of time adjusting actors to the Delacorte Theatre. She didn't call it "adjusting," she called it "playing around." Changes from one scene into the next proved difficult because some had to be re-choreographed; new music cues; the flag had to be cued separately. The inclusion of the song "Fall Asleep or Fall in Dark" sung by the Black actress Sybil Walker in a transition scene from the divorce court into the ladies-in-attendance at Katherine was brilliantly achieved. What Zimmerman does is create a world of text that exists in very human moments.

Directing at the Crossroads

The first correspondence from Crossroads Theatre Company about directing *And the World Laughs With You* by Karimah came March 16, 1993. At that time it was to be a rehearsed reading in the Theatre's annual New Play Festival, "Genesis 1993: A Celebration of New Voices." Because of illness I couldn't direct this reading. However, after the reading in May 1993, *And the World Laughs With You* was so well received, Crossroads Theatre decided to make it a part of their '93/'94 season.

The second correspondence arrived July 22, 1993. Rick Kahn, the Artistic Director, officially offered me the director's assignment and laid out the rehearsal plans. Rehearsals would begin January 4, 1994; the first preview would be February 1, 1994; Opening Night, February 5, 1994; and Closing Night, March 13, 1994. The second correspondence also informed me that Crossroads Theatre is a League of Regional Theatre (LORT) and must operate on several prescribed contractual agreements, including one of which I am a member, the Society of Stage Directors and Choreographers.

My director's contract was signed November 22, 1993. On the November 22, 1993 contract a rider was added including housing while I was in New Brunswick working on *And the World Laughs With You*. This proved to be more important than usual because during the rehearsal and performances the city witnessed some of the most devastating snow and ice storms in its history.

The design team and the artistic team began to take shape after three

237

readings of *And the World Laughs With You*. What exactly should the urban nightmare "look" like? How should the people who inhabit this nightmare "look?" What kind of dress do we often see on those who live in the nightmare? First, I met with Rick Kahn, the Artistic Director of Crossroads Theatre Company and Karimah the Playwright. The Dramaturg, Sydne Mahone, also participated. The first of a series of meetings took place during the month of August (at the North Carolina Black Theatre Festival); during the audition process (at West Bank Café) and at the Theatre. It was important that we all understood each other's vision; it was important that I understood the playwright's vision. Once we all agreed *And the World Laughs With You* is an urban nightmare, the design team could be selected. That design team consisted of Felix Cochran, set designer; Judy Dearing, costume designer; Shirley Prendergast, lighting designer; and Efrem Jenkins-Ahmad, sound designer. All the designers except Efrem had designed over a half dozen shows I'd directed over the previous ten years. They'd also designed for off-Broadway, Broadway, and dozens of resident professional theatres.

Selecting the Actors

Pat McCorkle Casting in New York City is an independent casting agency for theatres, film, and television. Her company casts all the plays presented at Crossroads Theatre Company. Their method of casting is basically straightforward. Their casting personnel reads the play, then they meet with the director, the playwright, and artistic director of the Theatre to discuss each character in the play. Those meetings took place at the McCorkle Casting office the first week of November 1993. Casting began November 11, 1993, and continued on November 12, 1993; November 18; and final callbacks of November 20, 1993. We auditioned about a hundred actors for nine roles.

After one of the auditions the director, the artistic director, the playwright, the set designer, and the lighting designer had an inspired meeting at the West Bank Cafe. I'm not sure if we'd been inspired by the wonderful acting talent or if we'd actually planned the meeting a week earlier. Felix Cochran had drawings and art work from American artists like Hughie Lee Smith and Red Grooms. He'd focused in on the nightmare aspect of the play. Red Grooms' buildings were slightly off reality. It was a fascinating concept. Shirley Prendergast and I talked a great deal about the film noir look one gets in some of the films of the Forties and Fifties. Somewhere a hydrant is spraying water, glistening the streets. We left that meeting with FILM NOIR URBAN NIGHTMARE.

The next day, November 23, 1993, I cast the play from the more than one hundred actors who auditioned. It's a very young cast. I don't think we had one actor over 30. The two leads were 12 and 13 years old. The older man plays the 12-year-old twenty years in the future, when he has become a successful surgeon. Specifically cast were Sharif Rashed, Kevin Davis, Ramon Melindez-Moses, Jean La Marre, Che' Williams, Laurence Mason, Anthony Thomas, Kalimi Baxter, Millicent Sparks, and Joy De Michelle Moore.

This was November 23, 1993. We'd have two more meetings at Crossroads Theatre Company before our January 4, 1994, rehearsal start. One would be for a set of playwright's revisions at the very end of November. These revisions did enhance a certain area of *And the World Laughs With You*, but in a larger context. The playwright changed a word here and a word there throughout the entire script.

On January 4, 1994, the first rehearsal of *And the World Laughs With You* was supposed to commence. It was cancelled because of a heavy snow and ice storm. I flew into Newark Airport from St. Louis (I was there directing *Checkmates* at St. Louis Black Repertory Theatre). I took a taxi from Newark to New Brunswick, New Jersey, only to find it cancelled. Actors and artists couldn't get to New Brunswick from New York City. Rehearsal began the next day.

Crossroads Theatre tries as much as possible to create a "family" atmosphere during the rehearsal process. On the first day of rehearsal all designers, stage managers, actors, and staff persons (all fifty-four of them) met for light repast. Then we had an official passing of the torch from the last show *Tell-Tale Hearts*. There were introductions, a circle of energy and prayer. There was a commitment from the Artistic Director, Ricardo Khan, that each and every department would work hard doing their jobs in support of the show. The director of group sales shared that she'd already booked over sixty groups to see *And the World Laughs With You* by Karimah.

To give a brief synopsis of the play, the action centers around an

The Impact of Race

11-year-old boy named Tyler. Tyler goes on a journey into the harshest sections of the urban ghetto in search of his mother, Winniefred, who left the comfortable suburban home they shared with his grandmother (Winniefred's mother) approximately six months earlier. Along the way Tyler meets several inhabitants of this world and each has a personal story of survival.

The one who makes the biggest impression on him is a 12-year-old boy who's quit school and lives by his wits on the streets running errands for drug dealers. He calls himself "Trump," he says, "After Donald Trump... I'm going to be a billionaire too someday." The boys strike up a friendship. Trump renames his new friend "Country" because a name like Tyler just won't work in this neighborhood. He shows Country/Tyler his gun and the $1,700 in cash he's carrying. He schools Country about the streets, even down to what it's like spending time with Sheneequa, the prostitute who conducts business in the abandoned building they're standing in front of. "She's just a crackhead skeezer," Trump says describing her.

While Trump visits Sheneequa and Tyler waits for him so they can start off together looking for his mother, he encounters Jimmy and Brew, two drug dealers looking for Trump because he's late with his delivery. Realizing the seriousness of Jimmy and Brew's visit, Trump coaxes Tyler when he returns to delay the search for his mother by visiting Sheneequa, allowing him time to drop off the money to Jimmy and Brew. For a few beats the stage is empty, then we hear Tyler scream. He runs out of the building followed by Sheneequa yelling, "Tyler! Tyler!" Sheneequa is Winniefred, his mother. The stage is empty for a few beats then Trump runs in frantic; it seems he misplaced the money he was supposed to deliver. Before our eyes an angry Brew shoots Trump in the back several times, killing him. This ends Act One. Trump's body isn't discovered for the rest of the action of the play.

The Second Act focuses mainly on the relationship between this 24-year-old mother and her 11-year-old son. Sheneequa, as she now calls herself, is an injured soul whose spirit broke under the strong hand of a repressive, abusive mother. Unable to bear any more after Tyler's father deserted her to marry another and move away, she's found independence living in an abandoned house, smoking crack and selling her services to support herself and her habit. We watch Tyler move from whiny boy to

240

manchild during the course of the action (consisting mainly of him pleading with her to change her ways and come back home). He realizes she's not coming back. He's left to pursue his life goal of becoming a doctor without her. She did give him the one gift she could, her sense of humor.

Cheryl Collins was brought on as my assistant. She's the director of her own theatre in Kansas. Bright, energetic. I was very generous with my time, attention and patience toward her. I placed her on a high level of authority in dealing with the cast, designers, stage managers, et al. We always met after rehearsals to discuss the day's work, brainstorm about present problems and anticipate developing issues. Sometimes these talks would only be a few minutes, other times — hours.

Much of the action of the play relied on the performance of two children. The boy cast as Tyler, Sharif Rasheed, was a veteran of many films, commercials and television shows (he was cast in a major role in Spike Lee's *Crooklyn*). He attended the professional children's school and his mother was at every tutoring session and rehearsal. Because the children had a one-hour commute each way from New York, four hours mandatory daily tutoring and required one hour for lunch (which his mother protected fiercely), that left only three or four hours a day the children were available to us. This limited our rehearsals severely. An assistant stage manager (interns) usually read for Trump or Tyler but it wasn't the same. The actor playing Trump, Che' Williams, was a natural but had very little theatre experience. He had very little theatrical work ethic. Coupled with the fact that he was Karimah's son and she'd written the play for him made dealing with him a little awkward. Che' and Karimah moved in from New York to the hotel across the street from the theatre. At rehearsals Che' was listless, easily distracted and quickly upset. He'd have his lines one day and be shaky the next. Working with Che' became a major assignment for my assistant Cheryl Collins.

In candid discussions with Che', Cheryl found out he rarely went to bed before one or two in the morning. That explained the listlessness and lack of concentration. During more intense discussion, Cheryl also found Che' feeling a bit slighted by all of the attention being paid to Sharif and his needs. Since he didn't have the experience or the work ethic Sharif had, he felt cast in the role of the bad child. Cheryl and Che' had an earnest talk about the theatre and what was expected of actors participating in it. It was his responsibility to come to rehearsal in condition to work. This meant he had to eat properly and get enough rest. He had to know his lines cold because the major action of the first act rested entirely on him. They talked about the character Trump and how he so affects the character of Tyler, that even after his disappearance Tyler's perception of himself and his future actions are substantially altered by Trump's influence on him.

Technical and dress rehearsals began a week before previews and included ten out of twelve rehearsals. Rich Khan and Sidney Mahone began to sit in on run-throughs. Linda Gravet (production manager, college professor, voice coach and cook extraordinaire) began to pull out actors who needed attention for voice work.

I wanted all the music cues and underscoring to be by the same artists—The Funky Natives. Efram Jenkins-Ahman, the in-house sound designer collaborated with me early on in choosing the right cuts for the right places. Collaborative adjustments went on all week.

The set was impressive. It was huge. The façade of an old dilapidated building in purple hues, a front stoop, a fire escape leading to the second floor balcony where Sheneequa stayed, a hydrant with running water that several characters used to wash and quench their thirst during the hot summer day/night. One of the lighting effects that I had Shirley Prendergast implement was to cast huge shadows from Tyler and Trump when they stood directly in front of the abandoned buildings. They looked like little lost boys in a big mean world.

The show opened to solid reviews. Crossroads felt it was a resounding success.

Management

For years I taught a management course at Columbia University. In the Spring of 1994, from late January through mid May, my course called "Critical Issues in Management" met once per week for two hours in the Hammerstein Center on the campus.

I had fourteen graduate students, all white. I mention their color because it's important to deal with who will be the American Theatre's future generation of theatre managers; and also to point out who can really afford the tremendous cost of tuition at major institutions.

Critical Issues in Management consisted of two case studies, each covering seven weeks. The first seven weeks examined the national productions as well as the Broadway production of *Checkmates* by Ron Milner. The second part covered the London production of the musical *King!* In each case I tried to show how the artistic impacted on the business management of the productions and vice-versa.

Part One — "Checkmates." A case study.
Total Cost: $850,000

I began with examples of productions in Chicago, Los Angeles, Atlanta, San Francisco, and Washington, D.C. It was important to know that in each of these productions the playwright, Ron Milner, gave the theatre no subsidiaries in his future productions. It was also important to know that *Checkmates* was not a touring production. Each city had its own cast. If a cast member from another production was hired that cast member had to arrange his own transportation and housing. From a management perspective the only constraints were playwright and the director.

The Impact of Race

The cast in each city was selected from the most visible local actors. This gave each production a tremendous local visibility. For example, at ETA in Chicago we cast Okora Harold Johnson and Linda Bright, two highly visible Chicago artists; in Los Angeles at Inner City Cultural Center we cast Denzel Washington, Paul Winfield, Loretta Greene, and the late great actress Gloria Edwards (we also had a second run at Westwood Playhouse with Paul Winfield, Roxie Roker, Marla Gibbs, Vanessa Williams and Richard Lawson); in Atlanta at the Jomandi the cast was Marsha Jackson, Thomas Jones, Ofemo Omilami, and Carol Mitchell Leon. In Washington, D.C. at Arena Stage *Checkmates* had a cast that consisted of Al Freeman, Jr., Ruby Dee, Elizabeth Van Dyke, and Thomas Jones. Again the reason for the local cast rather than a touring cast was lower production cost. The management of each production was handled by each local producer.

As a producer of these productions, taking into account New Federal Theatre's ownership of the option, I arranged all of the productions, including the Broadway one. First, the journey of *Checkmates* to Broadway, which had the distinction of being able to select the best cast members from the five productions of the play. From the Los Angeles Company Denzel Washington and Paul Winfield; from the Atlanta company Marsha Jackson; from the Washington, D.C. company Ms. Ruby Dee and Elizabeth Van Dyke; and from the Chicago company Okoro Harold Johnson. This casting made issues relating to management easier. Each actor had already played the roles or understudied them.

The main producers, James Nederlander, never saw any of the productions. Phillip Rose, one of the producers, saw the San Francisco production. It was on that basis that he convinced Nederlander to produce *Checkmates*. The producers hired Roy Somylo as general manager. Somylo hired his daughter as company manager. Since James Nederlander never appeared, Roy Somylo, the general manager, acted on Nederlander's behalf. In a sense Roy Somylo had no financial commitment yet called the shots because he signed the checks.

First, a major issue surfaced relating to what a beautiful Black woman should resemble. Second, Denzel Washington, the leading actor, had a contract that gave him approval of the leading lady. Third, Michael Harris and Heywood Collins, two young Black investors who helped finance the

244

Los Angeles and San Francisco co-production, wanted to be in on producing in New York. Nederlander suggested to Phillip Rose they put up $300,000 for producing credit. They said yes. A partnership agreement was drafted between their production company, Y NOT productions and Nederlander's company, GILSUL.

Roy and Philip had their own ideas on the leading lady. The director, the playwright, and the star disagreed. Denzel Washington wanted a leading lady who had no attachment to anyone connected with the producers, the director, or the playwright. He selected Marsha Jackson, partially because of her brilliant audition, her resemblance to his wife, and her excellent reviews for the Atlanta production of *Checkmates*.

The $300,000 from the two Black producers, Michael Harris and Heywood Collins was very slow in reaching the *Checkmates* bank account. Did they have the money? Heywood Collins, who arrived in New York City from Los Angeles two weeks prior to the first rehearsal, said his partner was out of the country but the money was good. Roy Somylo kept the novice producer away from any real business issues, i.e., theatre contracts, advertising agency contracts, production service agreements, etc. *Checkmates* opened August 4, 1988 and closed January 4, 1989.

The play *Checkmates* by Ron Milner, owned by New Federal Theatre took the route to Broadway via Black Theatres in Chicago, Los Angeles, Atlanta, San Francisco and a white theatre in Washington, D.C. It was produced by James Nederlander, Robert Nederlander, Phillip Rose, Michael Harris, and Heywood Collins. The producing entity was GILSUL, Inc. (a company owned by Nederlander). The budget was $850,000. It was not a limited partnership even though that's the customary method of financing a Broadway play. The commitment of Nederlander (GILSUL) to produce the play also meant they committed to finance *Checkmates*. New Federal Theatre; myself, the director; Ron Milner, the playwright, insisted its contract be with GILSUL.

A manager must protect the company and the producers by a first class attorney, a reputable accounting firm, and insurance. *Checkmates* had attorney Richard Ticktin; the accounting firm of Shapiro/Taxon/Kopell (Pauline Novick); and the insurance firm of MLW services (Dawn Keogh).

The manager must negotiate the salaries of the artist, director, and playwright. For Broadway Dramatist Guild, minimum for the writer (at that time) was an advance of $25,000; Society of Stage Directors and Choreographers control the director's fee. It was a minimum advance of $27,500. Each actor is covered by Actors Equity Association. However, a star's salary is based on how badly the production needs the star. *Checkmates* needed Denzel Washington $10,000-per-week's worth; Paul Winfield, $8,500 per week; Ruby Dee, $7,500 per week; and Marsha Jackson (the unknown) $1,200 per week.

The manager's worst nightmare occurred two months into the run. It was discovered by CBS News Los Angeles that Michael Harris was at 26 years of age a major international drug dealer, that he attempted to murder one of his associates, and that he wasn't in Europe but in jail in Los Angeles; and that he was one of the producers of the Broadway production *Checkmates*. Neither James Nederlander nor Roy Somylo had ever seen Michael Harris. Phillip Rose had met Michael Harris at the Arena Stage and they'd begun to talk about investments in other Phillip Rose productions. The media pounded on the Broadway production of *Checkmates*. Roy Somylo was inundated with questions he couldn't answer. He didn't know Michael Harris. He had to deal with the Federal Bureau of Investigation and the Internal Revenue Service. How should he, as manager, speaking for the producer, handle that? How much of the $300,000 had been spent? Of course, he would have to say all of the $300,000.

In this case the director is protected by SSDC; the playwright by the Dramatist Guild; the actors are protected by AEA. The manager works for the producer.

Part Two — "King: The Musical." A case study.
Total Cost: $6,500,000

The musical was set to open in February 1990 in London. The manager's first crisis arrived with the fall of the Berlin Wall in October 1989. The director was Gotz Friedrich, also director of Berlin's Deutsche Opera Theatre. However, when the Berlin Wall came down, making it possible for East and West Berlin to unite, Gotz's family (a wife and three kids) in East Berlin had to be dealt with. He couldn't abandon his new family (another wife and two kids) of almost twenty years in West Berlin. He bowed out as director of *King: The Musical* with less than eight weeks before rehearsals. I was his assistant director and producing consultant.

The general manager, Peter Armstrong asked me to handle auditions until a new director was hired.

The other problems were: the star Simon Estes lived in Switzerland; two of the producers lived in America; two lived in Switzerland; and the show was to be presented in London at the Piccadilly Theatre. A simple meeting cost $5,000 in transportation and per diems.

I brought Ron Milner in to write the new book to the musical. The music already existed. It was written by a white Brit, Richard Blackford. The lyrics to many of the songs were written by Maya Angelou, the American poet. I also brought in Diane McIntyre as Choreographer.

The new director came on board two weeks after the auditions and casting. The new director didn't like Ron Milner's book. Al Nellum, one of the producers, and I brought in Lonne Elder III. He wrote one version and even though the King family liked Elder's version, the director did not. He brought in the white American playwright Richard Nelson. The King family wanted out of this production. Maya Angelou asked that her name be removed from the project. Both hated Nelson's book. The producers felt Angelou had been paid and refused to remove her name. The new director felt he didn't need an American assistant director. The producers dismissed me from the production. Then, the new director was dismissed.

The critical issues facing the manager were: communicating with personnel in America, Switzerland, and other parts of England; living up to contractual commitment after individuals had been dismissed. Ron Milner, Lonne Elder, the new director, and myself were all dismissed.

A new director was recruited from the cast. Clarke Peters is an American actor who'd been living and working in England for over ten years. Peters took on the task with respect and care. He asked Lonne Elder to remain in England for another two months. He moved the opening back three months to April 1990. Diane McIntyre received full support for her preproduction work. She moved full speed ahead. The first ad appeared in the London *Times* November 1989.

The producers list eight partners on the legal partnership. Of the four main producers, two were creators, working on the production. The two were Simon Estes, the opera singer, who played Dr. King, and Richard Blackford, the composer. Of the other two, Peter Hagerty is a rock music producer and Hans Flury a businessman. Estes lives in the Netherlands. Other members of the partnership live all over the world.

As *King: The Musical* proceeded to its opening, two management problems arose: one, the original book writer sued to stop the production. Two, the King estate went to the press citing distortions of Rev. Dr. Martin Luther King's image. How would Peter Armstrong, the general manager, handle these two issues and at the same time manage this complicated production? The attorney for the production sought new answers on material for the stage based on dead or living persons. (I asked the class to examine the U.S. case against John Guare's *Six Degrees of Separation*.) The King estate's position on the musical became the production's critical management issue.

Thirty-Three Years of Production

Produced by Woodie King, Jr. and New Federal Theatre

1970/71 Season

Suddenly Last Summer—
   by Tennessee Williams,
   Dir. Woodie King, Jr.
Why Charlie Can't Win No Wars on the Ground & Misjudgement—
   by Earl Anthony, Dir. Bill Charles
   & Woodie King, Jr.
One—conceived & Dir. Dick A.
   Williams

1971/72

Black Girl—by J.e. Franklin, Dir.
   Shauneille Perry

1972/73

Dudder Love—by Walter Jones,
   Dir. Walter Jones
Jamimma—by Marta-Evans Charles,
   Dir. Shauneille Perry

A Recent Killing—by Amiri Baraka,
   Dir. Irving Vincent
Mondongo—by Ray Ramirez,
   Dir. Dean Irby
In My Many Names and Days—
   by Charles Fuller, Dir. Irving
   Vincent & Larry Neal

1973/74

Brisburial—by Ed Pomerantz,
   Dir. Richard Vos
Candidate—by Charles Fuller,
   Dir. Harold Dewindt
Commitment—by Joseph Lizardi,
   Dir. Carla Pinza
What the Winesellers Buy—by Ron
   Milner, Dir. Woodie King, Jr.

1974/75

Aid to Dependent Children—by Umar Bin Hassen, Dir. Helanie Head

Confession—by Ken Rubinstein, Dir. Ken Rubinstein

Drink Water—by Ifa Baez

Prodigal Sister—by J.e. Franklin & Micki Grant, Dir. Shauneille Perry

Sidnee Poets Heroic—by Amiri Baraka, Dir. Amiri Baraka

Taking of Miss Janie—by Ed Bullins, Dir. Gil Moses

Transition—by Ken Rubinstein, Dir. Ken Rubinstein

Cotillion—by John O'Killens, Dir. Allie Woods

1975/76

Bargaining Thing—by Dan Owens, Dir. Billie Allen

for colored girls who have considered suicide/when the rainbow is enuf—by Ntozake Shange, Dir. Oz Scott

Gilbeau—by Clayton Riley, Dir. Clayton Riley

Greatest Man on Earth—by Val Coleman, Dir. Ed Rambola

Section D—by Reggie Vel Johnson, Dir. Anderson Johnson

Tea—by Irwin Lerner, Dir. Gennard Montanino

Toe Jam—by Elaine Jackson, Dir. Anderson Johnson

1976/77

Defense—by Edgar White, Dir. Dennis Scott

Divine Comedy—by Owen Dobson, Dir. Clinton Turner Davis

Do Lord Remember Me—by James de Jongh, Dir. Reggie Life

Macbeth—by Orson Welles, Dir. Ed Cambridge

Perdido—by Soledad Santiago, Dir. Regge Life

Showdown—by Don Evans, Dir. Shauneille Perry

1977/78

African Interlude—by Martie Evans-Charles, Dir. Shauneille Perry

Block Party—by Joseph Lizardi, Dir. Joseph Lizardi

Daddy—by Ed Bullins, Dir. Woodie King, Jr.

Don't Let It Go to Your Head—by J. E. Gaines, Dir. Gil Moses

Initiation—by Rosemarie Guirard, Dir. Rosemarie Guirard

Mahalia—by Don Evans, Dir. Oz Scott

Night Song—by Patricia Lea, Dir. Walter Jones

Runners—by Ivey McCray, Dir. Novella Nelson

Season's Reason—by Ron Milner,
Dir. Ron Milner
As Long as You're Happy Barbara—
by Gary Lasdun, Dir. Otto
Pirchner

1978/79
A Black Retrospective:
  Anna Lucasta—by Phillip
  Yordan, Dir. Ernestine Johnson
  In Splendid Error—by William
  Branch, Dir. Charles Turner
  Raisin in the Sun—by Lorraine
  Hansberry, Dir. Ernie
  McClintock
  Take a Giant Step—by Louis
  Peterson, Dir. Oz Scott)
  Trouble in Mind—by Alice
  Childress, Dir. Shauneille Perry
Birdlan—by Barry Kaleem,
Dir. Anderson Johnson
Black Media—by Ernest Ferlita,
Dir. Glenda Dickerson
Flamingo-Flomongo—by Lucky
Cienfuego, Dir. Erick Santamaria
God of Vengeance—by Sholem Asch,
translated by Joseph C. Landis,
Dir. Stanley Brechner
Hot Dishes—by Maurice Peterson,
Dir. Irving Lee

1979/80
Amiri Baraka in Concert—by Amiri
Baraka, Dir. Norman Riley

Brewery Puppets—by Brad Brewer,
Dir. Brad Brewer
Crazy Horse Have Jenny Now—
by Louis Peterson,
Dir. Charles Maryan
Friends—by Crispen Langeria,
Dir. Leo Shapiro
*Glorious Monster in the Bell of the
Horn*—by Larry Neal,
Dir. Glenda Dickerson
Puerto Rican Obituary—by Pedro
Pietri, Dir. Jose Machado
Suspenders—by Umar Bin Hassan,
Dir. Al Freeman, Jr.
Take It from the Top—by Ruby Dee,
Dir. Ossie Davis

1980/81
Branches from the Same Tree—by
Marge Elliot, Dir. Arthur French
Connection—by Jack Gelber,
Dir. Carl Lee
Dance and the Railroad—by David
Henry Hwang, Dir. John Lone;
Ethnic Heritage Series
Git on Board—by Trazana Beverly,
Dir. Trazana Beverly
Grand Street—by Robert Reiser,
Dir. Elaine Kanas; Ethnic
Heritage Series
La Morena—by Beth Turner,
Dir. Raul Davila;
Ethnic Heritage Series
No—by Alexis DeVeaux,
Dir. Glenda Dickerson

Something Lost— by Anthony Wisdom, Dir. Richard Gant

Things of the Heart— by Shauneille Perry, Dir. Denise Hamilton; Ethnic Heritage Series

Trial of Doctor Beck— by Hughes Allison, Dir. Phillip Lindsey

When the Chickens Came Home to Roost and *Zora*— by Laurence Holder, Dir. by Allie Woods & Elizabeth Van Dyke

Widows— by Fundi Vandla, Dir. Vantile Whitfield

1981/82

Black People's Party— by Earl Anthony, Dir. Norman Riley

Boy & Tarzan Appear in a Clearing— by Amiri Baraka, Dir. George Ferenz

Child of the Sun— by Damien Leake, Dir. Harold Scott

Day Out of Time— by Allen Foster Friedman, Dir. Harold Guskin; Ethnic Heritage Series

Dreams Deffered— by Laurence Holder, Dir. Allie Woods; Ethnic Heritage Series

Keyboard— by Matt Robinson, Dir. Shauneille Perry

La Chefa— by Tato Laveria, Dir. Raul Davila

Louis— by Don Evans, Dir. Gil Moses

Love— by Carolyn Rodgers, Dir. Shauneille Perry

Paper Angels— by Genny Lim, Dir. John Lone; Ethnic Heritage Series

Shango Diaspora— by Angela Jackson, Dir. Abena Joan Brown

Steal Away— by Ramona King, Dir. Anderson Johnson

Who Loves the Dancer— by Rob Penny, Dir. Shauneille Perry

World of Ben Caldwell— by Ben Caldwell, Dir. Richard Gant

1982/83

Adam— by June Tansey, Dir. Don Evans

Champeen!— by Melvin Van Pebbles, Dir. Melvin Van Pebbles

Jazz Set— by Ron Milner, Dir. Norman Riley & Ron Milner

Liberty Call— by Burial Clay, Dir. Samm-Art Williams

Nuyorican Poets Cafe— by Tato Laveria, Dir. Tato Laveria

Portrait of Jennie— by Enid Futterman & Dennis Rosa, Dir. Dennis Rose

Trio— by Bill Harris, Dir. Nathan George

Upper Depths— by David Steven Rapport, Dir. Bob Kalfin

Wilderness of Shur— by Nicholas Biel, Dir. Gordon Edelstein

Woodie King, Jr.

1983/84

Basin Street (Storyville)—by
Michael Hulett & G. William
Oakley, Dir. G. William Oakley

Becoming Garcia—by Tato Laveria,
Dir. Carlos Gobera

Fraternity—by Jordan Budde,
Dir. Gideon Schein

Games—by Joyce Walker-Joseph,
Dir. Elizabeth Van Dyke;
The Women's Series

Hooch—by Charles Michael Moore,
Dir. Chuck Smith

Hospice—by Pearl Cleage,
Dir. Frances Foster;
The Women's Series

Incandescent Tones—by Rise Collins,
Dir. Marjorie Moon;
The Women's Series

Last Dance Man—by Alan Foster
Friedman, Dir. John Pychon
Holmes

Oh Oh Obesity—by Dr. Gerald
Deas, Dir. Bette Howard

Parting—by Nubai Kai, Dir. Bette
Howard; The Women's Series

*Searock Children Is Strong
Children*—by Paul Webster,
Dir. Paul Webster

Selma—by Thomas Butler,
Dir. Cliff Rocquemore

Shades of Brown—by Michael
Picarde, Dir. Joan Kemp-Welch

Trial of Adam Clayton Powell, Jr.—
by Billy Graham,
Dir. Diane Kirksey

Twenty Year Friends—by Sonny Jim
Gaines, Dir. Andre Mtume

1984/85

Americain Gothic—by Paul Carter
Harrison, Dir. Woodie King, Jr.

Long Time Since Yesterday—by
P.J. Gibson, Dir. Bette Howard

Thrombo—by Albert Bermel, Dir.
Leo Shapiro

Waltz of the Stork Boogie—by
Melvin Van Pebbles, Dir. Melvin
Van Pebbles

Welcome to Black River—by Samm-
Art Williams, Dir. Walter Dallas

1985/86

Appear and Show Cause—by
Stephen Taylor, Dir. Woodie
King, Jr.

December Seventh—by George
Ratner, Dir. Gordon Edelstein

I Have a Dream—by Josh
Greenfield, Dir. Woodie King, Jr.

In the House of Blues—by David
Charles, Dir. Buddy Butler

Long Time Since Yesterday—by P.J.
Gibson, Dir. Bette Howard

Ma Maw Blacksheep—by Stafford
Ashanti, Dir. Stafford Ashanti

*Nonsectarian Conversations with
the Dead*—by Laurie Carlos,
Dir. Latanya Richardson
Once upon the Present Time—
by Geri Lipschultz,
Dir. Geri Lipschultz
Second Hurricane—by Aaron
Copland, Dir. Tazwell Thompson
Williams and Walker—by Vincent
Smith, Dir. Shauneille Perry

1986/87

Boogie Woogie & Booker T.—by
Wesley Brown, Dir. Dean Irby
My Father and the Wars—by Robbie
McCauly, Dir. Robbie McCauly
*Lillian Wald: At Home on Henry
Street*—by Clare Coss,
Dir. Bryan Wortman
*Sovereign State of Boogedy
Boogedy*—by Lonnie Carter,
Dir. Dennis Zacek
The Meeting—by Jeff Stetson,
Dir. Judy Ann Elder
Time Out of Time—by Clifford
Mason, Dir. Al Freeman, Jr.

1987/88

After Crystal Night—by John
Herman Shaner, Dir. Max Mayer
From the Mississippi Delta—by
Dr. Endesha Ida Mae Holland,
Dir. Ed Smith
Mr. Universe—by Jim Grimsley,
Dir. Steven Kent

Trinity—by Edgar White,
Dir. Oz Scott

1988/89

A Thrill a Moment—by William M.
Stevenson, Dir. Ed Love
Good Black—by Rob Penny,
Dir. Claude Purdy
Jika—by Maishe Maponya,
Dir., Maishe Maponya
Tis the Mornin'—by Ruth Beckford
& Ron S. Thompson,
Dir. Ron Stacker-Thompson

1989/90

God's Trombones—by James Weldon
Johnson, Dir. Woodie King, Jr.
Goree—by Matsemela Manaka,
Dir. John Kani
Survival—by Fana Kekana, Thema
Ntinga, Seth Sibanda, Selaelo
Maredi, Mshengu, Dir. Jerry
Mofokeng

1990/91

The Balm Yard—by Don Kinch,
Dir. Shauneille Perry
Jelly Belly—by Charles Smith,
Dir. Dennis Zacek
Wizard of Hip—by Tom Jones,
Dir. Kenny Leon

1991/92

Chain/Late Bus to Mecca—by Pearl
Cleage, Dir. Imani

Testimony— by Safiya Henderson-
Holmes, Dir. Raina von
Waldenburg
Zion!— by Beverly Trader,
Dir. Thomas Jones II

1992/93
Christchild— by J.e. Franklin,
Dir. Irving Vincent
Robert Johnson: Trick the Devil— by
Bill Harris, Dir. Woodie King, Jr.

1993/94
*In Bed with the Blues: The
Adventure of Fishy Waters*— by
Guy Davis, Dir. Shauneille Perry
Looking Back— by Micki Grant,
Dir. Shauneille Perry
The Spirit Moves— by Trazana
Beverley, Dir. A Dean Irby

1994/95
Bessie Speaks— by China Clark,
Dir. Dwight R.B. Cook
The Matador of 1st & 1st— by Oliver
Lake, Dir. Oz Scott
*for colored girls who have considered
suicide/when the rainbow is
enuf*— Written and
Dir. Ntozake Shange

1995/96
*for colored girls who have considered
suicide/when the rainbow is
enuf*— Extension at Tribeca
Performing Arts Center, Aug.
16 — Sept. 24, 1995
Black Girl— by J.e. Franklin,
Dir. Anderson Johnson
Checkmates— by Ron Milner,
Dir. by Woodie King, Jr.

1996/97
Joe Turner's Come and Gone— by
August Wilson, Dir. Clinton
Turner Davis
Do Lord Remember Me— by James
de Jongh, Dir. Regge Life
The Last Street Play— by Richard
Wesley, Dir. Tom Bullard

1997/98
Incommunicado— Written and
Dir. Lee Gundersheimer
*My One Good Nerve: A Visit with
Ruby Dee*— by Ruby Dee,
Dir. Charles Nelson Reilly
Christopher Columbus— by Nikos
Kazantzakis, Dir. Lloyd Richards
Valentine's Day— by Val Coleman,
Dir. Ann Bowen

1998/99

The Trial of One Short Sighted Black Woman vs Mammy Louise and Safretta Mae—by Marcia L. Leslie, Dir. Paul Carter Harrison

Rose McClendon: Harlem's Gift to Broadway—by Vinie Burrows, Dir. Douglas Turner Ward

In Dahomey—by Shauneille Perry, Dir. Shauneille Perry

1999/2000

The Trial of One Short Sighted Black Woman vs Mammy Louise and Safretta Mae—(Remount) by Marcia L. Leslie, Dir. Paul Carter Harrison

Spermegga—by Clarice Taylor, Dir. Walter Dallas

Defending the Light—by Ron Milner, Dir. Jay Broad

James Baldwin: A Soul on Fire—by Howard Simon, Dir. Chuck Patterson

The Brothers Berg—by Richard Abrons, Dir. Jay Broad

The Dance on Widows' Row—Written and Dir. Samm-Art Williams

2000/2001

Conflict of Interest—Written and Dir. Jay Broad

The Conjure Man Dies—Written Rudolph Fisher, Dir. Clinton Turner Davis

The African Project:
Beautiful Things—Written and Dir. Selaelo Maredi
The Missing Face—by Osonye Tess Onwueme, Dir. Patricia White

2001/2002

Bringing Us Together to Take Back Our City (a benefit reading of 32 plays with 25 directors and 75 actors for victims of the 9/11 tragedy)

Urban Transition: Loose Blossoms—by Ron Milner, Dir. Woodie King, Jr.

2002/2003

A Last Dance for Sybil—by Ossie Davis, Dir. Ed Smith and Lloyd Richards

American Menu—by Don Wilson Glenn, Dir. Ajenes Washington

Whose Family Value!—by Richard Abrons, Dir. Philip Rose

Index

261